KU-528-216

MEDIA REGULATION, PUBLIC INTEREST AND THE LAW

MIKE FEINTUCK

EDINBURGH UNIVERSITY PRESS

To
Anna and Lisa

© Mike Feintuck, 1999

Edinburgh University Press
22 George Square, Edinburgh

Typeset in 11 on 13pt Goudy Old Style
by Hewer Text Ltd Edinburgh, and
printed and bound in Great Britain by
MPG Books, Bodmin

A CIP record for this book is available from the British Library

ISBN 0 7486 0997 0 (paperback)

The right of Mike Feintuck
to be identified as author of this work
has been asserted in accordance with
the Copyright, Designs and Patents Act 1988.

MEDIA REGULATION, PUBLIC INTEREST AND THE LAW

27 JAN 2005

LIVERPOOL JMU LIBRARY

3 1111 00810 4703

Contents

Acknowledgements

I am happy to have the opportunity to express my gratitude to all those who helped me complete this work.

I would like to acknowledge my colleagues here at the University of Hull, especially those who carried additional burdens during my study leave in the first semester of 1996–7, and in particular Cosmo Graham and Lisa Whitehouse who read and commented on a complete draft. All the defects that remain despite their efforts are my responsibility entirely.

I am also very grateful to Jane Feore, Commissioning Editor at Edinburgh University Press, who encouraged me to write the book, based only on a rather rambling paper given at the Socio-Legal Studies Association conference in 1996.

Last, but most of all, I must thank Anna and Lisa, who have had to endure my erratic moods and working hours connected with writing this book. Without their love, support and tolerance, it would not have been completed.

Mike Feintuck
Hull, March 1998

Abbreviations

ASA   Advertising Standards Authority
BBC   British Broadcasting Corporation
BBFC   British Board of Film Classification
BDB   British Digital Broadcasting
BSC   Broadcasting Standards Commission
CAP   Committee of Advertising Practice (of the ASA)
CAS   conditional access system (for DTT)
CRS   computerised reservation system (for airlines)
DCMS   Department of Culture, Media and Sport (formerly DNH)
DNH   Department of National Heritage (now DCMS)
DTH   direct-to-home (satellite broadcasting)
DTI   Department of Trade and Industry
DTN   Digital Television Network
DTT   digital terrestrial television
ECHR   European Convention on Human Rights
EPG   electronic programme guide (for DTT)
FCC   Federal Communications Commission (USA)
FOIA   Freedom of Information Act
FTA   Fair Trading Act 1973
GDP   gross domestic product
GII   Global Information Infrastructure
IBA   Independent Broadcasting Authority (now ITC)
IPPR   Institute for Public Policy Research
ITC   Independent Television Commission (formerly IBA)
ITV   independent television
LMA   *Ländesmedienanstalten* (in Germany)
MMC   Monopolies and Mergers Commission
NHS   National Health Service
OFT   Office of Fair Trading
Oftel   Office of Telecommunications
PCC   Press Complaints Commission
RA   Radio Authority
USO   universal service obligation

PART ONE

The Conceptual Framework

CHAPTER 1

Regulating the Revolution

– 1.1 INTRODUCTION AND OVERVIEW –

Our view of the world is arguably influenced more by the media than by our personal experience. We rely to a large extent on both the broadcast and printed media as communicators of politics, of culture and of 'information', and, as such, the media exercise great power in our lives.

Though both the 'popular' and 'quality' press continue to exert influence, increasingly, the broadcast media of radio and especially television have come to the fore. As long ago as 1967, it could be seen that 'television can be shown to stand out among mass media in its influence on our lives' (Blumler and Madge 1967: 5) while thirty years later television can be said to have become 'the defining medium of the age' (Herman and McChesney 1997: 2). With this in mind, it is both inevitable and proper that the focus of a study of media regulation should be pre-eminently on television, though, as will become apparent, even television exists in an increasingly multi-media and cross-media environment.

Television has enjoyed a meteoric rise to its present position of cultural supremacy. In Britain as recently as the 1940s, radio continued to be the dominant broadcast medium and cinema was hugely significant, with television, controlled entirely by the BBC, being viewed largely as an interesting and slightly amusing experiment. This position began to change dramatically and in 1953, when the BBC's live coverage of the coronation attracted the first genuinely mass audience for television, sales of television receivers soared. The power of the BBC both in radio and television had, however, reached its zenith, with the arrival of commercial television in 1955 marking the end of the Corporation's broadcasting monopoly.

The arrival of independent television (ITV), though seen as revolutionary and clearly a severe threat to the BBC's domination of broadcasting, in the longer term resulted only in a power-sharing arrangement, with public-service values co-existing reasonably happily with the degree of commercialism introduced. As recently as 1981, before the advent of Channel 4, television in Britain was still in effect a comfortable duopoly, with power shared between the BBC and the ITV companies. In the years since then, however, a fifth terrestrial channel has come on-stream and, much more significantly, new technologies, including cable and especially direct-to-home (DTH) satellite broadcasting, have changed the nature of British television.

New media technology does not, however, necessarily sweep away all that went before it but rather, at least in the medium term, new media seem to supplement and co-exist alongside the old. Book reading was not entirely replaced by radio listening, and books and radio have not ceased to exist with the advent of television, CD-Roms and net-surfing.

Indeed, the oldest form of mass media, newspapers, continues to sell at commercially viable levels in Britain and elsewhere. Whether any one newspaper has ever 'won' a British general election, as *The Sun* (11 April 1992) famously claimed, is debatable, but the continued use of this medium by those selling their wares, whether political or commercial products, and the continued existence, even under financial pressure, of a wide range of national daily and Sunday titles, should be sufficient to convince of the perceived ongoing power of the press.

In 1945, Britain had nine national daily and eleven Sunday newspapers, controlled by twelve different companies (Humphreys 1996: 77). By 1995, twelve national dailies (including Scottish titles) and ten national Sunday titles were shared between seven owners (DNH, 1995a: Annexe 2). While the total choice of title has therefore changed only slightly, the number of different owners has diminished markedly, and still more significant is the fact that five of these seven owners control only ten titles between them, leaving the remaining twelve titles, accounting for 63 per cent of newspaper circulation, in the hands of two controlling groups (DNH 1995a: Annexe 2).

The structural change over the last fifty years in the television and newspaper sectors sketched above, though important, tells only a small part of the story of change relating to the media market as a whole. Probably more significant has been the ongoing, technologically driven convergence of media, which has led increasingly to the blurring or breakdown of conventional sectoral divides between media, with digitalisation also rapidly eroding the demarcation between the media and telecommunications industries. Technological convergence has been mirrored by changing ownership patterns, with the development of giant cross-media empires cutting across the traditional divides between broadcast and print media. The influence of Rupert Murdoch – as controller via his News Corporation of 37 per cent of British newspaper circulation, a large stake in book and magazine publishing and total dominance of the British DTH broadcasting market via BSkyB – is the obvious and familiar example of this phenomenon.

Even this does not, however, indicate the full extent of change to date, for, just as news gathering and distribution, and cinema, especially in the English language, are now global enterprises, so cross-media empires now span not only sectoral but also national boundaries. For example, Murdoch's influence extends not only throughout Britain and his native Australia, but also into the massive North American market (Tunstall and Palmer 1991). The ability offered by satellite technology to transmit readily across long distances, whether intentionally or in the form of overspill of transmission, often has the appearance of rendering national boundaries irrelevant.

The three phenomena already identified – technological convergence, globalisation and horizontal and vertical integration – form the vital context for a discussion of media regulation in the modern era. However, descriptions of and commentaries on these developments are relatively plentiful and will not be reproduced here. Rather, this book focuses on the responses, actual and potential, to the challenges posed by these ongoing changes to the regulation of the media in the context of liberal-democratic theory and practice.

A fundamental distinction between democracy and other political systems is the expectation that arises from democracy that power will not be unlimited. Those who exercise political power are expected to be accountable to those who elect them, to their peers and to the courts, and should not only be subjected to giving an account of their actions, but also be liable to sanction if their behaviour exceeds limits established by the constitution. Those who exercise significant 'private' power, for example employers or corporate owners, will also, legitimately, have their powers limited by the state (Parkinson 1993). Given the degree of power that the media exercise by, in Blumler's words, providing 'the informational building blocks to structure views of the world' (quoted in Negrine 1994: 2), it is reasonable to expect that they too should be accountable; that their activities should be regulated.

The centrality of the media to democracy, as the primary information source, cannot be over-emphasised, and the very fact that democracy requires citizens to be informed, if they are to act effectively as citizens, serves as a prima facie justification for regulation; and, that the media are regulated is, state Herman and McChesney (1997: 11), true in all states. Whether it is through the kind of direct government control associated with communist or fascist states, or through apparently powerful, state-authorised agencies such as the Federal Communications Commission (FCC) in the USA, or through quiet accommodations such as under the D-notice or lobby systems in Britain, the state at all times ensures a degree of control or influence over the media. The range of regulatory techniques adopted at different times in different places will be considered, but the main thrust of this work is an argument that while regulatory techniques are continually being refined and reformed, a lack of attention is being paid to crucial prior questions.

In essence, it will be argued in this book that the rationales for regulation ('Why regulate?') and the objectives of regulation ('With what end in mind?') have been insufficiently addressed, with the consequence that regulatory techniques, no matter how sophisticated, do not have clear targets or a clear value system underpinning them. To some extent, success or failure of regulatory activities may be assessed by reference to the degree to which the regulatory regime achieves identified objectives or outcomes. Where clear objectives have not been set, perhaps as a consequence of failure to argue and articulate adequately the underlying *raison d'être* of the regulatory regime, success or failure become difficult to measure.

In the current context of rapid technological and structural change within media industries, the existing institutions of regulation are coming under increasing, and possibly terminal, strain. This book argues that important public- interest values continue to justify regulation, though they have often been weakly defined and protected in the past and risk being de-prioritised entirely in the course of the ongoing media revolution. A major concern of this book is therefore to develop a theoretical and institutional framework both for meaningful discourse regarding these values and for the development and implementation of policies which are effective in asserting and furthering the values thus determined.

Arising out of this agenda, this book has four primary objectives:

1. to identify rationales for media regulation and challenges posed to them by the ongoing media revolution;
2. to identify the values underpinning these justifications for regulation, and in particular to seek clarification of 'the public interest' in the context of media regulation;
3. to examine the existing and proposed structures of media regulation, assessing performance against democratic criteria; and
4. a synthesis of the second and third objectives, to identify values and institutional features that must be built-into any future regulatory regime.

Thus, Part One establishes the conceptual framework for media regulation, laying the foundation for studies of particular aspects of the British regulatory regime in Part Two. In Part Three, comparisons are made with other jurisdictions and conclusions drawn.

In essence, attempts to regulate the rapidly changing media environment can be equated to undertaking a somewhat hazardous journey through unknown and shifting terrain. Before commencing such an expedition, the prudent traveller will want to be clear about the desired destination, will need a map showing, as far as it is known, the lay of the land, will want a compass with which to orient themselves and the map, and will need to consider the most appropriate mode of transport. This book attempts to equip the traveller with sufficient information to allow informed choices to be made in respect of all these aspects of the journey. In discussing the objectives of media regulation, a range of destinations will be considered and an attempt made to help in ascertaining which are the most desirable in terms of democratic values. The map will be provided in the form of a discussion of current and projected future changes in the media and their regulation, hopefully indicating a way through this difficult terrain to desirable destinations. By discussing the principles which underlie decisions to seek a particular destination, a compass is provided; a means of orienting ourselves and maintaining the direction towards an ultimate objective. Finally, the discussion of various regulatory techniques comprises a range of choice as to modes of transport from where we are to where we might like to be.

This book seeks to offer a range of choice in respect of all of these travellers' requisites and, though it does suggest that some destinations may be more desirable than others and some routes and modes of transport more appropriate than their alternatives, it is primarily concerned to inform the decision-making process over these aspects by identifying the dangers in the terrain and the principles which may help to avoid pitfalls. It is, on the whole, a map and compass rather than a prescriptive guidebook, though in its capacity as a map it does not attempt to illustrate every hump and hollow but rather to indicate the general contours and most significant landmarks. The ultimate decisions as to the destination and the techniques to be used to get there lie with policy makers and regulators, though it is to be hoped that their choices will be informed by the matters discussed and the approach adopted in this book.

Though this book is written by a lawyer, the study of the law relating to media regulation will not be an end in itself. It is obvious that the law is implicated heavily in the process of regulation; however, its various roles and functions stand in need of close analysis. Clearly, the legality of the actions of those who regulate derives from their empowerment through law and their adherence to limits imposed by statute or other legal devices. However, of particular significance in the context of this book is a concept which encompasses, but extends beyond, legality; namely, 'legitimacy'. This relates to what can be considered as a set of requirements and expectations of an arguably 'higher order' than the legal limits on power established by statute or case law. It relates to adherence to a set of values or expectations which, in the jurisdictions which will be considered, derive from a common liberal-democratic inheritance. The accountability of those who exercise power, a crucial theme of this book, has aspects of both legality and legitimacy: claims of legitimacy frequently rely heavily on claims of being accountable, though such accountability may be as much through political and social mechanisms as through the potential for legal challenge.

As will be discussed later in this chapter and in Chapter 6, fundamental values can generally be discovered within the constitutions of individual states or indeed of transnational bodies such as the EU. In countries such as the USA, or any of the vast majority of Western democracies that have modern, written constitutions, it is likely that many of the values enshrined can, at least superficially, be gleaned fairly readily from an examination of constitutional documents, including perhaps a bill of rights. Though they will always remain subject to contemporary reinterpretation, these values provide a clear starting point when seeking to evaluate the legitimacy of subsequent action. In Britain, almost uniquely, the absence of a modern, written constitution renders this task more difficult, though not necessarily impossible, and the proposed incorporation into domestic law of the European Convention on Human Rights (ECHR) by the Labour Government elected in 1997 (Home Office 1997a), may go some way to assist in this respect. In the interests of understanding how systems of media regulation operate and the roles that the law plays, it will be necessary to examine the range of constitutional fundamentals that inform systems of media regulation in different jurisdictions under different constitutional arrangements. It is argued in this book that an awareness of the constitutional context is crucial, not only in terms of understanding and assessing how the system of regulation operates, but also in providing a basis for the establishment of rational, meaningful and clear justifications and objectives for the regulatory enterprise.

The remainder of this chapter seeks to develop a little further each of the themes identified above. By way of completing the context for this work, it is necessary to consider the power of the media and the significance of the claim of freedom of communication – a fundamental expectation in liberal democracies – though only briefly, given the extensive literature which already exists in these areas. The phenomena of globalisation of media and media empires and the implications of technological convergence will also be examined, and the tension between commercial imperatives and public service values in the media will be opened up, a theme to be explored more fully in Chapters 2 and 3. From there, preliminary consideration will be given to the rationales, objectives, techniques and outcomes of various regulatory approaches, laying the ground for more detailed discussions in Chapters 4 and 5. Finally, this chapter will introduce the vision of the legal and constitutional context for media regulation which will inform much of the rest of this book.

– 1.2   Communication and Power –

– 1.2.1   Freedom of Communication –

Claims of freedom of communication and resistance to regulation form the theoretical basis on which much of the power of the media has been built. McQuail (1992: 9) establishes a historical progression in the relationship between restriction and freedom of the media, tracing it from suppression (by the state and religious authorities) and selective prohibition, to limited permission 'in the name of liberty and business', to, in the modern era, prescription in pursuit of educational objectives and, finally, to libertarianism in what he refers to as 'a market-based claim to unhindered freedom of operation'. Though not by itself particularly revealing as to the theoretical underpinnings for claims of freedom of communication, this historical progression needs to be borne in mind, especially when considering Keane's thesis that present-day arguments for media freedom largely remain based on the philosophies and issues of the revolutionary period of the late eighteenth century, which focused on obtaining freedom from historical state repression. The very different political, social, economic and technological context in which debates over media regulation take place at the end of the twentieth century may, in the absence of new philosophical underpinnings, allow the claims for freedom of expression, so central to liberal thought in eighteenth-century Europe and America, to be subverted to the interests and purposes of the corporate giants who control the modern media (Keane 1991).

The ability to communicate beliefs, ideas and views is held to be central to democracy, yet in all democracies limits are placed on the freedom to communicate. Even in the USA, where the First Amendment guarantee of freedom of expression has the appearance of supreme authority, the courts have stated a willingness, albeit in very limited circumstances, to prevent those wishing to publish material from so doing. Although the *Pentagon Papers* litigation (1971) resulted in a majority of the Supreme Court bench finding against the Executive's desire to prevent publication by the *Washington Post* and *New York Times*, the Court made it clear that there may be circumstances in which they would uphold such a claim to 'prior restraint' (Rudenstine 1996).

Prior restraint, the formal prevention of publication, appears the most severe of restrictions on communication. However, in Britain, a wide range of other significant restrictions exists, ranging from general laws of obscenity, blasphemy, defamation and incitement to racial hatred, through to media-specific measures such as the non-statutory regime of cinema censorship enforced by the British Board of Film Classification (BBFC), the Video Recordings Act 1984 and the notorious temporary ban on broadcasting the voices of members of proscribed Irish organisations under powers granted by the Broadcasting Act 1990. In addition, those working in the news media must remain aware of the laws of breach of confidence (central to the *Spycatcher* litigation), contempt of court and, of course, the reformed but still wide-ranging Official Secrets Acts. (See generally Robertson and Nicol 1992.)

The technicalities of these laws are not of concern for the moment and it is sufficient to note that, despite the rhetoric of freedom of speech, there exists a wide range of limits on what can be communicated by either the media or individual citizens. Indeed, it can be argued that in Britain freedom of communication exists, as do many other 'fundamental' liberties, merely as a residual liberty; what is not unlawful by virtue of statute or case law is permissible, with no special protection or privileges attaching to the media in Britain. This stands in stark contrast with the position in the USA, where the starting point is the guarantee of freedom of speech contained in the First Amendment to the Constitution and any abridgement of it must be specifically justified. McQuail illustrates the American judicial attitude to the press and its regulation with a quote from a US Supreme Court judgement (*Associated Press* v *US* (1945) 326 US 1) where Judge Frankfurter stated that:

> In addition to being a commercial enterprise, it [the press] has a relationship to the public interest unlike that of any other enterprise for profit . . . The business of the Press . . . is the promotion of truth regarding public matters by furnishing the basis for an understanding of them. McQuail (1992: 36)

In practice, as will be seen in Chapter 6, such an awareness of the role of the media in democracy has not entirely prevented the US state from regulating media activity, and particularly broadcasting, though regulatory intervention has been limited essentially to structural and economic matters rather than control of the content of media output, which continues to enjoy First Amendment protection. Indeed, even the pornography industry, heavily restricted in Britain, continues to enjoy constitutional protection in the USA (cf. Abel 1994 and Itzin 1995).

The transatlantic difference in norms pertaining to freedom of communication can in part be explained by reference to the late eighteenth-century struggle for freedom from colonial rule in the USA, and the post-revolutionary constitutional settlement which reflects the values of its time and contrasts markedly with the British model established by the victors of the 'Glorious Revolution' one hundred years earlier. The degree of difference is still remarkable, however, given the shared philosophical heritage deriving from mainstream liberal-democratic thought.

Barendt (1985) presents three different lines of justification of freedom of expression from within this paradigm. Though best viewed as 'ideal types', and clearly presented with some difficulty when faced with the kind of issues and events relating to racist material and pornography discussed by Abel (1994), Barendt's identification of distinct theoretical justifications is helpful in isolating different threads of thought which may be hidden within or beneath general claims of freedom of expression.

The first category that Barendt considers is 'arguments from truth', which he associates closely with the utilitarian philosophy of John Stuart Mill. According to such arguments, open discussion is crucial to the discovery of truth and thus, if speech or communication is restricted, the discovery and publication of true facts and accurate judgements will be stifled or limited. The value of such discovered truth may be inherent and autonomous or its value may derive from utilitarian arguments regarding the general development of society. Barendt notes a difficulty here in relation to an assumption that truth of beliefs and claims is capable of objective verification. However, this problem may not necessarily be seen to undermine the line of argument entirely, if it is interpreted in terms of considering that most contentious beliefs can be categorised as 'possibly true' or 'probably false'.

Leaving this issue aside, a further, essentially utilitarian line underlying arguments from truth can also be discerned. This is the idea that defence of freedom of expression in pursuit of truth helps to ensure that no single set of values is allowed to dominate society; the constant potential for challenge to dominant values demands continuous rational justification of such values by those in power. However, it must be questioned whether the publication of any possibly true statement is always to be defended as a result of adherence to arguments from truth. For example, there is the possibility of truth in overtly racist literature, though such material may be caught by laws regarding incitement to racial hatred or the like, which appear to 'trump' the basic claim to freedom of expression. Similarly, while publication of leaked government documents might appear to be justified via arguments from truth, as they clearly contribute to the amount of knowledge or truth in circulation, they may still be restricted in the name of some

-11-

overriding national or public interest. Justifications for such restrictions tend to be based around a utilitarian concept of a broader public good that is furthered by them, and may be bolstered by secondary claims that protection for freedom of expression continues to exist because of the ongoing potential to debate and challenge the restrictions.

Arguments from truth can be seen to rest on a faith in the efficacy of a competitive market in speech or ideas, and it is readily apparent that, like all markets, it must be regulated or manipulated if effective communication, and therefore the market benefits, are to be realised. At its simplest, if two competing speakers talk simultaneously, it will be difficult to understand fully what either has to say; neither will contribute to effective or meaningful debate or ascertainment of truth. Thus, the freedom, to be effective, must be regulated by some agency. Similarly, if, like many markets, the 'market' in speech tends towards monopolistic or oligopolistic capture, then regulation will be necessary if the perceived benefits of the operation of the market are not to be lost.

The second approach to freedom of expression identified by Barendt appears to derive from an individualistic rather than utilitarian approach: 'arguments from self-fulfilment'. The basic argument here is that restrictions on expression inhibit individual growth as individuals will not develop unless free to formulate beliefs and political attitudes through discussion and criticism. This might appear to be a justification of broader application than only to freedom of expression; a case can be made for its extension to include other prerequisites of effective citizenship such as decent housing or education. One perceptible limitation of this line of argument is that it can readily take on the form of a negative freedom, liberty 'against the state', rather than a positive claim. It then becomes rather more of a hostage to fortune, being highly susceptible to judicial interpretation, though hopefully within the context of overarching constitutional standards. In the modern context, as will be discussed in due course, the question must be asked as to whether freedom of communication also includes liberty from the imposition of limitations by the exercise of corporate, private, as opposed to state, power.

The third distinct line of argument identified by Barendt is described as 'arguments from citizen participation'. Especially in the context of debates involving the US First Amendment, he finds it often argued that the primary purpose of freedom of expression is to enable individuals to understand political issues, thereby empowering them to participate effectively as citizens within the processes of democracy. Though this argument is generally expressed in terms of citizens' rights, an apparently individualistic model, Barendt notes that it is 'firmly utilitarian in spirit' (Barendt

1985: 20), being based around the good that will accrue for the majority of society from the pursuit of this policy. He goes on, however, to indicate some specific problems that may flow from this.

Within the context of a primarily representative (as opposed to partici-patory) model of democracy, this approach appears to allow elected representatives with a temporary hold on power to impose restraints on expression 'in the public good'. The only obvious response to this problem seems to be that certain 'rights', such as freedom of expression, are so important that they cannot be overridden easily by a government tem-porarily in power. Such repressive action might, especially with the aid of support from clear constitutional terms, readily be viewed as illegitimate and/or illegal. Alternative responses to this dilemma appear to fall back on either the individualistic, self-fulfilment argument or, possibly, a return to arguments from truth.

Clearly, none of the three lines of argument is without its problems, though they persist, often in varying combinations, as the key lines of argument justifying freedom of expression. Judicial decisions in both Britain and the USA, can often be found to contain elements of all three, though they tend to rely most often on concepts of 'citizen' or 'human rights', most closely associated with arguments from self-fulfilment and citizen participa-tion. Whatever combination of any or all of the three lines of argument is accepted, the centrality of freedom of communication to liberal-democratic beliefs is demonstrated, though disputes over its precise nature and extent continue. Ultimately, all three share an underlying belief in the value of allowing individuals and groups to have access to a wide range of informa-tion (both political and cultural), whether from the point of view of society ascertaining truth, or individual self-fulfilment, or citizens participating effectively in society. However, in modern, large-scale societies, this must be viewed primarily as an issue of mass rather than individual communication, and both transmission and receipt of effective mass communication, even in an era of international networks of personal computers, will require access to the mass media.

In light of the power of the media, discussed below, certain other values may compete with the claim to freedom of expression. In particular, claims to privacy, not to be harassed and the avoidance of defamation will be dealt with differently in different jurisdictions. For media regulators, however, another set of issues arises in the modern context. This concerns limiting the ability of corporate media giants to utilise the claim of freedom of communication to further their own commercial ends while acting in ways that run counter to maximising the provision of 'information' upon which the claim is premised. This is the concrete manifestation of the mismatch between late-eighteenth-century philosophical underpinnings and the late-twentieth-century context which Keane (1991) identifies. Examples of the problems created and of the generally futile attempts to resolve them via regulation are highlighted in later chapters, and confirm empirically the need, identified at a theoretical level by Keane, to develop a new and appropriate public-interest justification for regulation in the modern context.

In the specific context of broadcasting, Negrine (1994: 116) asks, 'How much freedom should broadcasters have, given that they have an almost monopolistic control over the means of mass communication?' It seems appropriate to answer this question in terms of setting the limits of media freedom in such a way as to ensure that their activities further, rather than damage, the public interest. The only problem with this response is in defining the public interest, the subject of Chapter 3.

– 1.2.2   THE POWER OF THE MEDIA –

Seymour-Ure (1996: 271) states that 'A history of media could easily slip into being a history of society as a whole. This in itself reflects the centrality of media in our lives'. With this caveat in mind, it is still necessary to consider the roles played and power exercised by the media before turning to questions of their regulation.

Much of the media's activity, especially in the areas of news gathering and distribution, is justified by reference to one or more of the theoretical justifications for freedom of expression expounded by Barendt (1985). The central role of the media in political discourse places it, or ought to place it, believe Herman and McChesney, firmly within the 'public sphere' (1997: 2–8). Habermas' construct of the public sphere and of the role of the media is summarised admirably by Dahlgren:

> In ideal terms, Habermas conceptualizes the public sphere as that realm of social life where the exchange of information and views on questions of common concern can take place so that public opinion can be formed. The public sphere 'takes place' when citizens, exercising the rights of assembly and association, gather as public bodies to discuss issues of the day, specifically those of public concern. Since the scale of modern society does not allow more than relatively small numbers of citizens to be physically co-present, the mass media have become the chief institutions of the public sphere. Yet Habermas' concept of the public sphere insists on the analytic centrality of reasoned, critical discourse. The public sphere exists, in other words, in the active reasoning of the public. It is via such discourse that public opinion is generated, which in turn is to shape the policies of the state and the development of society as a whole. (Dahlgren 1995: 7)

Tehranian and Tehranian (1995: 39) state that 'It is in the process of public communication on public policies that democratic institutions thrive', and it is clear that communications media can facilitate the objectives identified in arguments from truth, self-fulfilment and citizen participation, and have the potential to further the rational discourse enterprise identified in Habermas' public sphere. However, the media's activities can also be viewed in a less altruistic light, in terms of pursuing particular political agendas and in terms of manipulating material for commercial and/or political reasons. The power the mass media wield in a large-scale society, where individuals will communicate personally with only a tiny proportion of their fellow citizens, is clear, and, if this power is not constrained by adequate accountability mechanisms, it might be thought to be in breach of fundamental constitutional expectations. While the media are constrained by both the general law and media-specific measures referred to above, commentators consistently argue that this does not significantly inhibit the power and influence of the press and broadcasters on the grand scale.

In the modern context, the media must also be viewed as a huge, and increasingly global, commercial market. While all markets run the risk of domination by one or more major players, media markets appear to show a peculiar predisposition towards monopoly or oligopoly; the work of both Bagdikian (1992) and Herman and McChesney (1997) testifies to this, in the former case in the context of one country, the USA; in the latter on the global scale. If the media are to justify their existence and power in relation to any of the theories of freedom of communication identified by Barendt, or in terms of their contribution to the establishment and maintenance of the public sphere, then they must also establish that the commercial marketplace, in which they operate as profit-making enterprises, in turn contributes to the wider, democratic marketplace of ideas. The media, to continue legitimately to claim the power associated with freedom of communication and the domination of its channels, must contribute to the acquisition by citizens of a range of political and cultural 'information', from which they may engage, individually and collectively, in a triangulation process which ultimately allows them an informed view of the world. In this sense, the media may properly be viewed as a public resource. If the commercial imperative drives the media to a monopoly or near-monopoly of control, and this in turn results in a more restricted range of information or views being available where 'knowledge becomes ever less a common good and more and more the privileged possession of individual owners' (Hamelink 1995: 21), then this may be viewed as running counter to the democratic expectations on which freedom of communication is premised.

Schiller (1996) addresses the issues of the modern media context still more directly, illustrating again the inappropriateness of the claim to freedom of expression by the media where their activities appear to run counter to the democratic enterprise. Noting the increasing proprietorship of information in corporate, commercial hands, he comments that while 'Historically, the threat to individual expression has been seen to come from an arbitrary state' (43), 'What distinguishes this [present] era is that the main threat to free expression has shifted from government to private corporate power' (44). In addition, as Dahlgren (1995: 148) indicates, the institutional logic of mass media, and the television industry in particular, is not to further the public sphere, but to maximise profit. This is sometimes reflected in the statement that the central purpose of commercial media is not to deliver products to audiences but to deliver the audience, as a product, to advertisers. Given the power of the media and its centrality to democratic processes, if Hutton (1995: 9) is remotely near the mark in stating a 'growing conviction that an honest hearing in the press is the exception rather than the rule unless what is being said chimes with the transient preoccupations of editors and proprietors', it is clear that the media require regulation to ensure that they act in accordance with democratic principles; that the media support citizenship and the public sphere rather than undermining them.

However, in their role as the fourth estate, the media also claim to play a vital part in support of democracy by acting as a counterbalance to the state or government, especially in facilitating the calling to account of government. Again, this function appears to rely upon a degree of plurality in the approaches taken by the media and, in so far as ownership relates to editorial content, upon plurality of ownership. At the extreme, were the entire media to be in the control of a media magnate broadly or wholly sympathetic to the views of the government of the day, then the likely effectiveness of the media as a mechanism of accountability would be highly questionable. The net result would not be that far removed from the kind of situation in Nazi Germany or the Soviet Union (Siebert *et al.* 1956) where the state-controlled media could be viewed as an arm of the government rather than a counterbalance to it; as anti-democratic rather than furthering democratic objectives of scrutiny and accountability. Given the quasi-constitutional role that the media take on in this sense, the need for their accountability and the justification for their regulation are further emphasised.

Blumler and Madge (1967) suggest at least four aspects of the media's impact on citizens: at the time of elections; more generally in providing a picture of the political system; in establishing and serving group relationships and interests; and as a source of knowledge leading to civic action. The reform of housing law in Britain following the outcry created by the screening of Ken Loach's *Cathy Come Home* in 1966 provides a concrete example of the media's power to influence social reform. It would be rather pious, however, to consider the media only in the context of 'informing' and 'educating', to the exclusion of the third part of Lord Reith's formula, 'entertaining'. The media's activities must be considered in terms of both, in Corner's words, 'the public knowledge project' and 'the popular culture project' (quoted in Dahlgren 1995: 37).

In large-scale societies, to the extent that we share expectations, assumptions, values and, more broadly, a 'view of the world', this is the result of the entertainment industry which overlaps with, though is far from cotermi-nous with the media considered here. In so far as they are commercial activities, the visual and performing arts, together with leisure industries such as participatory and spectator sports and gambling (bingo, lotteries, betting shops and casinos), form part of this entertainment industry which, though often corporately related to, cannot be considered, by and large, to be part of, the mass media. The area of overlap is large, however, taking in much of television and radio output, the cinema and video market and the recorded music industry. Of these, control of coverage of major sporting events and television premieres of movies by BSkyB have formed the lever used by Murdoch to force the pace of change currently to be found in British television.

Whether viewed as a force towards social solidarity, as symptomatic or causal in the atomisation of society, or as a high-tech 'opium of the masses', dulling the effects of the painful cutting edge of capitalism, it is fair to conclude that the media, and television especially, have, over the last forty years, provided most of the experiences shared *en masse* by vast sectors of society. We have shared together in the drama of sporting triumph and defeat, in world records being broken, golfers holing putts and (especially) footballers missing penalties. We have watched together hundreds of births, marriages and deaths (and the occasional burying and discovery of bodies under patios) in our favourite soap operas. We have watched thousands of fictional and recreated crimes, natural and human-made disasters, and fights and battles lost and won. We have sometimes cried and laughed together in our thousands or millions as these events unfolded on our screens (or even on our radios), and though at the time we were alone or in our small family or social circle, they have formed the focal point of much of our intercourse with others in the days and weeks that followed. The coverage, or arguably media creation, of the 'national mourning' following the death of Diana, Princess of Wales, in September 1997 provided still further evidence of the power of the media to engage vast sectors of society, and indeed, arguably, contributed significantly to actual action on the part of those who chose travel to London to pay their respects under the eye of the watching media.

Conventional television, free at the point of reception, can be said to provide 'a cultural cohesion to the nation' (Negrine 1994: 198). The significance of the threat of cultural imperialism on a global scale posed by (US) English-language-dominated media therefore becomes apparent. But, whatever the messages transmitted by the media are, and however they are understood and acted upon by individuals, groups or nations, the mere fact that commercial broadcasting is able to support itself primarily from advertising revenue is indicative of the significant power of the medium in the eyes of those who have products to sell.

It is not though the purpose of this book to attempt to unravel the mysteries of the power of the media, or even, by and large, the social purposes for which this power is used. It is sufficient for present purposes to note that undoubted power exists, and to note also that 'in all societies the questions of who owns and controls the media, and for what purposes, have been political issues' (Herman and McChesney 1997: 11). As such, we must expect the state and machinery of government to take an active interest in media-related activities, and in particular to respond to the media's 'capability to define and present its own role to the public' (Schiller 1996: 125). However, as Eldridge et al. observe:

> The conceptualization of the mass media as being either 'the fourth estate' or 'agencies of social control' is an oversimplification. The role of the mass media at any time is shaped by factors particular to the period under consideration as well as the medium under study. (Eldridge et al. 1997: 13)

Via a brief historical account of the development, and attempts by the state to control cinema and the popular press, Eldridge et al. (1997: 23) conclude that it was only in the twentieth century that 'the market and the system of information control became central to the government's strategy to manage the media'. Though access to, and control of, information must therefore of necessity provide a significant part of the backdrop to our consideration of media regulation, it is equally important to understand the particular context in which such debates must currently take place. In the modern era, the globalisation of corporate media interests combines with rapid technological change to form what is, at the very least, a challenging environment in which to develop and implement media policy.

– 1.3 GLOBALISATION AND TECHNOLOGICAL CHANGE –

– 1.3.1 THE GLOBAL MEDIA EMPIRE –

Over recent years, much attention has been paid to the apparent domination of national media sectors, or indeed national cross-media, by individual corporate giants. In Italy, Silvio Berlusconi came to dominate the commercial television sector, and indeed challenged the primacy of the state broadcaster in the overall television market (Herman and McChesney 1997: 170–3; Tunstall and Palmer 1991: Chapter 8). In Britain, Rupert Murdoch was allowed to develop dominance in DTH satellite broadcasting while simultaneously building a holding approximating to one-third of the national newspaper market (Herman and McChesney 1997: 166–70; Tunstall and Palmer 1991: Chapter 6). However, regulators must remain aware that there is more to their task than 'regulating the bogey man' (Feintuck 1997a), truly the stuff of James Bond in *Tomorrow Never Dies* for, as Keane (1991: 154) notes, 'The obsession with media magnates has little in common with a politics of maximising freedom and equality of communication'. The scope of the regulatory endeavour is bigger even than the mightiest media magnate, and any individual magnate or corporation defeated on an individual basis will soon be replaced by another, or others, pursuing the same agenda and posing the same threats. There will always be more bogey men lurking in the woods or under the bed.

More typical than near or actual monopoly in media markets is a condition of oligopoly. In the USA, as charted by Bagdikian (1992), the entire media market in television, movies, newspapers and magazines has fallen increasingly into the hands of a small number of corporate giants. While such developments in themselves pose significant challenges for national regulators, for whom ensuring diversity of ownership has conventionally been an objective, a more fundamental problem has become increasingly apparent.

While regulation of media ownership has traditionally taken place at the national level, the media market has become increasingly international, both in terms of transmission of media products across national borders and in terms of ownership patterns. The former phenomenon, significant especially for the potential it offers in terms of outflanking 'the ultimate [national] regulatory sanction of revocation of licence' (Marsden 1997b: 2), has largely arisen out of technological developments (which will be addressed shortly) while the latter relates more to the development of increasingly international corporate structures in media markets, an aspect say Herman and McChesney (1997), of an increasingly global economy.

Though Seymour-Ure (1996: Chapter 5) identifies the existence of a significant role for foreign capital in the British (print) media even prior to 1945, he records also the changing patterns of ownership and particularly the rapidly changing shape of the market in the 1980s and 1990s, especially in terms of 'scope, scale, management, balance and volatility' (119). In earlier eras, only the news agencies operated in a truly international environment, while in modern times the likes of CNN and MTV are broadcast globally, and empires such as Murdoch's operate on a transcontinental scale. Such developments clearly pose problems for national regulators, given the limited significance of national affiliations for global corporations; however, they also carry a threat to conventional public-service values and standards in broadcasting, given that 'the major feature of the global media order is its thoroughgoing commercialism' and the resulting centrality of advertising. (Herman and McChesney 1997: 1).

The synergistic strength of cross-media corporations identified by Herman and McChesney (1997) is constantly increased by the processes of horizontal integration (within individual media sectors) and vertical integration (across media sectors) taking place on a near-daily basis. The result of these processes is the potential for even large media players such as the American broadcasters NBC and CBS to be shut out of the market by real giants such as Disney and Time Warner which can provide their own films to their own broadcast and cable television channels (Herman and McChesney 1997: 68). As yet, the potential for the total global domination of American-originated images is not complete, but the corporate structure for its achievement is largely in place (see generally Schiller 1996).

While such trends pose a clear threat to the diversity which appears to underlie much of the regulatory endeavour in relation to the media, it would be naive to believe that such developments have always run counter to the wishes of national governments. Certainly, there was no active government opposition in Britain to, and possibly even encouragement for, the involvement of newspaper groups in the early development of the ITV companies (Barendt 1993: 131) though subsequently, from the Television Act 1963 onwards, regulators were given the ability to limit cross-media ownership and control. However, Herman and McChesney (1997) argue persuasively that in many cases governments, especially those of the USA and UK, continue actively to encourage the transformation of home-grown media enterprises into worldwide players, in pursuit of the perceived benefits that will accrue both in terms of the national economy and in extending their sphere of influence.

The economic significance of the media market should not be underestimated, with Collins and Murroni (1996: 1) indicating that the media account for approximately 5 per cent of British gross domestic product (GDP). In an increasingly global economy, it should be no surprise, however, to find that much of the truly international media is US-dominated, though Herman and McChesney (1997: Chapter 3) note that even the buoyant, home US market is not immune to penetration by non-American media players.

While national economic benefits will inevitably prove tempting to governments, dependant for image and re-election on economic success, allowing or encouraging local media empires to grow to a size at which they can compete effectively on the global scale carries with it the risk of them having to be allowed to grow to a position where they may dominate the home market, posing significant challenges for domestic regulation. Given the undoubted significance of the media to national political, cultural and social life, such risks should not be underestimated. The problem is that, as Humphreys states,

> The main determinant of media policy in the 1990s seems to be policy makers' perception of what is in the economic interest. Unsurprisingly, given the 'structural power' of large media corporations, the 'economic interest' conforms with the said corporations' interests. (Humphreys 1997a: 19)

While conventionally the primary focus of the national regulatory endeavour has been on the resolution of conflicts at the domestic level, the growth of international media empires, combined with technological developments and what Herman and McChesney (1997: 41) refer to as the 'rapid reduction or elimination of many of the traditional institutional and legal barriers to cross-border transactions'; has changed the nature of the game. Certainly, the development of a Global Information Infrastructure (GII) has a sinister appearance for national regulators traditionally charged with a public-interest mandate. 'Can the undemocratic sort of capitalism that will finance the GII in fact produce a genuine participatory democratic arrangement?' asks Hamelink (1995: 16), or will its further development simply increase the ongoing trend identified by Schiller (1996) as the privatisation of information and therefore democracy?

Understandably, one reaction to the global media has been to shift the regulatory focus away from its traditional home in the nation state, and a growth in the role ascribed to international organisations in regulating the media. However, international cooperation in a field such as this is difficult, and in Europe, though the EU appears potentially to have a key role in establishing the regulatory agenda for the region as a whole, it has as yet failed to establish its position fully and may have some difficulty in keeping up with the rapid pace of development. Though these issues will be returned to in Chapters 4 and 6, it should be noted at this stage that, from a democratic perspective, the EU's activities in relation to the media may be limited by the fact of its primary focus being based upon economics rather than, say, citizenship. In addition, both Harcourt (1996) and Doyle (1997) draw attention to the problems of institutional inertia and entrenched perceptions of national interests within Member States, apparent within the EU's attempts to develop a coherent and effective media policy.

- 1.3.2 TECHNOLOGICAL DEVELOPMENT AND CONVERGENCE -

While the changing corporate structure of the media industries reflects in part a general move towards an international or possibly global economy, the rapid change in recent years has also been related to the significant degree of technological change and development. The development of Teletext services, in which newspaper groups hold a significant stake (Peak and Fisher 1996: 167), the availability of newspapers on the Web, plus the delivery of television, interactive home shopping and banking services together with conventional point-to-point telecommunications services via fibre-optic cable, are all indicative of this process. Another obvious and current manifestation of such development is the imminent arrival of digital terrestrial television (DTT) in Britain, which will be examined shortly. However, the degree of technological development and its impact, and especially the reduction of a wide range of material to digital bit-streams, extends far beyond DTT and represents a fundamental challenge to our view of, and methods for regulating, the media.

The 1980s saw the advent of computerised typesetting and gradually improving quality of colour printing in newspapers, and though the former especially was viewed as revolutionary in the newspaper industry, like the introduction of hot metal or linotype production twenty years earlier, it was of relatively minor significance to the typical newspaper reader. The first significant and concrete manifestation of the technological revolution for the British media 'consumer' came with the advent of DTH satellite broadcasting.

After a false, dual-track start by British Satellite Broadcasting and Rupert Murdoch's Sky, satellite television in Britain really began after the two merged or after, according to Seymour-Ure (1996: 114), the former was taken over by the latter, in November 1990 to form BSkyB. Since then, the British viewer has grown accustomed to, if not content with, the domination of live coverage of Premier League soccer, World Cup cricket and overseas test match series, major boxing events, and the first television showing of movies, by subscription channels or, on occasion, pay-per-view facilities. While this has in itself formed a significant change for British broadcasting, and signalled the final demise of the BBC/ITV duopoly, it has also acted as a catalyst for further change and a fundamental reappraisal of the place of the BBC.

At the same time, cable companies offering combined telephony and television facilities have sought, with limited success, to break into the British market. By the end of 1996, there were only 1.65 million domestic cable television customers in Britain (*Financial Times*, 11 December 1996) compared with an estimated one-quarter of domestic households having access to BSkyB's satellite services. However, it can be argued that in the long run it is likely to be fibre-optic cable rather than satellite broadcasting, that represents the potential future for the media. Fibre-optic cable offers the potential for the delivery to individual households of television and radio, networked computer facilities, interactive services such as home banking, shopping and video on demand, combined with telecommunications (telephone and fax) facilities. Indeed, the ultimate potential of digitalisation, allowing the transfer of all such material down a single line, seems almost boundless. Keane (1991: 160) suggests that amongst the more significant aspects of digitalisation are its ability to facilitate the transfer of data between media, to decrease the relative cost of information processing, and, most crucially, he states, to move away from the conventional broadcasting model to a more individualised, user-selected, 'narrowcast' model of communications.

Tehranian and Tehranian (1995: 39) describe how from the scribes attached to religious orders, to the rise of the secular, scientific universities with the advent of printing, 'each new communication technology in history is accompanied by the rise of a new communications elite that masters the use of that particular technology and thus assumes a leading role in developing new mediating ideologies and institutions'. An indication of the potential for the digitalised media to become dominated by the technical experts of the computing industry is provided by Marsden (1997a) in noting the attempt by Microsoft, Intel and Compaq to set the technological standards for DTT.

However, in the early days of such an era, it is difficult to predict with any certainty the final extent of the impact of technological convergence. It may be that 'mass media' will be rendered obsolete as every individual becomes their own 'home publisher', and we will no longer want or need access to mass circulation material, choosing instead to access selectively that which we want to read or watch, the end consumer setting their own agenda or scheduling rather than depending on the newspaper editor or the television programmer.

While acknowledging the beliefs of those such as Negroponte (quoted in Herman and McChesney 1997: 106) that 'the monolithic empires of mass media are dissolving into an array of cottage industries' as a result of electronic publishing via the developing 'information superhighway', Herman and McChesney believe that further development in this direction depends on long-term and widespread extension of fibre-optic cable networks. Therefore, they conclude persuasively, 'the Internet and the digital revolution do not pose an immediate or even foreseeable threat to the market power of the media giants' (107). They go on to note that the future commercial potential of the Internet is likely to be maximised only by those who can best advertise their products through other, more widely accessible channels (i.e., existing big-league media players), demonstrating again the synergistic strength of cross-media empires. The same authors consider also that while access to the Internet remains limited to an elite in almost all societies, such developments will further exaggerate social stratification. The same point is raised by Charlesworth and Cullen (1996: 27) who note that the so-called information revolution may 'simply bypass some sectors of society' and may lead to 'further concentration of information access, and as a result political and social influence, with those social groupings which already enjoy a disproportionate degree of power'.

Whatever the future, certain immediate consequences are already apparent. Digitalisation in television broadcasting means a final end to frequency scarcity, as will be discussed in Chapter 2, the most long-standing justification for the regulation of broadcasting. The potential for digital compression to create hundreds of new channels within a spectrum previously restricted to carrying five analogue television channels, suitably separated to avoid cross-channel interference, offers the potential for either vastly increased choice or 'wall-to-wall *Dallas*'. If, however, access to such extra facilities comes only at a price to the individual viewer, such facilities will not be available to all but only those prepared and able to pay. If the arrangements for broadcasting these extra television services are not 'free at the point of use' (free-to-air), thus exaggerating social hierarchy, the development risks undermining the degree of cultural cohesion imported by conventional mass media, especially if it leads to a reduction in the perceived legitimacy of, and therefore funding for, public-service broadcasting. At the same time, if the evolving situation is not adequately regulated, the range of channels, and therefore the choice of content available, may be controlled by those who control the delivery mechanisms. Both Murdoch's removal of the BBC from his service provided to Asia via the Star satellite (Herman and McChesney 1997: 74) and the decision in February 1998 by Murdoch's HarperCollins publishing house to pull the publication of the memoirs of Chris Patten (last British governor of Hong Kong), in order to avoid alienating the Chinese government and therefore to maintain Murdoch's potential for penetrating this developing and potentially massive new media market, may be an early sign of things to come.

Regulators, seeking to avoid adverse consequences flowing from such developments, may consider the adoption or adaptation of mechanisms already familiar from other fields. In telecommunications, and following other privatisations in Britain, limited universal service obligations (USOs) were imposed upon the new operators, requiring, for example, basic telephony services to be maintained in the form of unprofitable call boxes in rural areas to cater for those who did not have the means to fund a telephone in their own home. Clearly, such methods do not provide the full benefits available to those who are able to buy in the full service, just as access, even free access, to a computer facility networked to the Internet in every village hall would not provide the same benefits or access as equipping each home with such a machine. The imposition of such a USO to supply an unprofitable service and avoid the potential for cherry-picking by private enterprises acknowledges, however, in the case of utilities, the legitimacy of state intervention in markets where 'the public interest' demands it, and a willingness, on the part even of economically libertarian governments to make economic adjustments in pursuit of a limited form of social justice. Though the transfer of such measures to the media environment may therefore be of interest, USOs remain in practice a limited concept, arguably insufficiently focused on, or giving insufficient emphasis to, equality of citizenship. The kind of baseline services likely to be provided under USO obligations are unlikely to be sufficient to ensure that all citizens have access to a sufficiently wide range of media to enable them to participate in society as citizens.

In any case, in terms of broadcasting, a straightforward adoption of USOs in the call-box form applied to basic telephony services is not suitable. It is highly doubtful that those not owning, say, DTH satellite-receiving equipment would be prepared to gather routinely in a public place to watch television, though pubs and clubs have become popular venues for occasional events, especially soccer coverage. In practice, it might be necessary to impose 'must carry' requirements upon those controlling delivery mechanisms, demanding that they carry basic services, free at the point of use, alongside subscription or pay-per-view services. In addition, perceived threats to traditional publicly funded, non-commercial enterprises such as the BBC might be defended against in the new commercial environment by the imposition of 'play or pay' duties, under which broadcasters not subject to the full range of public-service broadcasting requirements may be required to pay a levy to help fund the delivery of free-to-air non-commercial services. These options will all be considered in due course, but for the moment it is helpful to note that the changed technological and commercial environment has already forced a shift in regulatory focus, towards those controlling delivery and reception of broadcast media rather than on the content of programming or the ownership of broadcasting companies. It is a move away from regulation of structure and content, towards regulation of behaviour in the media marketplace. One concrete example of this phenomenon has already arisen in the context of the introduction of DTT, discussed further in Chapter 4. Though it has already been noted that the introduction of DTT may, in time, be overshadowed by the widespread use of fibre-optic cable to deliver an integrated telecommunications/broadcasting/computer network, the switch from analogue broadcasting to digital has raised questions that will remain relevant whatever form the new market takes in the future. Limited attempts to restrict the anti-competitive potential of control of technological gateways in the distribution infrastructure can be found in European and British regulatory responses discussed later; however, as will be seen, it is possible that such attempts to limit power in relation to such 'pinch points' will be unlikely to prove effective unless they form part of a broader and coherent policy of regulation of the media market as a whole. As has been suggested elsewhere, regulating this small if crucial part of the market will be ineffective unless the shape of the media market as a whole is also regulated (Feintuck 1997b and 1997c).

Schiller (1996: 40) argues that the radio spectrum, via which conventional broadcasts have been routed, is in effect a 'public natural resource' and certainly, in an age of mass communication, this argument draws strength from the significance of broadcast media in fulfilling expectations of the public sphere. To the extent that even in a freedom-of-communication culture such as the USA, the state has acted to regulate broadcasting (and, as will be discussed later in this Chapters 2 and 3, broadcasting has consistently been more heavily regulated than print media), this principle has been fundamental in legitimising intervention. To date, however, the information revolution, especially as manifested in the Internet, has not been claimed for the public, but rather left to the whim of its commercial developers.

As already acknowledged, it is impossible to predict with certainty the extent to which the new information infrastructure will prove central to communications in the future, but, to the extent that it does prove to form an essential part of democracy, the same public-resource argument must apply. Regulators will need to be empowered to act to restrict the utilisation of this medium as a commercial asset if and when the commercial imperative infringes on its democratic function. The problem, of course, is that the longer regulatory action is delayed, and the more entrenched becomes the commercial ethos for the information infrastructure, the more difficult it will become to legitimate public-interest intervention and to limit the private property rights of the controlling corporations. A further problem for regulators, identified by Klingler (1996), definitional by nature, also arises out of the breakdown of conventional sector divides between traditional broadcasting to a mass audience and individual point-to-point communication, with 'narrowcasting' now forming a hybrid communications medium. Taken together with the international nature of modern communications media, such issues appear to reaffirm the need for reconsideration and clarification of the principles which underlie any regulatory intervention.

Such issues must be addressed as part of the development of what McQuail (1992: 307) terms 'a revised agenda of public interest concerns'. Part of this process must involve the reclamation of the public sphere, and the re-legitimation of public intervention in matters of democratic concern. Such concerns must include rectifying 'the mistaken trust in the therapeutic powers of unbridled technical expertise' (Keane 1991: 179), if the anti-democratic consequences of 'technocratic capitalism' (Tehranian and Tehranian 1995: 41) are to be avoided.

– 1.4   The Revolution and the Law –

– 1.4.1   A Broader Concept of Law –

It is obvious that the law is heavily involved in media regulation: it forms a network of rules which are applied or not applied; it offers mechanisms for resolving disputes and for challenging decisions; it says what is lawful or unlawful; it may prescribe and impose sanctions where rules have been broken; it is the instrument via which government policy is translated into enforceable reality; it establishes authorities and grants power to them. Law is, however, about much more than judges deciding cases and the words and interpretation of statutes, the classical subjects of traditional legal scholarship.

The range of issues raised for the public lawyer, whose focus is upon constitutional and administrative law, are widespread in the context of media regulation. These issues include, but extend beyond, the intricacies of individual court decisions in judicial review cases involving regulatory bodies, the network of often interrelating and overlapping regulatory institutions and the role of government in relation to them, and the existence of both statutory and non-statutory regimes. All of these provide obvious focal points, and it is also possible to identify readily concerns arising out of the different approaches which are likely to be adopted by national and international bodies which may approach issues from different jurisprudential, constitutional and economic perspectives.

For the uninitiated, it may therefore be surprising to find that while adequate legal commentaries are readily available (e.g., Barendt 1993;

Robertson and Nicol 1992), with only limited exceptions surprisingly little analysis has been carried out by British public lawyers. Amongst the honourable exceptions have been Lewis (1975), Elliott (1981) and Prosser (1997) who each focused upon aspects of the broader public law agenda in the context of broadcasting licence allocation. While Gibbons (1991) has taken the time and trouble to pursue a more wide-ranging analysis, his work has now been largely overtaken by the rapid pace of events (though a second edition of his work is due to appear in 1998). More recently still, Hitchens (1994 and 1995a) has made a significant contribution in scrutinising recent developments and indicating the need for a more thorough and considered policy review, a process to which this book is intended to contribute. In addition, Marsden (1997a and b) has begun to make a telling contribution from the perspective of competition law. However,

> The net effect of these contributions, while enlightening in many ways, is to leave largely untouched the underlying issues, focusing as they do primarily upon specific developments and occurrences rather than the broader issues and rationales which underlie the subject. Put more specifically, rather like the activities of government and the media regulators, the focus of commentators has tended to be on amendments to the institutional structure, and the outcomes of regulation and proposals for its reform rather than upon giving serious consideration to the underlying rationales for the regulatory endeavour. (Feintuck 1997c: 1.3)

Such tinkering with the fine detail is unlikely to equip us adequately to address the challenges posed by the ongoing media revolution. It seems largely futile to examine regulatory policies, mechanisms and outcomes without first reflecting upon the objectives, deriving from principles, in turn born of the rationales for intervention.

The range of rationales in play indicate immediately a significant role for the media specialist, the political scientist, economist, sociologist and many others, but the lawyer, arguably, must justify their interest, especially given the hitherto dominant tradition amongst British legal academics of confining themselves to the cataloguing or chronicling of the legal rules in play, in the absence of any contextual or conceptual analysis. However, a wider view of law can be applied.

While public lawyers clearly have an interest in the administrative law and practice applicable to an area such as media regulation, they must also place this in its constitutional context, and scrutinise legitimacy and rationality as well as mere legality. Such an approach demands not only the examination of technical rules, but also an examination of their relationship to fundamental constitutional and democratic values. It is this more holistic approach to public law that is adopted in this book. A conventional public law analysis of the institutions of media regulation can offer much, in terms of both substantive and procedural comment. However, there is a sense in which such critique becomes vacuous if not integrated with an understanding of the values which inform any such regime.

At the heart of liberal-democratic theory is a concept of citizenship, to be discussed in the specific context of media regulation in Chapter 3. If citizenship implies effective participation in society (Barbalet 1988), in an era in which effective participation has come to rely increasingly upon access to the media as the primary arena for political and cultural communication, it can be argued that access to the media, certainly in terms of receiving its output but also, arguably, in terms of inputting (see Barendt 1993: Chapter 7), has become a prerequisite of effective citizenship. Even if, as in this book, the focus is predominantly on citizen access to the media in terms only of simply receiving a diverse range of media output, the public lawyer, in addition to considering the nature of rules and norms existing in this field and the quality of the administrative process, must also recognise that equality of access to the media (as an aspect of equality of citizenship) should be utilised as a yardstick when examining existing and proposed regulatory mechanisms.

In the absence of adequate clarity regarding the rationales and objectives of regulation, it is unlikely that the policies, mechanisms and results of regulation can be analysed meaningfully. Therefore, it can be argued that it is necessary to step back from the intricacies and specifics of institutional design, and focus instead upon the justifications, principles and goals of media regulation.

The law provides standards against which the behaviour of those who govern and those who are governed can be measured, though it would be foolish to believe that the law is the whole story; lawfulness is important, but remains only one aspect of legitimacy. While the law may be changed by the government of the day provided only, in Britain, that it can command a majority in Parliament, governments are concerned with not only legality, but also legitimacy. They may remain within bounds established by the law but will seek also to maintain a public perception of legitimacy in their actions. They will wish to be seen as remaining within legitimate, as well as legal, bounds, and the former is often both much more indistinct and far-reaching than the latter. In Britain, as will be demonstrated, where the constitution is often unclear as to what constitutes legitimate action, it may be necessary to have recourse to general fundamentals of liberal-democratic theory and to often nebulous notions such as 'the rule of law' in determining legitimacy. Thus, the well-rounded public lawyer must have an awareness of both the detail of the law and the framework of institutional morality within which it operates. A broader concept of law is required.

In the mid-1980s, drawing extensively on the work of Karl Llewellyn, Harden and Lewis (1986) established a four-fold classification as the basis for their discussion of law in the context of their study of the British constitution. These four 'law jobs' move beyond a narrow definition of 'law' into a broader model that will inform the remainder of this book. In essence, Harden and Lewis note that Llewellyn identified four tasks which must be accomplished for any group, large or small, to continue in existence as a group.

The first of these is probably the easiest to understand. Dispute resolution, or 'the disposition of the trouble-case' is often viewed as the archetypal law job, and is certainly the one most immediately recognised as 'legal' by the layperson. This involves the resolution of felt grievances and disputes, and may be associated closely with the classical, British, courtroom process of the resolution of a bipartite dispute by reference to a tripartite procedure with an authoritative judge adjudicating. In the modern context, the judge in robes may be replaced by a tribunal panel or an arbitrator, but the nature of the task and process remains essentially the same. That said, the kind of polycentric dispute which may occur in an area such as media regulation may not lend itself well to this model of dispute resolution.

The second law job Harden and Lewis identify is referred to as 'preventive channelling'. This involves a range of procedures and institutions, ranging from the customary to the innovatory (the latter perhaps taking legislative form) which organise individual and collective activity to produce and maintain, in Llewellyn's terms 'a going order instead of a disordered series of collisions' (quoted in Harden and Lewis 1986: 67). Though by no means the exclusive domain of the lawyer, the establishment of norms and institutional structures for the ordering of social activity is central to their activity.

The third law job, 'the constitution of groups', concerns the establishment and allocation of authority. This establishes the location of legitimate institutional power, for example of rule-making, arbitration or executive power, and furthers the broader objective of organising social life.

The final law job relates closely to, but extends beyond, the second and third. 'Goal orientation' involves processes for determining the desired direction for society to take, either very broadly or more specifically, for example identifying the direction to be taken by the media.

A discussion of media regulation necessarily involves the consideration of all aspects of this 'extended concept of law', but even then, it remains necessary to be aware of a broader phenomenon that is much harder to define. The kind of powers and functions envisaged by the law jobs cannot always be defined by reference to 'black letter' law – lawyers' shorthand for the law as found written in statute and judgements. Rather, it is often possible to find examples of norms and standards being developed outside the scope of, or within the open texture of, the framework of 'hard law'. The concept of the 'living law' (identified by Ehrlich 1922) helpfully encompasses such practices, identifying them as legal (within the scope of Llewellyn's definition) despite the absence of the trappings of formal legal form.

Thus, the regulatory power enjoyed by the BBFC, ASA or PCC in relation to the media has a legal nature, is clearly within the scope of the law jobs, despite the absence of any apparent legal foundation in terms of statute, as is the pattern of interventions in newspaper takeovers and mergers, in which the development of norms and practices through the exercise of discretion is much more significant than the widely drawn statutory measures which grant the discretion. Similarly, the influence exercised by government ministers, or the informal accommodations they reach with the 'media establishment', take on the characteristics of law, in terms of the law jobs, without having any black letter law basis. The allocation of power, and its exercise, often through essentially corporatist arrangements with no apparent legal foundation, are just as much the concern of the public lawyer as the courtroom process of judicial review (Birkinshaw *et al.* 1990). It is just as important that those who exercise the public power of regulation should be accountable as those who exercise the power of the media.

– 1.4.2   THE LAW AND THE CONSTITUTION –

It is possible to view a constitution in at least three different ways.

First, and most obviously, it can be viewed as a map of power, of utility when it is necessary to navigate the organs of the state. It allows the identification of the location of various powers, such as those of the legislature, the executive and the judiciary. In this sense, the constitution can be viewed essentially as fulfilling a 'descriptive' function.

In addition to this descriptive aspect, further scrutiny of the constitution will reveal that it also contains a 'normative' element. By this is meant that in addition to identifying the location of various powers, the constitution will also establish limits on the legitimate exercise of power. For example, the constitution may specify matters on which the legislature may not make law, or establish principles which the executive and legislature must not breach. It may also lay down special procedures which must be pursued for the revision of the constitution itself, or for the revision of the make-up of the legislature.

In addition to their descriptive and normative elements, constitutions contain material which is not entirely descriptive or normative. The kinds of constitutional rights enshrined in the US Bill of Rights may be considered normative in nature, in that they do suggest limits on the legitimate activity of the executive, legislature and judiciary. However, they are also subject to judicial interpretation, and in carrying out this interpretative function the judiciary may appear to act in pursuit of a broad set of values which underlie the constitution. In this third sense, the constitution can be said to be 'value laden', and within all the jurisdictions which will be considered in this book, broadly speaking, a common set of familiar liberal-democratic values can be found to underlie them.

The particular form of the constitution of any state will be determined by its history, and in particular is likely to be subject to change dramatically following a major constitutional upheaval or crisis such as revolution, civil war, occupation by a foreign power, or the gaining of independence from a colonial power. In Britain's case, it is peculiarly difficult to discern the precise content of the constitution, the difficulty deriving to some extent from the relative stability that has existed in British constitutional arrangements since the seventeenth century. Unlike its European neighbours, Britain has encountered no significant constitutional crisis in the last three-hundred years, and as such, has had the opportunity to avoid the necessity of a significant review of the constitutional arrangements.

While the avoidance of revolution and the like might be considered to be a benefit, the resulting absence of a recent fundamental reappraisal of the constitution makes life difficult for those seeking to understand the British constitution at the end of the twentieth century. A bill of rights, dated 1688, may be thought to be rather past its sell-by date, given the degree of social, political and economic change in the intervening three-hundred years, and indeed the Labour Government elected in 1997 has plans to introduce the ECHR into domestic law by way of filling part of the apparent gap (Home Office 1997a). Clearly, other acts of Parliament and international treaties also carry constitutional significance, and the European Communities Act of 1972, committing Britain to membership of the EEC, has resulted in the transfer to the European institutions of a degree of competence, in certain areas specified by the Treaty of Rome and now those of Maastricht and Amsterdam.

In addition to these statutory and international documents, judge-made law, via both statutory interpretation and common law development, serves in Britain to fill many of the gaps found in the documentary material. Indeed, it can be argued that in the British context, judicial interpretation is a more significant aspect of the constitution than elsewhere, given the greater scope for manoeuvre granted to the judiciary in the absence of a clear, modern, constitutional statement. However, on the other hand, the apparent latitude provided for judges by the flexibility inherent in the unwritten constitution may also prove problematic. The lack of clarity in their constitutional position and adherence to the principle of the supremacy of Parliament (under which British judges are unable to review the propriety of acts of Parliament against constitutional standards) has led to the British judiciary enjoying a far less buoyant position and a far less creative role than, say, their US counterparts.

A final 'source' of the constitution in Britain is a series of unwritten, and sometimes ambiguous, constitutional norms or conventions which can be said to illustrate, and represent a manifestation of, the values underlying the constitution. The central one of these is adherence to the concept of the Rule of Law, frequently identified, along with Parliamentary Supremacy, as one of the twin pillars on which the British constitutional arrangements rest. Debate over the meaning of the Rule of Law in contemporary Britain persistently starts from the writing of A. V. Dicey, whose work at the end of the nineteenth century took place in the context of very different social, economic and governmental traditions to those that have predominated in the latter half of this century. Attempts to clarify the concept's meaning have largely come from academics rather than judges, and although writers such as Harden and Lewis (1986) have sought to identify a contemporary meaning for it, ascribing to it the qualities of a 'principle of institutional morality' rather than mere lawfulness, the concept continues to lack clarity and specificity in use (see Jowell 1994).

Though all of these various documents and concepts provide fragments of the information to be found, typically, in the constitutional documents of other states, Britain has no single, modern constitutional document. Thus, the common reference to an 'unwritten constitution' is both partially accurate and partially misleading. Some of Britain's constitutional arrangements can be found in writing, though others, especially the often inexplicit conventions, can prove difficult to pin down with any confidence. The Labour Government elected in 1997 proposes to introduce wide-ranging reform, which may significantly change the constitutional landscape. In addition to the devolution of certain powers to Scotland and Wales, reform of the House of Lords and the incorporation of the ECHR into domestic law, the government also proposes to have Parliament pass a Freedom of Information Act (FOIA), which, in granting citizens legal rights of access to certain government-held information, may be viewed as having constitutional implications.

An FOIA appears to promise improved access to information for citizens and media alike yet, ultimately, it must be viewed as a potentially important adjunct to, rather than a substitute for, a pluralistic and universally accessible media: for most citizens, their information will continue to come predominantly from the media rather than directly from individual requests for information under an FOIA. Whether the programme of constitutional reforms proposed by the Blair government serves to bring any greater degree of clarity in terms of fundamental constitutional values remains to be seen, though it is not entirely without promise. Crucial to this agenda, however, will be the role to be played by the judiciary, who have the power to breath life into the reforms or leave them stillborn.

While public lawyers may be unimpressed by this brief overview of the constitution, others may at this stage need some clarification as to why this is relevant to the regulation of the media. In essence, it is important to be aware of the normative and value-laden aspects of the constitution in that they, as the embodiment of liberal-democratic values, provide the framework within which media activity and regulatory activity take place. Where administrative law, in the form of Broadcasting Acts, other specific measures and delegated powers associated with bodies such as the Independent Television Commission (ITC) are in place, so this law operates within the parameters established by the constitution. At a broader level, and especially where regulation takes place without the presence of explicit hard law, the values or expectations, and hence the objectives of the regulatory regime(s), though specific to the media, must derive from more general norms and expectations of an essentially constitutional nature, and legitimacy of action must be measured against these standards. In particular, as identified above, legitimacy (as opposed to mere legality) of action presupposes limited (as opposed to unlimited) power, and accountability in the exercise of power, which are in themselves fundamental assumptions attaching to the exercise of power in a liberal democracy.

 Chapters 4, 5 and 6 will all consider specific examples of media regulation in which the law is implicated. This will be treated in the context described above, and will address both procedural law and the substance of decisions. Judicial review actions in Britain tend to focus on procedure, with judges traditionally being reluctant to strike down administrative action on substantive grounds. However, it can be argued that an exclusively, or even predominantly, procedural approach to review, as important as procedures are, may not reflect adequately the underlying values and expectations that should inform regulation in an area such as the media. In Britain, such principles may need updating to mesh successfully with the expectations and environment of the modern era. It seems likely that a clarification and reassertion of broad constitutional values must be combined with specific, statutory measures (both substantive and procedural) in pursuit of defined goals, if media regulation is to be a worthwhile enterprise in the current climate.

As commentators such as Barendt (1993) and Humphreys (1996) illustrate, it is necessary to view apparently narrow aspects of media regulation in their constitutional context, as it is invariably the case that historical circumstance, combined with constitutional form and tradition, will have established the environment in which media regulation takes place. When consideration is given to media regulation in other jurisdictions (as in Chapter 6), it becomes especially important to remain aware of the different constitutional backgrounds and traditions to regulatory activity.

Certain key themes and issues have emerged in the course of this introduction. Central to these is the need to identify and articulate with clarity the underlying rationales for media regulation, for without such definition, reform of the regulatory system is likely to achieve little of substance in relation to preserving or furthering democratic values. The degree and pace of change in the media identified in this chapter indicate the need to break with the tradition of ad hoc, incremental and reactive reform, and to move beyond what Negrine (1994: 97) refers to as 'prescriptions . . . set out in previous eras'. The extent to which this proves possible will depend on conceptual clarity, especially in relation to the particularly nebulous and slippery issue, 'the public interest'.

CHAPTER 2

The Market, Public Service and Regulation

– 2.1 THE MARKET AND PUBLIC SERVICE –

Implicit in the foregoing discussion has been a tension that will run through the rest of this work, namely the struggle within broadcasting between market and public-service values. A failure to identify, acknowledge and address this tension is likely to undermine any attempt to regulate. The public-service tradition in Western Europe has served to insulate the media partially from what are perceived as the worst excesses of market forces. Certainly, European (and especially British) television output as a whole is generally compared favourably in terms of diversity and quality with the US equivalent, which has developed in the absence of a public-service broadcasting tradition. That the insulation from market forces is only partial, however, is evidenced by the experience of Italy (see Chapter 6) and also perhaps suggested by the arrival of Channel 5 in Britain, though this example must be viewed alongside the continued existence of four other channels which remain very much within public-service traditions.

It can be argued that the British experience demonstrates that there is not necessarily any evidence to suggest that the arrival of a competitive market in broadcasting brings identifiable benefits. Indeed, the experience of the BBC/ITV duopoly suggests that the arrangement resulted in positive outcomes in terms of producing an enviable range of quality programmes, even if it remained within a culturally 'mainstream' tradition, subsequently extended somewhat by the arrival of Channel 4.

Despite this relative success, the potential for privatising the BBC, the archetypal public-service broadcaster, was actively considered by the Conservative administrations of the 1980s, alongside the privatisation of other utilities such as gas, electricity, water and telecommunications (see Chapter 5). While the evidence of some of these privatisations suggests that benefits may have accrued to citizens (as consumers) as regards extended choice, reduced costs and even improved quality of service provision, there seems every chance that no such benefits would accrue from a wholly privatised broadcasting system, at least unless substantial and effective regulation were to accompany such a reform. In particular, in relation to the media, a particularly high premium is placed on diversity of output, and though there is no reason in principle why a privatised broadcasting system should not continue to provide a range of diverse, high-quality products, such an outcome would not be assured by market forces. Indeed, the opposite, in the form of homogenous, lowest-common-denominator programming has largely been the outcome of the American experience of minimalist regulation.

The commercial potential of broadcasting is clear, and, in countries such as the USA has been acknowledged from the earliest days of radio. In the UK, however, broadcasting remained an entirely not-for-profit enterprise until the introduction of commercial television in the mid-1950s. Until that time, British broadcasting, in the form of the BBC, had been unashamedly imbued with a particular, Reithian set of 'public-service' values: to inform, educate and entertain. While the introduction of ITV merely replaced a BBC monopoly with a duopoly, with commercial broadcasters still heavily constrained by public-service requirements imposed by the legislation and regulation of the time, the more recent flourishing of national and local commercial television and radio, and the further expansion of channels provided by the introduction of satellite and cable broadcasting, have posed severe challenges to the comfortable public-service ethos which used to predominate.

There is a sense in which this is nothing new, given, for example, the launch of BBC Radio 1 as a direct response to the popularity of offshore, 'pirate' pop music stations in the 1960s, and although pirate broadcasting did not come to be legitimised in the way in which Italy's pirate local commercial television channels eventually were (see Chapter 6), the role of unlicensed, commercial broadcasters in forcing the pace of change upon official, national, public-service broadcasters is closely paralleled. It is legitimate to ask what role remains for the BBC, or a broadcaster of that kind, in an era where the range of channels is potentially unlimited and an increasing number of viewers may see little point in funding an organisation via a licence fee when they can, instead, choose what they want to watch (and pay for), and, via video on demand or near-video on demand, when they want to watch it, from the range of commercial channels on offer.

In the past, the quality of commercial broadcasting in Britain has been guaranteed to some extent by regulation, demanding a minimum range of programmes and imposing limits on advertising time, but also, arguably more significantly, by the ITV companies having a monopoly over television advertising revenue. The absence of competition for this source of income has allowed the ITV companies, though arguably producing more populist programming than the BBC, to maintain high production standards and to compete directly with the BBC in the medium-brow markets and in sports coverage. It is not the purpose of this book to consider the quality or relative merits of programming as such, though it is important to take on board that the predominance of cheap, down-market programmes is a consequence feared by many who view with trepidation the increasing commercialism seen and predicted in television.

As has already been noted, television is a central, arguably *the* central, entertainment medium for most of the British and indeed Western population. To the (presumable) delight of those who are entertained by chat shows, quizzes, soap operas and sport, an era is promised in which this diet will be constantly available, uninterrupted by news, current affairs or 'serious' programmes with informative or educative intentions. In fact, of course, it is already pretty much here, given that with the assistance only of a remote control, the British viewer could watch continuously, all day, every day, carefully avoiding any programme which aspired to anything more than straightforward entertainment.

However, in an environment in which an increasing number of commercial broadcasters must compete between themselves for advertising revenue, and assuming that the potential amount of such revenue does not grow proportionately to the number of commercial broadcasters, the battle for slices of the advertising cake is likely to become increasingly hard-fought and destructive. Audience maximisation will be the key to attracting advertising, and if what holds or increases audience share is soap opera, violence, topless darts, or chat shows, then that is what commercial broadcasters will offer; if such programming is cheap to produce, so much the better. For unique products with wide-ranging popular appeal, such as major sporting events and movie premieres, commercial broadcasters will be able to increase revenue as a result of both associated advertising and increased receipts from subscribers or pay-per-view users. Such charging at the point of use will mean, however, that the product will be available only to those who can afford it.

There may well remain niche markets for broadcasters offering more wide-ranging and challenging cerebral fare, but simple economics suggest that they will prove expensive for the viewer if supplied on a subscription basis, in view of the likely relatively small take-up. Given their limited appeal, it may be difficult to justify their funding or support from the public purse. The end result of this process is that while cheap popular programming will be relatively readily available, informative and educative programming and broadcasting of 'special' events will remain available only to those who can afford to pay premium-rate subscriptions. Access to the media will therefore reflect and reinforce social stratification.

This is not to argue that all viewers should be forced to take in an unremitting diet of wholesome, informing, educating and entertaining programmes, as provided by the BBC in its monopoly years. This appears, to modern eyes, overly paternalistic and also to ignore the realities of the digital age. Now that we have multi-channel technology available, there is, to borrow one of BSkyB's advertising lines, 'No turning back', and if public-service broadcasting is to survive, it must do so in the context of a mixed-media economy. However, if those charged with regulating the media do not wish to end up at the market-driven destination just described, with the broadcast media simply a buttress to social hierarchy and furthering social exclusion, offering choice only to those who can afford it, then they must consider the way forward carefully and look at the map and compass and the alternative roads ahead, if they are not to find themselves following an itinerary that inevitably leads them to a destination that few would visit voluntarily.

– 2.2 REGULATION: WHY, HOW AND TO WHAT END –

In adopting an analytical perspective that focuses on 'the social values at stake' (Blumler 1992: 5) in broadcasting regulation, Blumler identifies three current issues that might impact upon these values. First, a set of questions as to how and to what ends the expanding private sector in television can be regulated, and how effective such regulation can be. Second, the direction to be taken by public-sector broadcasters, whether and how to continue to provide a comprehensive service or to opt for a narrower range of programming. Third, to devise mechanisms of accountability for both broadcasters and regulators, appropriate to current conditions.

Though focused on broadcasting, the issues raised in Blumler's agenda may be applied across the whole range of media, in the increasingly cross-media environment. Some of the social values at stake and the threats to them have already been indicated. The rest of this book, though declining on grounds of lack of expertise to engage except peripherally with the second area of questions, is focused closely on Blumler's first and third agenda items, and the remainder of this chapter is devoted to introducing some of the issues to be addressed, before they are examined in more concrete form in later chapters.

– 2.2.1 WHY REGULATE? –

Some of the justifications for regulating have already become apparent in the previous discussion; in particular, the threats of monopoly and of increasing commercialism should be clear. As Schiller (1996) and others have demonstrated, the privatisation of information and communication is proceeding apace, and the option for regulation merely to stand still and fail to find mechanisms to avoid the adverse consequences of commercial and technological 'progress' is not available, unless it is deemed acceptable to sacrifice citizenship and democracy to the unbridled forces of the global economy and technological revolution. The age of public-service monopoly in broadcasting has long gone, and a 'mixed economy' appears inevitable. In Dahlgren's terms, 'what is needed is re-regulation, to counteract the negative aspects of market forces and optimize the positive role they can play' (Dahlgren 1995: 15).

However, it is not sufficient to assume the existence of meaningful rationales for regulation simply in terms of reactions to perceived threats. If any regulatory regime is to prove effective in steering away from these perceived dangers and towards a more desirable position, it is crucial that the underlying rationales and positive objectives are spelled out with adequate clarity. In an era in which government is driven by a hands-off approach and promises the withdrawal of the state from traditional roles, it becomes particularly important to identify and establish justifications for continuing state intervention in the media market.

As Keane demonstrates admirably, censorship, or non-liberty of communication, can be carried out equally by either state power or corporate power (Keane 1991: Chapters 1 and 2) and, given that 'the dynamics of democracy are intimately linked to the practices of communication, and [that] societal communication increasingly takes place within the mass media' (Dahlgren 1995: 2), the exercise of such democratically significant power must be subject to accountability, whether regulation of communication is carried out by public or private power-holders.

The arguments for freedom of communication, discussed in Chapter 1, while appearing to militate against regulation, in practice lie beneath one primary justification for intervention; the implication being that effective communication depends on the effective regulation of communication. This is not as paradoxical as it might appear. Just as having two people talking simultaneously does not make for effective communication, two radio stations broadcasting on the same frequency or interfering with each other's transmission is equally unsatisfactory. Thus, much state regulation of broadcasting from the 1920s until relatively recently was premised largely on the necessity to avoid cross-channel interference via the allocation (licensing) of adequately separated frequencies within the available, finite spectrum. As has already been indicated, this 'frequency scarcity' rationale for intervention has lost much, or possibly all, of its currency in the modern era in which digital compression and developments in cable and satellite have vastly, almost infinitely, increased the potential for the number of channels. Of course, no such justification ever applied in relation to regulation of the press, and it is therefore perhaps helpful, in the search for fundamental rationales for regulation, to consider the typology established by Siebert *et al.* (1956) in relation to the press.

In their seminal work, Siebert *et al.* offer a typology of media systems – authoritarian, totalitarian, libertarian and social responsibility – and demonstrate the historical relationship between forms of government and approaches to regulation of the press. Both Humphreys (1996) and Negrine (1994) point towards a failure in this typology, developed from an American perspective, to reflect the significance of public-service models in Europe when applied to broadcasting. Equally, however, both testify to the significance of this work more than forty years on.

Siebert *et al.* establish the authoritarian model as relating to an essentially pre-democratic era, in which the press was either owned or heavily regulated by a ruling class or group. In Humphreys' terms (1996: 8) this amounts to the effective subservience of the press to the state. The 'totalitarian' model is associated by Siebert *et al.*, writing in the Cold War era, with direct state control of the media, as in Nazi Germany or the Soviet Union.

The final two categories established by Siebert *et al.* are more familiar to modern, Western eyes. The libertarian model represents a situation in which the media are lightly regulated and little licensing or censorship exists. This is most closely associated with a free marketplace of ideas, and views press freedom and the ability to make profit from it essentially as a property right. The social responsibility model, however, emphasises instead the role of the media, as a public resource, in 'informing the debate'. This appears to take on additional significance in relation to broadcast rather than printed media, perhaps because of the extra power attributed to broadcasting, but it also links to the frequency scarcity justification for intervention. If the (broadcast) media are to serve society effectively, they must be both diverse and regulated, thereby justifying both regulation of ownership and/or public ownership. There is a marked shift between the libertarian and social responsibility models, the former emphasising the private-property basis for press freedom, the latter prioritising the public or collective interest in the media. In the present context of technological change and the concurrent hegemony of market economics, Humphreys (1996) identifies a switch back to the historically earlier, libertarian model of media regulation.

While the work of Siebert *et al.* is focused predominantly on the press, their work, like that of Barbrook (1995) in relation to the French media, is helpful in identifying historical trends. However, it is necessary in this connection to

LIVERPOOL JOHN MOORES UNIVERSITY
LEARNING SERVICES

differentiate between the printed and broadcast media. The social responsibility model has significantly informed the development of public-service broadcasting and the rather heavier regulation of broadcasting in general than is found in relation to the press. The justifications for this higher level of regulation for broadcasters are expanded upon in Chapter 3, but appear, in brief, to be premised largely upon the extra power attributed to broadcasting as a result of its accessibility, immediacy and intrusiveness. For the moment, it is sufficient to note that Barendt (1993) identifies at least part of the justification for the heavier regulation of broadcasting as resulting from the relative newness of television and radio, which has presented governments with an opportunity, historically long gone in relation to printed media, to regulate actively. Thus, as Barendt goes on to demonstrate, the heavier regulation of broadcasting compared with the press is largely contingent upon historical circumstance, constitutional form and tradition, rather than resting upon clearly defined principles.

What is evident, however, from all the writing is the truth of Herman and McChesney's observation that regulation of the media has always been viewed as a legitimate activity for government, to which we might add that only the forms of intervention, as opposed to the fact of it, change, and that significant deregulation is therefore likely to be more apparent than real. That said, Humphreys (1996 and 1997a) expounds convincingly on a claim that recent reforms, especially in European media markets, have been driven by a process of 'competitive deregulation', with jurisdictions reforming regulation so as to attract or maintain levels of inward investment (see Chapter 6). This would be consistent with what McQuail (1992: 143) identifies as 'A more general "liberalizing" and deregulation political-economic trend', though the real extent of the withdrawal of the state should perhaps be treated somewhat sceptically; experience tends to suggest that the state never withdraws, but simply re-forms, replacing, perhaps, formal regulatory powers with informal and less accountable networks of influence (see Birkinshaw et al. 1990). If significant deregulation might therefore be unlikely, 're-regulation', adopting new forms in line with currently dominant political norms and expectations, is much more plausible. However, this is not to say that an answer to Dahlgren's plea for re-regulation already exists. In the absence of close consideration of underlying values, principles, objectives and policies, and the analysis of outcomes, any system of media regulation will quickly become anachronistic in a period of rapid change. It can be argued that incremental change as a result of ad hoc responses to changes in media structures has typified British and other systems of media regulation, leaving a pressing need now for a more fundamental review.

Having identified a number of different historical traditions in media regulation, it is now necessary to attempt to summarise the particular justifications for regulation currently in play, all of which, in one form or another, have been flagged up earlier in this or the previous chapter. These can be reduced, in essence, to four rationales:

1. effective communication;
2. diversity, both political and cultural;
3. economic justifications; and
4. public service.

'Effective communication' has already been discussed in the context of frequency scarcity, but more generally, the freedom of speech ideal manifested, for example, in the US First Amendment and the ECHR (though at present implicit and limited in Britain), suggests that freedom of expression and communication (both transmission and receipt) are central to democratic expectations. In the modern context, in which meaningful freedom of communication depends heavily upon access to mass media, effective communication has come to rely increasingly upon the media. Were all communication to be channelled or controlled exclusively through state-controlled media, this would run counter to the liberal-democratic ideal of freedom of communication. However, the same argument would seem to apply were the media to be effectively under the control of one or a handful of media owners; a situation of private monopoly or oligopoly.

Effective communication therefore appears to imply not only unobstructed communication but also, in the interests of democracy, diverse communication. In Britain, however, almost two-thirds of national newspaper circulation is shared between two news groups, *News Corporation* (37 per cent) and the *Mirror Group* (26 per cent) (DNH 1995a: Annexe A). If at the same time such a group were to have substantial holdings in broadcasting, albeit within limits established by the Broadcasting Acts, this could further restrict the range of views presented in the media and therefore effective communication. If, in addition, the same group were to control technological gateways in distribution, such as those present in the DTT market, then a still more virulent form of the problem would be presented. Given that effective communication – whether approached via arguments from truth, self-fulfilment or from citizen participation – appears to require the presentation of a wide range of views in the media, then domination of the media by one or a few players, who may control editorial content, threatens effective communication simply because it threatens diversity in the viewpoints which can be transmitted and received, and thereby may undermine the potential for citizens to engage effectively in a process of triangulation.

This line of reasoning leads naturally into a second identifiable under-lying rationale for media regulation, namely diversity. This is clearly related to effective communication rationales, but may also be presented as a separate, freestanding justification which in itself contains two strands.

The first of these connects with the point just made. Political debate, supposedly the lifeblood of democracy, appears to need a free flow of ideas via which informed participation can take place. If one or two owners dominate press ownership and use this position to control editorial content, there is likely to be limited scope for heterodox views. In Britain, with the domination of newspapers by two groups and with only 3 per cent of national circulation (DNH 1995a: Annexe A), in the form of *The Guardian* and *The Observer*, of an arguably left of centre orientation, it is highly debatable whether any meaningful political diversity exists in the news-paper market. However, as McQuail (1992: 142) demonstrates, referring to Hoffmann-Riem's writing, 'the diversity principle lies at the heart of broadcasting arrangements in Europe', at least as manifested in the various public-service broadcasting traditions.

A note of caution is needed regarding the term 'diversity', which is used here to refer to a range of perspectives reflected in media output as a whole; in this sense, 'pluralism' in content is used synonymously in this book. However, on occasion, 'pluralism' or 'diversity' of media ownership will also be referred to, and, particularly when possible relationships between ownership patterns in the media and the range of views reflected in output are discussed, the reader must be careful to ensure that the correct meaning is understood. As will be discussed later, there *may* possibly be strong contingent relationships between diversity of ownership and diversity of output, or between monopoly of ownership and homogeneity of product in terms of political perspective or lack of diversity in programme range, but such relationships remain contingent rather than necessary. In addition, care should be taken to distinguish between what McQuail (1992: 149) refers to as 'horizontal diversity', or 'the number of different programmes or programme types available to the viewer/listener at any given time' and 'vertical diversity' in terms of the 'number of different programmes (or types) offered by a channel (or set of channels) over the entire schedule'; the latter is intended throughout this book.

Political diversity in output overlaps with, but is reasonably distinct from, a second strand, cultural diversity, where the special remit provided to Channel 4 to cater for minority interests serves to identify part of the issue. There would be wide-ranging agreement that the provision of programming relevant to varying groups, based on race, gender, age, sexual orientation or other social variants, is a positive development. 'Alternative' or non-mainstream television is thought to serve a particular function in reducing social exclusion, and this essentially provides the justification for the insertion of specific requirements to this effect in Channel 4's licence. Proponents of choice would presumably support variety as an end in itself, while others would identify the underlying objective as being the reduction of social exclusion. From whichever perspective, diversity in media output appears to be a positive objective.

In an international context, the cultural diversity justification for regulation takes on a further dimension, with the identification of the mass media as a crucial factor in the continuation or demise of national culture. In Britain, S4C and certain BBC services cater for the Welsh language, while in other countries, for example in France, cultural imperialism, in the form of mostly US cinema and broadcast media, is viewed by some as a threat to individual national and linguistic cultures. The same phenomenon can be seen in a still more virulent form in those states positioned geographically in the USA's 'back yard' (Herman and McChesney 1997: Chapter 5).

This might be considered a particularly dangerous threat in developing countries, but it can also be observed in smaller, highly developed Western states. In a small country such as the Netherlands, with a language little spoken in the wider world, the requirements of international trade and distinctiveness from its mighty neighbour Germany have both contributed to a high degree of education in and exposure to English, and it is now possible that, within a few generations, Dutch may become very much a second language to English, much as Welsh is in much of Wales or still more as Scots Gaelic is even in the Western Isles.

As Thomas (1995: 179) states, 'A language at a given time is kept in existence by a group of people speaking to each other in that shared set of terms; and clearly in modern conditions, a language that does not have access to the media is doomed, for the media are an extension of people speaking to each other'. He goes on to say that the existence of media in the minority language 'normalizes the status of minority-language speakers, [and] raises their self-esteem'. Thus, the high priority attached by linguistic minorities to the existence of media in their language, for example in Wales or Catalonia, is not surprising. Thomas believes, however, that the proliferation of broadcasting channels as a consequence of digitalisation may in practice serve only to marginalise, or further marginalise, minority-language services, given the degree of investment that will be required to establish services in the new, digital medium.

While the French demonstrate more resistance than most to Anglophone cultural imperialism (Americanisation), the first faltering steps have been taken by the EU towards a cross-European response to this phenomenon. The Television Without Frontiers Directive of 1989 (Directive 89/552), in addition to seeking to establish common transmission across Member States, also requires Member States to ensure that broadcasters transmit a proportion of European-produced programmes, and indeed a 'predominance of European work'. The Advanced Television Standards Directive (Directive 95/47) adds to this in terms of seeking to harmonise technical standards for television receiver equipment. Inevitably, however, in as linguistically fragmented an organisation as the EU (even discounting non-recognised, minority languages), and given the cultural diversity across Europe, a meaningful internal market in broadcasting probably remains something of an ideal rather than a reality.

Thus, regulation for cultural diversity remains as a significant justification for state and international intervention in the media. It seems unlikely that, even if widespread access to the information superhighway occurs, this phenomenon will contribute to such diversity. On a global scale, access will remain markedly unequal; it will tend to produce fragmented rather than mass media; it is likely to be (US) English-language dominated; there is no guarantee of diversity in terms of worthwhile products. There are, of course, arguments to the contrary, but the issues just identified seem powerful enough to suggest that the need to defend cultural diversity will not be diminished by advances in information technology; indeed, the concerns might reasonably be expected to be heightened.

Before leaving diversity as a justification for regulation, it is necessary to note the potential tension between this justification and intervention premised on paternalistic concerns regarding the nature of material, especially as regards sexually explicit and violent material. The range of material which may be broadcast in any jurisdiction may be significantly limited, as in Britain, by reference to concerns regarding 'taste and decency' or in particular the protection of minors. Clearly, such censorship can be viewed as cutting across the objective of diversity, and it should therefore be expected that such a power will be exercised accountably.

In addition to the effective communication and diversity rationales for intervention, a third thread in current justifications for media regulation can be clearly identified. Defences of the market economy, and the competition law intended to support it, are based upon perceived benefits that accrue from the operation of competitive markets. It is claimed that markets are efficient, when compared with other delivery mechanisms, at delivering what society wants or needs. However, the demands of profit-producing cost-efficiency may run counter to expectations of social justice. This factor, in relation to public services, and especially those services to which all have an entitlement or need as a prerequisite of effective citizenship, may require heavy intervention in markets, or even the replacement of market mechanisms, for the delivery of those public services which can be characterised as 'public goods'. This issue will be addressed further in Chapter 3; it is sufficient to note for the moment that in an age of payment-card facilities for subscription or pay-per-view services, the extent to which broadcasting meets the definition of a public good is debatable. However, as discussed shortly, there also remains a significant public-service element attached to the media, especially broadcast media, which appears to justify continued intervention in media markets.

As has been suggested earlier, the perceived economic benefits which accrue to the country as a whole from flourishing media industries also appear to be influential in determining government policy towards media regulation. Thus, a recurrent theme in the British government's 1995 White Paper on media ownership (DNH 1995a) was the national economic interest in allowing and encouraging British media players to develop in the international media market; to develop national 'champions' equipped to compete in the international tournament. However, this growth of British-based media giants, large enough to play effectively on the international stage, must in turn be viewed with caution, given the threat this phenomenon may pose to diversity in the British market.

The tensions between different versions of economic rationales for intervention, for example between the nurturing of national champions and the preservation of domestic competition, can be seen in the legal framework, and in particular in the media-specific measures which supplement or modify the underlying general framework of competition law. In essence, the thrust of these measures can be seen to be the amelioration of the effects of commercial activity in so far as these impact adversely upon the perceived public-service values of the media, and in particular broadcasting.

Humphreys (1996: Chapter 4) demonstrates clearly how different versions of public-service broadcasting have existed across Europe, indicating that the Reithian model is not the only manifestation of a public-service ethos. The lowest common denominator across these various models appears to be a commitment to delivering 'a wide-ranging quality service to the whole population' (117) though Humphreys also identifies non-commercialism as an essential common aspect of public-service broadcasting systems. This is not to say that public-service broadcasting may not include a commercial element: the British experience of ITV demonstrates that, as opposed to the audience maximisation model of the USA, it has been possible to have a commercial television service competing with the archetypal public-service broadcaster (the BBC) but competing in terms of quality of programming rather than audience maximisation. Whether ITV programming will retain its quality and range in the face of increased competition for advertising revenue is a question that has already been raised.

Whether a viable model of public-service broadcasting can be developed that will continue to flourish in an increasingly commercial environment, supported by the politically dominant market-oriented views of the age, is a key matter for debate. As Blumler notes, public-service broadcasters may be torn between two equally risky options: 'On the one hand, they may be tempted to try to offer a fully comprehensive service, even when diminished resources could limit their chances of doing that well. On the other hand, they will not wish to slip into the marginal role of merely filling whatever gaps are left untended by the commercial broadcasters' (Blumler 1992: 4). However, this debate must in itself be placed in the context of competing underlying rationales for state intervention in the media. The ongoing replacement in broadcasting of a public-service ethos by a clear commercial imperative provides, arguably, a justification in itself for regulation, though, as Negrine (1994: 200) suggests, 'once the changes are being implemented, it will be too late to retrace our steps and recapture the Reithian ideal'. However, though is implausible to propose a return to a pre-1950s model as a viable objective for regulation, it is not necessarily the case that public-service values must be discarded in their entirety, or consigned to the margins of broadcasting as in the USA.

The Labour Government, elected in the landslide victory of May 1997, has committed itself to the reduction of social exclusion, in particular via improvements in the education system. Presumably, in this context education is seen as a key to effective citizenship, but, the government must, logically, acknowledge also the significance of the media in this citizenship agenda: even the well-educated citizen would have difficulty in participating effectively in society in the absence of accessible media.

As with the still broader concept of the public interest, the extent to which public-service values are clearly identified and articulated is likely to be a key to whether meaningful objectives can be established for the regulatory regime. It is clear from the foregoing that there are inherent tensions both between and within the four basic rationales for media regulation. In particular, conflicts exist between the economic imperatives and the important public-service objective of diversity. In the terms of Congdon et al. (1995: 7), 'Profit-maximisation and political pluralism are different and not necessarily complementary objectives' and 'there can be little confidence that unregulated commercial broadcasters are much concerned to maintain pluralism . . .'.

It is unlikely that these tensions and conflicts can be resolved neatly; however, it is essential that the problems be addressed rather than ignored. Government, or arguably society, must make clear its basis for intervention and state which rationales for regulation will be prioritised, if meaningful objectives for regulation are to be defined, and if regulators are to act consistently in the pursuit of clearly defined objectives and effectively in their capacity as stewards of the public interest in the media.

– 2.2.2 How to Regulate –

If, and only if, meaningful rationales for regulatory intervention can be determined, is it possible to move on to a policy-making process which identifies objectives and establishes techniques for achieving them.

The recent history of media regulation and its reform has occurred in the context of a perceived breakdown of the public sphere (Dahlgren 1995; Blumler and Gurevitch 1995) and the intertwining of state and civil society (Keane 1991: 107; Harden and Lewis 1986). The environment thus created has allowed the growth of corporatism, or 'government by moonlight' (Birkinshaw et al. 1990) in which government and powerful private entities reach accommodations and symbiotic relationships in a secret world, hidden from public scrutiny and outside the scope of traditional account-ability mechanisms. The effects of such powerful but unaccountable relationships in an area such as the media, which touches so acutely on democratic concerns, cannot readily be quantified, given the inevitable lack of transparency in their operation. It is quite possible, however, that apparent withdrawals of the state from regulatory roles may in reality merely be the replacement of public, overt, regulatory activity by hidden, unaccountable, corporatist influence, and the secret furthering of symbiotic interests by government and the media establishment.

As is the general case in Britain, the policy-making process relating to the media has not been transparent. Indeed, it can plausibly be argued that no recognisable policy-making process has existed; certainly, Hitchens (1995a) indicates the highly reactive nature of policy decision-making in recent years, reflecting Elliot's analogy of 'chasing the receding bus' made almost fifteen years earlier (Elliot 1981). Goldberg and Verhulst (1997) note limited moves by the British Government towards addressing technological con-vergence in the early 1980s, but also a very clear reversion to a sectoral approach and a strong deregulatory approach to both broadcasting and telecommunications from 1984 onwards.

Despite the publication of numerous government White Papers in recent years – three in 1995 alone (DNH 1995a, b and c) – these have invariably amounted primarily to statements of government policy rather than rigorously argued discussions of alternatives. The review undertaken prior to the 1995 White Paper on media ownership (1995a) is correctly viewed by Hitchens (1995a) as being located firmly within the incrementalist tradition. Certainly, no clear vision of an overarching media policy along the lines suggested by Negrine (1994: 203) has been developed, and it may well be that Britain finds itself in the same situation described by Klingler (1996: 69) in relation to the USA, of seeking to apply regulatory structures and devices from the 'Bronze Age of information services' (the 1930s –1970s!) in this 'information moment'. However, the absence of clearly or rationally identified objectives has not prevented the growth of a range of regulatory institutions with an interest in the media.

On a statutory (if often discretionary basis), the generalist competition authorities (such as the MMC, OFT and the Secretary of State) carry out regulation generally triggered by structural thresholds being met, alongside both the relevant Directorates General of the European Commission, with their more behavioural focus on competition, and specialist British media-related bodies such as the ITC and the Radio Authority (RA) which exercise powers under the Broadcasting Acts. In addition, behavioural and content regulation is carried out via a range of bodies which include the ITC, RA, Oftel and the BSC, and the courts may intervene in relation to statutory and common law matters involving secrecy and breach of confidence, obscenity, blasphemy, defamation and contempt of court.

Beyond such black letter law-based mechanisms for regulation, and in addition to the market forces that regulate the structure of media markets, a further range of non-statutory or hybrid bodies also regulate behaviour and content. These include the self-regulatory PCC and ASA, the Royal Charter based BBC (though the BBC is also confined by the terms of its Licence Agreement) and the BBFC, which acts as censor on a non-statutory basis in relation to the cinema, but exercises statutory powers over home-video classification under the terms of the Video Recordings Act 1984, the latter being in itself a prime example of highly reactive regulation introduced in response to an unproven outcry, including judicial statements, regarding the impact of 'video nasties'.

A couple of particular points need to be made in relation to the above. First, as will be discussed in Chapter 5, that privacy, though the subject of statutory provision in many jurisdictions, is not so protected in Britain at present, though data-protection measures and the proposed incorporation of the ECHR may be of relevance in certain situations. Second, that it is difficult to categorise the D-notice system, by which government and the media establishment engage in a process of embargoing certain information. Though D-notices have no legal foundation, Birkinshaw (1996: 172) notes

that failure to agree to or comply with the imposition of a [
mean exclusion from the circle of trusted recipients of inforn
other words, removal from the 'cosy collusion' (Birkinshaw 199
lobby system.

The D-notice system may appear superficially to be an ex
media engaging in self-denying ordinances; however, on closer examination, especially of the underlying power coordinates, it can be viewed as an
example of the exercise by government of, in Daintith's terms (1979),
'dominium' or the exercise of influence via the use of power relationships, as
opposed to 'imperium' or exercising control via the use of formal powers.
The peculiarly British D-notice and lobby systems, symptomatic of the
problems raised by the absence of freedom of information legislation and
general lack of transparency in government, raise the crucial issue, to be
explored in Chapter 5, of the extent to which those who exercise power in
and over the media are, and should be, subject to adequate degrees of public
scrutiny and accountability.

Hoffmann-Riem (1992a: 175) establishes a bipartite model of regulatory
techniques, referring to 'imperative' regulation, or the imposition of specific
standards and requirements on the media, and 'structural' regulation,
which attempts to reflect in ownership patterns and market behaviour
certain public-service values. For the moment, however, it is perhaps more
helpful to adopt a tripartite classification, consisting of structural, behavioural and content regulation, as this better illustrates the range of distinct
approaches to regulation. In shorthand, 'content regulation' refers to
limitations being imposed on what cannot or must be broadcast or
published, while 'structural regulation' refers to limits on the extent of
that which can be owned within any market by any one corporate entity,
and, in effect, 'behavioural regulation' generally serves to limit how
property held can be used in relation to its impact on actual or potential
competitors.

Certainly, a confusing array of regulatory approaches is in evidence.
Structural regulation is commonplace and embodies the approach taken by
British competition law. The emphasis here is on corporate structure,
seeking to avoid the anti-competitive consequences of the domination of
media markets by one or more major players. However, structure rather
than behaviour has to date remained an important focal point, with an
established market share (typically 25 per cent) triggering the potential for
intervention by the authorities. By way of contrast (at least until such time
as the Competition Bill 1997 passes into law), EU competition law con-
centrates directly on effects or behaviour, with Articles 85 and 86 prohibit-
ing, respectively, 'the prevention restriction or distortion of competition'

and 'abuse of a dominant position'. While it is clear that markets require constant regulation if they are to provide the benefits attributed to them, the restrictions on ownership and use of market power established by competition law, however, only form part of the bigger regulatory picture. Behavioural and content regulation also exist, in the form of both statutory and self-regulatory schemes, as referred to above.

The apparent objectives of different parts of the regulatory regime vary between the prevention of monopoly (or perceived abuse of market power); the protection of differing versions of public-service values; the provision of choice, in terms of product, political viewpoint and cultural diversity; and the application of essentially paternalistic censorship. In practice, however, it seems that the debate over objectives has increasingly been focused on consumer choice of media product, at the expense of broader, citizen-oriented expectations such as those underlying the public-service tradition in broadcasting or the imposition of universal service obligations (USOs) in relation to utilities. Not only does this place an undue emphasis on a particular version of one rationale for regulatory intervention, but it also, in so far as it really allows consumer choice to determine the ultimate shape of the media market, may create a high degree of uncertainty as to outcomes. For example, it is unclear whether, given real choice, the consumer would ultimately be tempted most by the charms of DTT, or satellite services, or broad-band cable facilities. Traders in each might ply their wares, but ultimately this could result in an undesirable trade war, replicating in a new forum the battle of formats in the early 1980s between VHS and Betamax in the home video market, a battle which resulted in much consumer uncertainty and dissatisfaction before VHS finally won through. Though the present government is following the decision of its predecessor to facilitate the development of DTT, it is by no means certain that this is what the consumer market would or will prefer. If serious about the creation of market choice, a government may find itself, as Marsden (1997b) suggests, with no logical alternative to regulating for a range of acceptable, alternative delivery platforms, though even this must be carried out in such a way as to integrate the regulation of control of platforms alongside transmission, production and conditional access systems (CASs) as part of the larger media market.

Content regulation is also widespread. In terms specifically of standards in British public-service broadcasting, the key mechanism employed is the insertion of positive programme requirements into broadcasting licences. In addition to considering programming proposals in the process of franchise allocation (see Chapter 4), and general statutory requirements regarding political impartiality and balance, the ITC is required to ensure that the broadcasters it licenses provide 'for example, original programmes, children's programmes, religious programmes, programmes "of high quality", programmes which will appeal to a wide variety of tastes and interests' (DNH 1995a: Para. 2.11). That said, Curran and Seaton (1997: 303) note that, symptomatic of a shift in attitude towards, and change in the status of, public service broadcasting, is the fact that although the arrangements under the Broadcasting Act 1990 for the allocation of Channel 3 licences required 'quality programming', 'not only was this undefined, it only occupied two paragraphs in the Act', while 'By contrast, conditions governing the financial arrangements for the auction of franchises took up fifteen pages'. In the modern context of a mixed economy in broadcasting, such a statutory focus is perhaps inevitable, though the consequent dangers of losing sight of the underlying public-service ethos must be recognised.

Congdon et al. (1995: 70) note that 'The aim of regulation of market share is primarily to restrict influence, but it ought, within a general competition framework, to provide the necessary – though not sufficient – condition for access and for content diversity'. This is important, both in highlighting the absence of any necessary, direct connection between regulation of market share and ensuring diversity of content, and at the same time in emphasising that regulation of market share serves only as a surrogate for regulation focused unashamedly at the ultimate objective of freely available and diverse content.

It may be advisable for a degree of regulatory emphasis to be shifted to focus on market structure and perhaps behavioural aspects of control of delivery mechanisms, given the significance of technological 'gateways' in the new, digital markets. However, when focusing on this new area, the regime must remain aware of the broader market and public-service contexts and be informed by clearly identifiable objectives arising out of clearly defined rationales for intervention. To intervene is not necessarily to deny market forces, but to give effect to them in pursuit of a modern regulatory agenda. Almost nowhere does a market survive which is not regulated, and in an area such as the media, which shows such clear tendencies towards monopoly, regulation is the necessary partner of market forces if the perceived benefits of the market are to accrue. The application of different modes of regulation – structural, behavioural and content – is not in itself unreasonable but, unless co-ordinated by reference to clearly articulated guiding principles, may lead to confusion, uncertainty and a lack of direction for the regulatory system as a whole.

– 2.2.3   THE OUTCOMES OF REGULATION –

It seems reasonable to assess the success or failure of regulatory policies by comparing the outcomes achieved with whatever objectives for regulation may be derived from the underlying rationales for regulation. Regardless of regulatory output (for example, evidence of increased regulatory activity), if the results or outcomes of regulation are not consistent with the policy objectives established, and with the identified rationales for regulation, then the regulatory regime stands in need of fundamental review.

In terms of the four rationales for media regulation set out earlier (effective communication, diversity, economics and public service), some preliminary conclusions can now be drawn, focused for the moment on the second rationale, diversity, where 'diversity' is used to refer to both pluralism of ownership and its contingent relationship to diversity in the political orientation of media output. From this perspective, it might be concluded that regulation in Britain has to date failed, at least in relation to the press.

Noted earlier were both the increasing concentration of ownership and the decrease in political pluralism in the British press in the post-war era (see Humphreys 1996; Negrine 1994: Chapter 3; Seymour-Ure 1996: Chapter 3). Humphreys (1996: 76) demonstrates that in Western Europe, if the proportion of the market controlled by the two largest newspaper publishers in each country is applied as the indicator of concentration, only the French-language press in Belgium and the Irish press demonstrate concentration of ownership as great as or greater than the British press. He accounts for this largely in terms of national characteristics, that is, in particular the view taken on the role of the state in relation to the media, which in turn derives from variations in constitutional and state tradition.

If regulation for diversity can be seen to have failed in this sense, then press concentration must also be viewed in the increasingly relevant context of cross-media domination and control of television channels. It has already been stated that Rupert Murdoch's News Corporation has managed to obtain control of 37 per cent of the British national press, while his BSkyB is in effect the only player in Britain's fast-growing DTH satellite broadcasting market. That the presence of BSkyB in a consortium seeking a multiplex licence for the forthcoming DTT service was found unacceptable by the licensing authority (see Chapter 4) may be considered good news from the perspective adopted here, as it seems to avoid the extension of the group's influence into the delivery of programming in this new market. However, it should be noted that, given BSkyB's experience and expertise in relation to the decoding equipment associated with DTH satellite broadcasting, the likelihood is that a Murdoch-related company will have a major stake in the development and marketing of CAS decoder equipment, allowing the group a significant role, despite it's exclusion from the multiplex licences.

What is apparent within the British market, therefore, is an example of expansion towards a point of dominance, not only within individual media markets such as the press or DTH satellite television, but also across the overall market. Not only this but, if unchecked, Murdoch has the potential to control if not the means of carriage (multiplexes), then the means of receipt of programmes by the viewer. Clearly, based on the experience of the British press, if dominance of this kind is permitted, there is absolutely no guarantee that more media will result in more or even existing levels of diversity, in either a political or cultural sense.

A similar phenomenon can be seen in Italy, with the growth of Silvio Berlusconi's Fininvest empire, to the extent that there, the control of the media was believed to be connected with Berlusconi's temporary rise to the position of the country's premier. This will be explored further in Chapter 6, but it should be noted here that the Italian experience should serve as a warning as to the necessity to ensure that regulation moves beyond the 'symbolic-ritualistic' function which Hoffmann-Riem (in Blumler (ed.) 1992: 198) associates with Italy. Though, as will be demonstrated in Chapter 6, Germany also has its examples, Berlusconi and Murdoch represent Europe's two prime examples of the ability to develop cross-media empires which can not only exert dominant influence within individual sectors such as the press and television, but also grow to the size where they threaten overall domination of the national media market taken as a whole, and are able also to exert considerable power on an international basis.

It would be wrong, however, to assume that the above demonstrates the total failure of the media regulation regime in Britain. Certainly, there is little evidence of diversity being extended, and growing concentration of ownership appears to pose a significant threat to perceived economic benefits attaching to markets. In addition, as access to media output via satellite and cable technology becomes increasingly significant, so the risk of social exclusion from the democratic benefits presented by the media increases. However, though this latter threat is increasingly imminent, much of mainstream broadcast cultural and political output is still at present effectively free at the point of use, and the range of programming available amounts to a reasonably good standard in terms of public-service values. There must be significant doubts, however, as to whether the regulatory structure will withstand the further shocks of increased technological development and convergence, and greater growth of cross-media empires.

It is clear though that the track record to date should not necessarily inspire optimism in this respect.

The nature of the ongoing media revolution appears to demand a reorientation of the regulatory endeavour towards structural and behavioural objectives. In addressing this issue, however, regulators and policy-makers must remain aware that if the ultimate objective is a freely available, citizenship-enhancing diversity in media output, it is democratically legitimate (and probably necessary), if not politically fashionable, to employ the kind of imperative, content-oriented controls to which Hoffmann-Riem refers. There is no doubt that structural and behavioural modes of regulation fit more easily with the dominant market paradigm, yet in relation to citizenship-related objectives, they can serve only as a surrogate for devices aimed directly at the apparent main objective: diversity.

CHAPTER 3

In Search of the Public Interest

– 3.1 THE COMPETING VALUES –

The various rationales and objectives for regulatory intervention outlined in Chapter 2 may seem contradictory and inconsistent. They appear to start from different bases, pull in different directions, exhibit tension between each other and reach conflicting conclusions. In part, these contradictions are merely an accident of history, a reflection of the piecemeal way in which policy has responded to the historical development of different industries as opposed to 'the product of rational differentiation between media within the framework of an integrated plan' (Curran and Seaton 1997: 329). However, the very fact that no planned, medium- or long-term media policy or planning process has existed (Hitchens 1995a) appears to arise out of the failure to resolve inherent tensions and identify if not a desirable destination, then at least a general direction in which to travel. The central thrust of this chapter is to seek to assist in the identification of a meaningful, overarching rationale for regulation of the media, to clarify or replace what has been the nearest thing as yet to serve as a guiding principle, the concept of 'the public interest'.

Much regulatory activity, not only of the media, but also for example of utilities, is justified by reference to a claim of the public interest. It might be expected that this basic justification would be clarified by reference to objectives that are deemed to further this concept. However, where the concept is itself inadequately defined, it is difficult to identify objectives with adequate specificity and still more difficult to assess whether outcomes are meeting the various criteria which may be embodied in 'the public interest'.

The term 'public interest' is used in relation to the entire range of media regulation issues. From particular issues such as privacy and media intrusion, through to general matters of the relationship between the state and the media, something called 'the public interest' appears to have informed the policy of all British governments. Even in terms of a fairly specific issue such as privacy, as will be seen in Chapter 5, it is not easy to be certain what the public interest demands, though the concept is certainly not coterminous with what the public, or certain sectors of it, might be interested in.

McQuail (1992: 3) provisionally identifies the term 'public interest' in the media context to refer to 'the complex of supposed informational, cultural and social benefits to the wider society which go beyond the immediate, particular and individual interests of those who communicate in public communication, whether as senders or receivers'. As he acknowledges, however, this remains 'both vague and contentious' and requires further attention. Indeed, definitional problems appear to be major obstacles to the development of a meaningful construct of the public interest, though even where attempts have been made to define the concept, they tend to incorporate rather than resolve tensions between competing versions of it. An example may be helpful here in demonstrating the inherent contradictions that may be contained within 'the public interest' as presently applied.

Under the terms of Paragraphs 9–13 of Schedule 2 to the Broadcasting Act 1996 (considered more generally in Chapter 4), the ITC and the RA are charged with applying a test of public interest when considering the acquisition of commercial broadcasting licences by cross-media corporations already controlling one or more newspapers. The criteria to be applied as indicative of the public interest as set out in Paragraph 13, include:

a) the desirability of promoting –
   i) plurality of ownership in the broadcasting and newspaper industries, and
   ii) diversity in the sources of information available to the public and in the opinions expressed on television or radio or in newspapers,
b) any economic benefits . . .
c) the effect of the holding of the licence by that body on the proper operation of the market within the broadcasting and newspaper industries or any section of them. (para. 13, Sch. 2, Broadcasting Act 1996)

In effect, this paragraph incorporates all the various rationales for regulation identified in the previous chapter, and the tension and conflict between these competing public-interest claims is obvious. The regulators will have to balance potential economic benefits against the values of plurality and diversity and the effects on competition, thus incorporating the competing interests and leaving to the largely unstructured discretion of the regulator the choice of which to prioritise.

The same tension is revealed in the Conservative Government's 1995 White Paper on media ownership (DNH 1995a: 16):

Television, radio and the press have a unique role in the free expression of ideas and opinion, and thus in the democratic process. The main objective must therefore be to secure a plurality of sources of information and opinion, and a plurality of editorial control over them. Another important objective is to provide an environment to enable United Kingdom broadcasters, equipment manufacturers and programme makers to take full advantage of major market opportunities.

Thus, as was suggested in the previous chapter, plurality may have to be compromised to allow British media corporations to grow sufficiently to enable them to compete effectively with other players in an increasingly global market. However, it is not just at the national level that such tensions are revealed. As Doyle (1997) demonstrates, in the EU context the objective of pluralism (implying diversity of output) has for pragmatic reasons given way to the competing approach, in which regulation of ownership or control, an easier concept to define than diversity of output, is the primary approach of the regulatory enterprise. 'The public interest' appears, therefore, to be a concept subject to ready capture and reinterpretation.

To a certain extent, the somewhat schizophrenic approach to regulation demonstrated by these examples perhaps reflects the split personality of the media in claiming to serve simultaneously both the advertiser and the audience, whose interests will not always coincide (Keane 1991: 55; Blumler 1992: 2). Tensions between competing elements of the portmanteau concept of 'the public interest' must be resolved and decisions taken regarding which element or version should win out. Allowing different areas of regulation to give preference to different versions of the concept will produce inconsistency, and failing to identify and justify the grounds on which one version of the concept is preferred to another will render the process opaque. However, if consistency and transparency are to be achieved, it seems necessary to reinvent 'the public interest' in terms of an overarching principle which will guide regulators towards consistent outcomes.

Of the problems identified between the existing models, the most fundamental tension appears to be in the relationship between the media and the state. The public-service tradition in the regulation of British broadcasting has already been identified as being a version of the 'social responsibility' model (Siebert *et al.* 1956) for regulation of the press. As such, this implies a significant role for the state in establishing the framework within which the media will operate. However, Curran and Seaton (1997) demonstrate not only that the conception of public service has been susceptible to change, but also that the relationship between state and media has also been subject to fluctuating pressures, differing identifications of the public interest and differing conceptions of the extent of legitimate state activity.

As was discussed in Chapter 1, McQuail (1992:9) traces the conflict between state authority and media freedom through suppression and prohibition, to permission and then prescription, before a recent shift to more libertarian values. It is clear that the public-service tradition in broadcasting is historically associated most closely with the prescriptive epoch yet exists today in a more libertarian environment. While it is important to be aware that that the public interest in media is not synonymous with public-service broadcasting, the public interest is given probably its most concrete manifestation in the form of public-service broadcasting in the Western European tradition, of which the BBC is perhaps the paradigm case.

Attitudes towards the BBC, subject to a broad, supportive consensus around the Reithian tradition in the 'prescriptive' 1940s and 1950s, continued, if not unhindered then ultimately unbroken by the arrival of strictly regulated commercial television. However, the position changed markedly in later years, and the Annan Report (Annan 1977) is generally considered a landmark. It tends to favour a more restricted, less interventionist role for public bodies such as the IBA (Negrine 1994: 106) and favours the pursuit of a range of programming, catering for the interests of the diverse groups in society rather than 'seek[ing] to offer moral leadership' (Curran and Seaton 1997: 304). In discarding much of what remained of the Reithian, paternalistic inheritance, the Annan Report moved the basis for British broadcasting and its regulation from relatively familiar to uncertain and unstable ground. In Curran and Seaton's terms.

> The Annan Report's reinterpretation of public service unintentionally left British broadcasters defenceless against the threats posed by recent technological developments. By so transforming public service it left no grounds to manage or control the impact of the inevitable introduction of cable, video or satellite broadcasting. (Curran and Seaton 1997: 304)

In shifting the orientation of public-service broadcasting so that, in effect, it began to take on the characteristics of 'a poor mimicry of the market' (Keane 1991: 155), the distinctive character of public-service broadcasting began to be lost, and with it perhaps the understanding of why it had existed.

While the basis for public intervention in broadcasting therefore became uncertain, broader concerns regarding the relationship between the state and the media were amplified. A somewhat shrill clamour, largely from government, for broadcasters to ensure political balance or impartiality mounted in the 1970s and 1980s, with programme producers and BBC governors finding themselves under increasingly direct pressure. On the one hand, this indicated a need for the media to be protected against the interference of the state, enabling it to fulfil its role as 'the fourth estate', while on the other, it suggested the need for active regulation to guarantee pluralism in media output.

To some extent this dilemma was avoided rather than resolved by an increasing application of consumerist logic to the media. The provision of pluralism would be ensured, it was argued, by the operation of market forces through which consumer choice would demand, and, facilitated by ongoing technological developments, would be supplied with, diversity. Whether consumer choice is likely to deliver on this promise will be explored shortly.

The inconsistencies in state/media relations abound. On the one hand, British governments have consistently refused to fund newspapers in order to promote diversity of output; on the other Channel 4 was created to enhance diversity, and was funded by a levy imposed upon other commercial broadcasters. The attempts to revive the ailing British film industry, associated with Channel 4's remit, was part of a long sequence of ad hoc interventions seeking to bolster the British cinema on cultural, economic and especially employment grounds. The Eady Levy, introduced in the late 1940s, through which cinema box office takings were taxed to enable support to be given to the British film industry, was an attempt to fund support via a levy on the most successful, mostly American, films. This essentially protectionist measure survived until 1984, even though, as Curran and Seaton (1997: 326) note, by then it was mostly supporting 'British' films being produced by notionally British companies that were essentially American.

The willingness of governments to intervene in relation to cinema and broadcast media has, however, never been paralleled by a willingness to regulate the press. Though Broadcasting Acts and the Annan Report frowned upon foreign holdings in British broadcasting, foreign ownership and control of British newspapers have been permitted on a grand scale. At the same time, while broadcasters in Britain have been constrained in their activities by licence requirements, or in the BBC's case Charter terms, the government has been shy of intervening in relation to the activities of the press, declining to impose statutory standards in relation to privacy (DNH 1995b) or to act decisively to halt the promotion of one medium (satellite broadcasting) via another (newspapers) owned by one cross-media group (Barendt 1993: 135; Sadler 1991).

The apparent contradictions between governmental approaches to printed and broadcast media can be explained on a number of different grounds. The limited scope permitted to the BBC to cover hard news in its formative years, in response to the press industry's anxieties regarding competition, led, claim Curran and Seaton (1991: 329), to broadcasting being seen 'as a medium of entertainment for which "cultural" and not "political" standards were appropriate'. Such a justification appears weak in the modern era where news content in television and radio appears to grow at a similar rate to the concurrent reduction of hard news in popular newspapers.

Another version is that while changing patterns and degrees of regulation of the press have occurred over a long historical period, broadcasting has a much shorter history and has developed in an era in which the state, at least until very recently, has in general played a more active and interventionist role. Thus, the history of the broadcast media cannot be traced through the phases of development identified by Siebert *et al.* (1956) but, from its earliest days in Britain at least, has been regulated within the social responsibility paradigm; identified as a public resource and therefore legitimately the subject of state intervention.

Barendt (1993) identifies at least four different perspectives from which the differential regulation of broadcast and print media may be justified. The first of these is the familiar, if now outdated, frequency shortage type of argument referred to in Chapter 2. The need to ensure adequate and clear access to the airwaves for state services such as the police and military initially formed a justification for intervention and state regulation, permitting the state to allocate frequencies.

This is a particular version of a second, public resource, argument. However, in an era in which other services and utilities previously identified as public resources, such as the utilities, have been privatised, there seems little to stop the state, as in the USA (Schiller 1996: 83), selling off blocks of redundant analogue frequencies as new technologies take over. Though proposing to reform the charging basis for the radio spectrum, the Government's 1996 White Paper (DTI 1996) did not at that stage envisage a secondary trading market in spectrum developing. In any case, even full-scale privatisation would not necessarily result in the Government abandoning entirely the regulatory endeavour, but rather would be likely to see Government distancing itself from regulation via the creation of statutory regulatory agencies such as those introduced for the privatised gas, electricity, water and telecommunications industries. Indeed, the new role ascribed to Oftel in relation to DTT, under the Broadcasting Act 1996 (see Chapter 4) suggests that steps are already being taken in this direction.

A third theory expounded by Barendt, like the first derives from historical circumstance and draws upon the work of Bollinger (1990). Barendt suggests that as the printed media are relatively unregulated, it has become necessary, in order to ensure a degree of diversity and plurality in media output, to regulate more heavily the arguably more influential newcomers to the media world, the broadcasters, subjecting them, for example, to requirements of political impartiality. This is related to the logic of what is the fourth, and arguably the most clearly articulated reason for heavier regulation of the broadcast media, stated by the US Supreme Court in the *Pacifica* case (FCC v *Pacifica Foundation* (1978) 438 US 726). The majority of the Supreme Court bench in *Pacifica* justified greater state intervention in relation to television broadcasting by nature of the medium's peculiarly pervasive and intrusive potentials. The immediacy and, in relation to children and the vulnerable especially, the accessibility of television, together with its direct reach into the home, provides one strand of reasoning underpinning the heavier regulation of broadcast rather than printed media.

There is an essentially paternalistic line being adopted here, reflecting the kind of roles performed in the UK by the BBFC and BSC in relation to sex and violence in the cinema and television, which is at odds with more libertarian approaches towards the role of the state. Technological developments such as the 'V-chip', designed to filter out and restrict children's access to such material, may have an impact on this argument, especially in the current essentially deregulatory, libertarian era. However, the relative difficulty of controlling access to similar material available via the Internet, if not the subject of similar censoring devices, may provide an argument for similar restrictions on computer-generated material, though policing of such purported restrictions would appear to be nightmarish in terms of practicalities, the identification of a responsible originator of material and jurisdictional issues being among the problems.

However, it seems likely that the print media will continue to be more lightly regulated than broadcasting. Newspapers will continue to point towards their historically hard-fought and won freedoms, while the broadcasters, born into an age of state regulation of public resources, have no such historical credentials. The practical reality is that governments have had, and have taken, the opportunity to regulate broadcasting in a way which has not been available or perceived as legitimate in relation to the printed media in the modern era. What Barendt demonstrates is that the justifications for heavier regulation of broadcasting are largely contingent: contingent upon historical circumstance and constitutional form and tradition, rather than resting upon clearly defined principles.

That said, while views may differ as to the extent to which state intervention in media markets is legitimate, both paternalists, who seek a 'properly informed' public, and libertarians, who emphasise choice, share an objective of diversity in media output. The common ground is that diversity is desirable; the difference is in response to the question 'Why?' Put simply, diversity of media product is viewed, respectively, as a function of a well-informed public equipped to participate effectively in society, or as a function of a citizenry endowed with the maximum of choice as an end in itself. If diversity in media output is universally valued, and if it cannot necessarily be guaranteed without regulation, then media regulation targeted at diversity appears to be justified.

However, this conclusion is likely to be disputed by those associated with a belief in the efficacy of market forces to respond to the wishes of individuals and provide the range of products that they wish for (see Veljanovski, 1989); if market forces can deliver choice, then no or minimal regulation will be prescribed. The problem from this perspective is that if markets do not deliver a range of choice that fulfils these demands, then it may be necessary to intervene to produce the required diversity.

In considering the regulation of cable television in Britain, Veljanovski (1987) succinctly summarises the weaknesses in the traditional, paternalistic concept of public service associated with broadcasting in Britain and epitomised by the BBC. Veljanovski dispenses with the frequency scarcity argument for regulation, identifying it as 'an artificial one created by government' (276) and claiming that a viable alternative would be the identification of broadcasting frequencies as private property, to be traded at will, with disputes to be resolved by private litigation.

He then goes on to discuss what he considers to be the only remaining plank of the concept of public-service broadcasting, namely the maintenance of standards in programming via, in Hoffmann-Riem's terms, 'imperative' regulation. He doubts and questions the validity of both the paternalistic line, 'that people should not be given what they want but what they need', and the market failure approach that 'there are inherent structural defects in markets for television programming and distribution which necessitate government involvement' (Veljanovski 1987: 277).

This latter argument appears to revolve around the claim that, for commercial television, the essential purpose of broadcasting activity, profit-making, is heavily dependant upon supplying audiences to advertisers which in turn provide revenue to the broadcasters. The role for the regulator in this context is to avoid a battle for audience maximisation that results in lowest-common-denominator programming which drives down programme standards and diversity. Veljanovski's point here though is that the end product of the regulatory system that produced the BBC/ITV duopoly in Britain in reality resulted in direct competition for audience share between the BBC and the commercial broadcasters, and a resulting homogeneity of product, despite the two schools of broadcasting not having to compete for advertising revenue. Why? Because, says Veljanovski (1987: 278), 'Parliament will not increase the licence fee if the BBC is not seen to offer a significant proportion of the viewing public what they want', and therefore the BBC is forced to engage in a ratings war, despite not being driven by the advertising revenue imperative.

If Veljanovski's argument is sustainable, then regulatory failure on the grand scale is observable. In so far as the public service ethos associated traditionally with British television can be defined, then, if Veljanovski's conclusions are correct, it is not being furthered by the regulatory approach adopted.

Without diverting from our agenda too far, it is necessary to consider whether this is indeed the case. Certainly, there is significant overlap in programme type: ITV's *World in Action* and BBC's *Panorama* have consistently been broadly comparable, and it is true that ITV companies produce serious new programmes and, as has been demonstrated in relation to Formula 1 motor racing, are perfectly capable of producing sports coverage of as high a quality as that of the BBC. In addition, the previously distinctive voice of BBC2 is increasingly comparable to the output of Channel 4. One exception to this pattern of similarity in conventionally regulated television is, however, without doubt, Channel 5, which appears to produce an unremitting diet of down-market programming. A clearer contrast emerges, however, in the context of radio, where the five national BBC channels continue to provide a varied, high-quality output catering for popular and minority tastes and interests. Though local and national commercial radio stations seek out and appeal to niche audiences, with varying degrees of success, neither individually nor collectively do they provide the range of output, and particularly the in-depth analysis and news coverage, offered by BBC radio.

There is perhaps an analogy here which needs to be considered when reading Veljanovski's conclusion (1987: 279) in relation to cable television that 'The direct link between consumer and cable operator afforded by pay-cable ensures that the programmes shown cater to a greater extent for the preferences of viewers (rather than those of the regulator or advertisers)'. Pay-television, whether delivered via cable, DTH satellite or DTT devices, certainly caters for niche interests, and the growth of consumer attraction to BSkyB's channels in Britain can undoubtedly be attributed to its delivery of extensive and exclusive sports coverage (especially live Premier League soccer) and television movie premieres. Undoubtedly also, on a global scale, CNN has begun to change the face of television news coverage and has indeed forced the BBC to introduce, in its twenty-four-hour news service, a development which can be viewed as mimicking the CNN approach. However, there is no evidence to suggest that programmers broadcasting via the new delivery mechanisms have as yet produced, or are likely to produce, anything to compare with the range of services and in-depth analysis and informative or educational content of the services offered by the regulated, public-service broadcasters.

There is undoubtedly a market demand for the kind of product offered by BSkyB, but there is also a strong claim that the public would regret the passing of an age where, in addition to such programming, the quality and range of product associated with the BBC and also conventional, regulated, commercial television in Britain is universally available. This view will inevitably be ascribed the pejorative epithet 'paternalistic', however, if television is viewed as anything more than simple entertainment. If it is recognised that television is our primary source for a view of the world, then it seems legitimate to intervene to ensure that it continues to fulfil this function effectively, and that the unquestioned value of entertainment is not allowed to predominate entirely over the potential informative and educative aspects of the medium. If a viable basis for universally accessible public-service broadcasting is not maintained alongside commercial niche broadcasting, television will be relegated to a medium of pure entertainment, with the broader democratic values currently enjoyed sacrificed on the altar of consumerism.

It is important to heed the lesson Keane draws from an analysis of the press, that it is dangerous to be 'too sanguine about the capacity of market competition to ensure the universal access of citizens to the media of public communication', as such an attitude can too easily fail 'to grasp the many ways in which communications markets *restrict* liberty of the press' (Keane 1991: 46, original emphasis).

Though the case just outlined for the defence of public service broadcasting seems persuasive, it could be rendered still more so if it were possible to identify with reasonable clarity precisely what exactly the public-service ethos in broadcasting amounts to. In drawing comparisons with regulation of the privatised utilities, Prosser (1997: 253) notes that in both cases the regulation of the industries is underpinned by 'social obligations'. He states, however, that 'public service broadcasting is a far more developed concept than the other forms of public-service obligation' (241) and, as such, it might be expected that the concept would be more readily identified.

In considering the institutional structure and approach to independent broadcasting, Prosser (1997: 255) rightly acknowledges, however, that 'the concept of public-service broadcasting is extremely difficult to define'. He goes on to adopt as 'the nearest thing to a definition' a list of principles drawn from the Home Affairs Committee report The Future of Broadcasting (1987–8), which includes:

> Universal service, freedom of broadcasters from direct governmental intervention, provision of a service which should inform and educate as well as entertain, and programmes which should cover a wide and balanced range of subject matter in order to meet all interests in a population. (Home Affairs Committee 1987–8)

This list is helpful, but in itself requires the addition of a point which Prosser makes when considering specifically the interplay between media-specific and general competition law structures in the context of the regulation of broadcasting. He emphasises that 'it must always be borne in mind that the aim of these controls is not simply maintaining fair competition but also maintaining diversity of information' (Prosser 1997: 253). Though it is not stated explicitly, this agenda also appears to require an acknowledgement of the potential for public-service media to alleviate the risk of unregulated media contributing to social exclusion.

In adopting this as a statement of principle, apparently paternalistic arguments in favour of public-service broadcasting or of regulation of broadcasting in the public interest are bolstered by reference to a fundamental democratic expectation: namely that citizenship, or full and effective participation in society, is dependant upon universal access to adequate sources of information. There is no evidence to suggest that an unregulated, truly commercial market in broadcasting would fulfil this promise. Though some might suggest that computer technology and the information superhighway will in due course supersede the presently limited information provided by broadcasting, the realisation of this dream appears some way off at present. Though such developments must be monitored, and taken account of when regulating communications as a whole, they do not as yet undermine the case for effective public-service broadcasting, given the limited and extremely hierarchical access to such high-tech alternative services at present and in the foreseeable future.

What is helpful, however, in considering high-tech responses to access to information, is that they draw our focus outwards to the realisation that the issue must be viewed in a regional, international or arguably global context. Satellite broadcasting and measures such as the EU's Television Without Frontiers Directive (89/552) and the Council of Europe's Convention on Transfrontier Broadcasting (see Coleman and McMurtrie 1995) are already challenging the strength of national sovereignty in this area of regulation. The commercial reality, as demonstrated by Herman and McChesney (1997), is that technological convergence has combined with corporate restructuring to provide the potential for domination of media markets, on a global scale by unashamedly commercial, (US) English-language-dominated, and often American-financed, media giants. Vertical and horizontal integration, and technological convergence mean that not only domination of individual, national media sectors is threatened, but that these genuinely cross-media or multi-media giants may dominate broadcasting not only in terms of programming, but also in terms of delivery mechanisms. It is therefore right for regulatory responses seeking to defend public-service values to be pitched not only at the national, but also at the international level.

– 3.2 The Objectives of Competition Law –

Given that the threat of market domination is traditionally the stuff of competition law (anti-trust law in the USA), it might be expected that competition law would derive from a particular economic model and that it would therefore provide a clear model of the public interest.

The underlying assumptions (Whish 1993: 1–12) are that a state of perfect competition results in both allocative efficiency and productive or cost-efficiency and maximises society's overall wealth as a consequence. It is also believed that competition leads to innovation. According to this, neoclassical model, the number of firms competing and/or the degree of contestability of the market is the crucial factor in arriving at a state of perfect competition, with, in practice, the focus being on avoiding the market distortions created by monopoly or oligopoly and avoiding market closure. Alternative perspectives can be brought to bear, however. For example, emphasis may be placed not on the number of firms, but rather on the degree of entrepreneurial rivalry and innovation as the key indicators of competition; or the fundamental assumption that markets are competitive can be challenged by demonstrating the inherently monopolistic tendencies displayed in real markets.

It is, however, the neoclassical model that is the dominant influence on competition law, and from this perspective, by way of contrast with a state of perfect competition, a situation of monopoly will permit profit maximisation at the expense of allocative efficiency and suppliers not forced by competition to minimise costs may also be productively inefficient. The risk of monopolistic situations arising is at its highest where significant barriers to market entry are found and where markets are not contestable. Whish appears to accept that, in reality, monopolistic or oligopolistic competition, rather then either perfect competition or true monopoly, is very much the norm, and this appears to be as true in media markets as elsewhere. Indeed, it can be plausibly argued that the focus of the competition law endeavour should more appropriately be 'workable competition' than the 'ideal type' presented by the theoretical construct of perfect competition.

It has already been noted that media markets, if unregulated, appear to have strong tendencies to fall into oligopolistic patterns. That said, in practice of course, broadcasting in most Western countries (the USA being a major exception) has been subjected to partial state monopoly for much of its history. As Whish (1993: 7) states, generally 'It might be that social or political value judgements lead to the conclusion that competition is inappropriate in particular economic sectors', and this was indeed the case for broadcasting and most of Britain's nationalised utilities until the Thatcherite 'revolution' of the 1980s. Specifically in relation to the media, Barendt (1993: 121) states that public monopolies may in practice provide the best guarantees of plurality in media output.

It therefore has to be accepted that competition law, and the regulatory framework for media regulation more generally, is not based solely upon foundations of economic theory of competition. It appears to incorporate, if not to acknowledge fully, the existence of social objectives beyond competition as an end in itself, and does not simply assume that market forces will deliver all that democracy expects of its media; in Whish's terms, competition law does not operate in a vacuum and may have a range of objectives beyond those identified in the economic model. A strict adherence to competition theory raises difficulties in relation to externalities (social costs) and, particularly in relation to media regulation, these must include, crucially, the consideration of ensuring the maintenance of 'that variety of sources of information which is necessary for an effective democracy' (Barendt 1993: 122).

Thus, in addition to pursuing the outcomes associated with 'perfect competition', competition law may have a range of other specific objectives, including protecting the product user against the power of the monopolist; assisting governments in achieving policy objectives in terms of regional, employment or price inflation policies; and at the international level protectionism, or, in the case of the EU, the pursuit of an integrated single market. Significant difficulties exist, however, in relation to market definition, especially as regards industries such as the media in which both the outer boundaries (for example, where 'media' meet telecommunications) and internal, sectoral divides are increasingly blurred by technological convergence and corporate conglomeration.

It is clear, as Whish (1993: 672) suggests, that pure economic theory does not provide all the answers to media regulation from the perspective of democratic expectations. In Marsden's terms, the communications industries must be acknowledged as 'a uniquely sensitive industry prone to market failure' (Marsden 1997b: 2), and helpfully, Ogus (1994) identifies the public-interest grounds for regulation in terms of both economic criteria and, in particular, the problem of addressing 'public goods', referred to in Chapter 2.

As an example of market failure, Ogus (1994: 33) identifies 'public goods' in terms of two characteristics: 'first, consumption by one person does not leave less for others to consume; and, secondly, it is impossible or too costly for the supplier to exclude those who do not pay from the benefit'. Classically, public-good qualities have been associated, as Ogus exemplifies, with services such as national defence systems, which provide the benefit of collective security and from which someone who avoids, or is not obliged to pay, taxation cannot be excluded. However, the traditional public-service model for broadcasting, in the form of the BBC, also fits this definition almost exactly in terms of both characteristics. It is obvious that my tuning in to BBC1 does not affect anyone else's ability to do so, while the second characteristic, in terms of the BBC, boils down to licence fee evasion and the prohibitively high cost that would be involved in any serious (as opposed to symbolic) attempt to stop it. Such a situation appears to render conventional, analogue public-service broadcasting unsuitable for the simple application of market forces, especially given that universality of access is one of its fundamental objectives and appears to justify either heavy intervention in markets or perhaps even public ownership of public-service broadcasters. However, in relation to digital transmission, as has already been demonstrated by the introduction of subscription and pay-per-view arrangements for cable and DTH satellite services, technology provides the ready ability to exclude those who will not, or cannot pay for the services. In this sense, modern broadcast media may no longer be considered under the traditional model of public goods and alternative justifications for regulatory intervention will need to be found, especially in an age in which market forces are given paramount importance.

Whish (1993: 16) offers a rather depressing observation in relation to both general competition law and media-specific measures: that there has often been 'no overall conception of the function either of competition or competition law'. In practice, Barendt (1993: 123) believes that the law has often proved unhelpful in ensuring diversity or plurality in the media, having failed to take a sufficiently radical approach: 'Conventional competition regulation preventing, for instance, new combinations without disturbing existing patterns of ownership may not be enough to ensure this goal'.

However, just as competition law does not operate in an environment free of everything but economic theory, so also regulation of the media should not be free from constitutional input. Barendt sets out examples, from Germany, Italy and the USA, of the constitutional courts stepping in to support legislative attempts to further media pluralism. Most notably, he refers to the role of France's Conseil Constitutionnel in establishing constitutional status for the principle of plurality of sources of information (Barendt 1993: 127). The extent to which constitutions make either a potential or actual difference to regulatory outcomes in relation to the media is very much the subject of Chapter 6.

Barendt (1993: 143) goes on to state that the principal of plurality of media sources is now becoming recognised also at the transnational level.

Despite the overall intention of the EU's competition policy being to encourage the development of a harmonised and integrated single market, Merger Regulation (Art. 21(3)) specifies plurality of the media as a legitimate interest which Member States may seek to protect provided that steps taken remain consistent with Community law. In terms of positive regulation for diversity, however, Doyle (1997) demonstrates how in practice the EU's agenda appears to have been watered down, from originally focusing on pluralism, to a new and more limited emphasis on ownership.

It should be clear from the foregoing that competition law involves a range of objectives which encompass largely the same range of factors as have been considered previously when surveying competing constructs of the public interest. Though it appears to derive from a clear economic model, the form it takes and its application in practice appear to be influenced as much by social-policy objectives as by pure economics. Add to this the difficulties involved in defining 'the market' in relation to the media and elsewhere, and the potentially conflicting goals of programmers and distributors (Marsden 1997b: 11), and it should not be surprising that competition law appears to have absorbed, rather than clarified, the inherent contradictions and tensions between the competing strands that comprise 'the public interest' in media regulation.

Whish (1993: 13) suggests that in the detail of competition law which has the apparent objective of protecting smaller firms against potentially predatory larger rivals, the bigger picture might reveal a view of the promotion of economic equity rather than efficiency. Underlying this, he identifies unconstrained economic power, such as that exerted by monopolists or huge conglomerates, as being 'a threat to the very notion of democracy'. The avoidance of unconstrained power has already been identified (in Chapter 1) as being essential to liberal-democratic theory, and therefore an issue of the highest constitutional significance. From Barendt's account, there appears evidence to suggest that clarification of the underlying rationale(s) for media regulation might best be achieved via a consideration of the constitutional fundamentals. Not surprisingly, however, nowhere are these fundamentals likely to be more nebulous than in the UK, where the public interest in media regulation is not set out and is, as will be demonstrated in later chapters, largely subject to potential definition by only the executive rather than any higher constitutional authority.

– 3.3 The Seductive Charms of Choice –

It has already been noted that the privileging of choice offered attractions to libertarians not only on principle, but also as a pragmatic solution to the dilemma of state intervention in the media, identified above. While digital broadcasting technology appears to offer the potential for almost unlimited choice of channel, critics of unmitigated market forces note that 'channel abundance is no guarantee against concentration of ownership or against homogeneity of content, which can result from competition for the same mass audience' (McQuail 1992: 175).

Choice is certainly significant in liberal-democratic theory, though whether as an end in itself or instrumentally as a means to achieving or fulfilling other ends is open to debate. What is not open to question, however, is that choice in this context must be informed choice. Choice based on inadequate information cannot be considered choice in any meaningful sense. Equally, meaningful choice must be between a range of attractive, desirable, differentiated options; the choice between fifty or a hundred remarkably similar options is scarcely worthy of the name.

Given that the media provide essential elements of our view of the world, the role of the media in facilitating meaningful choice must not be underestimated. In order for citizens to make considered choices, based on adequate information, it is generally considered necessary for the media to deliver a wide range of perspectives; media plurality as a prerequisite of meaningful choice. The argument must now become 'how, by what structures and mechanisms, can media plurality be maximised and en-sured?' Not surprisingly, the hegemony of individualism in British politics throughout the 1980s and 1990s has emphasised individual choice, but also supported market mechanisms as the best means of facilitating it.

Clearly, law can have an important instrumental role to play in ensuring such choice, and a relatively rare consideration of the relationship between 'choice and the legal order' is provided by Lewis (1996). The present author focuses on choice specifically as instrumental in pursuit of citizenship, rather than the more general goal of human agency pursued by Lewis, though this difference in emphasis renders Lewis's approach no less relevant.

Lewis (1996: 114) states that 'The market order is . . . a system of free exchange governed by rules which governments enforce, but it should not be subject to arbitrary and coercive intervention by government in relation to the details of exchanges between individuals'. In essence, Lewis is claiming that choice, in a democracy, is not confined to 'high politics' but to everyday relations, and that the law has an important facilitative, as opposed to coercive, role to play.

He goes on to note the potential benefits and risks of market competition and the roles of government in this context. Processes of privatisation, contracting out or market testing, in relation to what were previously public services, delivered by public monopolies, have introduced a degree of competition into such areas and, claims Lewis, 'All these experiments chime with the logic of choice, diversity and experiment and many of them are to be welcomed at face value' (1996: 120). He accepts, however, that the evidence from consideration of such reforms to date has been mixed in relation to the degree to which choice has been extended. For example, in the area of the introduction of quasi-market forces into state-funded schooling, there is little doubt that the range of measures deriving from the Education Reform Act 1988 have in reality done little or nothing to enhance meaningful choice and have also, in practice, moved the decision-making power largely out of zones of accountability via conventional democratic mechanisms, relocating the power to choose not with 'consumers', but with those delivering schooling who may be subject only to the flimsiest accountability mechanisms. There is also evidence in this area to suggest that the exercise of such choice as does exist is uneven, tending to reproduce or heighten social hierarchy (Feintuck 1994).

The apparent failure of some such experiments, hower, does not prove that the underlying logic of choice and diversity through competition is fatally flawed. It does, though, serve to illustrate usefully that whatever constitutional value is attached to choice per se, must be weighed against competing values such as accountability and equity. The sort of liberty and citizenship envisaged in liberal democracy includes choice, but not to the exclusion of other values.

Lewis goes on to conclude that in relation to the consideration of the role of choice in Western societies, 'What has been missing is a clear and public philosophical programme grounded in a contemporary catalogue of human rights operating alongside a set of congruent social and economic objectives interpreted through processes of institutional fact-finding and dialogue' (1996: 126). This is undoubtedly correct and, for better or worse, the media have a crucial role to play in this process. If citizens, diverse as they are, are to make meaningful inputs into this process, they require access to a media market which is in itself diverse, allowing them to absorb and triangulate information provided from a range of perspectives. In the absence of access to media, citizens will not be in a position to exercise informed choice. Given its essential nature in relation to democracy, the media cannot be treated like a commodity; the democratic premium on diversity and universal availability means that these features cannot be left to chance. In the modern, market context, however, Schiller (1996: 126) claims that 'Substituted for these elemental human aspirations is the promise of consumer choice – a choice that is not genuine – and a hopelessly narrow standard of production efficiency'.

While the role of choice in media markets is uncontested at one level, in that choice should be maximised for all citizens, at another level a crucial question remains as to how best to deliver this choice. Would a laissez-faire media market best deliver this plurality or diversity, or are alternative, interventionist regulatory mechanisms required?

Lewis (1996: 123) states that 'Regulation is almost always a second-best enterprise' but goes on to accept that 'There are many reasons for regulating desired goals into existence' (124). He states that 'There is no denying the pace of continued regulation. What is more evasive is a clear unifying philosophy' in the context of 'the untheoretic, pragmatic approach to regulation in the UK' (125).

While 'the principle of freedom of communication presupposes an abundance of channels and choices as desirable conditions of a free and democratic society' (McQuail 1992: 175), the strong tendency of media markets towards oligopoly has already been noted, and the potential risk to diversity in media output thus indicated. It seems therefore that a valid case for media regulation remains; freedom for media market players, though apparently desirable in principle, is clearly an area in which it is necessary, in Lewis's terms, 'to regulate desired goals into existence'. What those desired goals might be, and how best to achieve them, is very much the focus of this book. If meaningful citizen choice is given a high priority and this requires access to a diverse range of media, then it will be necessary to limit the freedom of those who play in the media market. The form and structure of such regulation, especially in terms of whether its focus will be primarily structural, behavioural or content-oriented, can be chosen meaningfully only when the goals are adequately clarified.

It should be noted, however, that in so far as behavioural regulation is adopted, this will imply the restriction of the property rights of those who own or control the media infrastructure; a theme to be returned to in Chapter 7. If justification is required in relation to the restriction of property rights in the media, it can be found in the fact that in relation to many commodities, the consequences of market forces will not have fundamental, democratic repercussions but in relation to others, including the media, a minimum standard of service will be deemed essential in the interests of citizenship. In relation to services such as power and water, such interests receive a degree of protection via the imposition of USOs, although even here a high premium will be placed by citizens on price and service efficiency in relation to what is a largely undifferentiated product; I may choose between gas suppliers, but the product will remain essentially the same. In relation to the media, however, the universal availability of a wide range of products has, in itself, the status of a democratic prerequisite, and the same product will not necessarily be available from a range of suppliers. Thus, both the commodification of media, pointed towards by Schiller (1996) and many other commentators, and the associated handing over of media distribution to unmitigated market forces, must, in the name of democracy, be resisted.

– 3.4   Resolving the Tensions Between Competing Rationales: The Current State of Play –

The existing oligopolistic situation in the British media suggests that attempts to date to ensure plurality and diversity have failed, at least in so far as pluralism in ownership is concerned. That said, at present a fair diversity of product, in broadcasting at least, is still available to everyone via existing public-service broadcasting mechanisms. Monopolisic control of major sporting events and movie premieres, albeit significant in itself, is somewhat marginal to the overall scheme of things, though it is perhaps significant as a portent of things to come.

As will be seen throughout the next two chapters, various forms of competition law, both media-specific and general, have become increasingly significant as mechanisms of media regulation. While it might be expected that the objectives of such mechanisms would be primarily economic, given the theoretical foundation of competition law, in practice, intervention in the name of competition is used as a tool available to government to be applied in the pursuit of a range of objectives, sometimes to do with national economic objectives (for example, addressing price inflation), sometimes with international objectives (for example, protectionism or integrationism in Europe), or sometimes with broader social/political objectives (for example, the preservation of jobs by allowing newspaper takeovers where the alternative would be closure). The problem, of course, with this latter approach is that the employment objective may cut across the objective of plurality of media ownership. Earlier in this chapter, examples were provided of how both government policy documents, and their manifestation in legislation have incorporated rather than resolved potentially conflicting objectives.

On occasion, intervention via competition law might be resisted by those commercial enterprises whose growth or sales are affected by limits on expansion imposed and enforced by the competition authorities; they may claim, in the media context, that such restrictions run counter to their right to free expression. Though the US courts have addressed this issue, it may prove more difficult in the UK where constitutional principles are less clear. Certainly Barendt (1993: 166) demonstrates that American courts have identified this as a matter of limiting property or profit-making rights, rather than an issue of freedom of expression, and have privileged plurality of media above these claims. That said, Marsden's analysis (Marsden 1997a) of US regulation of the pay-television market suggests that regulatory interventions have derived from a strongly consumerist paradigm, which may be thought ultimately to accept rather than challenge the commodification of media. It would not be surprising if this were also to prove the basis upon which any future EU initiatives were also to be based, with any resulting benefits for citizens as citizens being purely contingent upon benefits granted to them in their more limited capacity as consumers.

The application of consumerist rhetoric to media markets and the potentially perverse results it may produce have been noted. If choice of product is an objective, either as an end in itself or as a prerequisite of citizenship, then the media market must be regulated against the operation of free-market forces which, by themselves, would be likely to produce oligopoly or monopoly, and therefore run counter to an objective of plurality or diversity. In addition, from a different perspective, free-market approaches to media markets raise issues which, while not of significance to proponents of consumerism, appear to fall within general constitutional expectations. Equality of citizenship appears to presuppose a degree of equality of access to media output, and, if a significant part of the range of media product is available only to those with the means to buy it, the principle of equality of citizenship appears to be breached. The question of where the line should be drawn, where something akin to USOs need be applied and where they need not, is returned to in Chapter 7.

It is therefore apparent that, short of the adoption of a totally laissez-faire approach to media markets and an acceptance of the likely inegalitarian, anti-democratic consequences, intervention will take place in pursuit of economic or social objectives; though overt adoption of the rhetoric of social objectives remains somewhat unfashionable, even under New Labour, being associated with active attempts at social engineering in the tradition of 'Old' politics. The combination of the application of New Right consumerist rhetoric and New Labour's shyness over identifying and pursuing social objectives has allowed the development and continuation of a retreat away from traditional public-service ideals in the media, particularly in broadcasting. Certainly, it would now be unimaginable to find senior politicians supporting anything approaching a public monopoly, or even a publicly regulated duopoly, in broadcasting, a situation which persisted not so very long ago.

Alternative devices for intervention and regulation, such as the imposition of levies or granting of cash aid by government, have generally been considered inappropriate in Britain, at least in relation to the newspaper industry. Concern over being associated with either state control or state censorship has seemed to underlie government's reluctance to become involved in financing the newspaper market in pursuit of diversity, despite the fact that it would be perfectly possible, as in the Netherlands and Scandinavia (Humphreys 1996: 105–6) to engage in such a practice, perhaps through an intermediate body, without adverse inferences being drawn. Admittedly, though, differences in state and constitutional traditions would need to be addressed.

Ultimately, the devices utilised to regulate the media, and the conception of the public interest which they have been intended to pursue, have been arrived at on a pragmatic, inconsistent and historically contingent basis. As such, it is difficult to discern a common thread running through these regulatory devices other than a commitment to ensuring, to a minimum extent at least, a degree of diversity in sources of information. Though the diversity objective is often found in combination with competing objectives, all of the mechanisms for intervention identified so far contain diversity or plurality as one aspect. Even the consumerist, anti-interventionist rhetoric assumes and takes on board the concept of diversity of product in its privileging of choice as the key objective.

It can be debated whether the existing situation of oligopoly fulfils the demands of diversity. Whatever the answer to this question, however, the ongoing processes of technological convergence and development of cross-media empires suggest that the status quo will be unlikely to remain in place. The forces of convergence and conglomeration imply a great threat even to such diversity as presently exists, and for those who instinctively have a problem with this likelihood, some rational basis for regulation towards other ends must be found.

This lowest common denominator in existing regulation may prove helpful in considering the basis for a new construction of the public interest. Diversity of output appears to be central to all the regulatory approaches, though at times can be countered by other objectives in opposition to it. What appears to be needed is a clearer understanding of *why* diversity of output is the common element across all the regulatory approaches, before a meaningful rationale can be discerned, and in turn a structure of objectives and institutional arrangements for their attainment can be established. It can reasonably be expected that this rationale will have something to do with the needs of democracy and of citizenship.

– 3.5   Citizenship as the Public Interest? –

When the French Conseil Constitutionnel, considering the 1986 Broadcasting Bill, in effect gave constitutional status to the principle of plurality of sources of information, and when the Italian and German courts have ruled also that competition law applicable to commercial broadcasting should be sufficiently strong as to safeguard 'plurality of opinion' (Barendt 1993: Chapter 6), the constitutional significance of media regulation is highlighted. It appears to be constitutionally necessary to protect, in Barendt's terms, 'that variety of sources of information which is necessary for an effective democracy' (122). Unfortunately, many commentators leave the argument at this point, apparently content in having identified the public interest. However, this plurality of information sources should not be viewed as end in itself in this context, but rather, according to Barendt's typology (Barendt 1985), as a means to achieving truth, self-fulfilment or effective participation in democracy by citizens.

McQuail (1992: 22), however, does take this further, identifying, after Held (1970), a tripartite typology of public-interest theories. The first of these, the preponderance theory, identifies the public interest with the preferences of a simple majority of the public, appearing to be consistent with market logic but failing to reflect what McQuail (23) refers to as 'the broader notion that public interest means something more than the sum of individual preferences'. The second approach, the common interest theory, refers to 'cases where the interests in question are ones which *all* members are *presumed* to have in common, with little scope for dispute over preferences' (original emphasis). Typical examples provided by McQuail of areas in which such theory may be applied include utilities, and matters such as defence and policing, which commonly fall under the classification of 'public goods' discussed earlier. The difficulty identified by McQuail in relation to this approach is that while it facilitates the assertion of certain general objectives as legitimate, including access to media as channels of public communication, it 'does not demonstrate the necessity (or demand) for meeting any particular claim'.

The third of Held's categories discussed by McQuail (1992: 23), the unitary theory, he states, amounts to 'the assertion of some absolute normative principle, usually deriving from some larger social theory or ideology'. In this connection, McQuail notes that unitary theories in relation to the public interest in the media can derive from quite different bases, for example from an ideological belief in either public or private ownership of media, or from claims to education, protection of minors, or of national language and culture. While acknowledging the weaknesses associated with the application of unitary theory which McQuail notes, in particular potential 'insensitivity to popular wants' and even more problematic, he states, 'their frequently authoritarian, paternalistic or ideologically contestable character' (25), it seems reasonable to state that a unitary approach to media regulation based explicitly upon citizenship as its organising ideal would not, within liberal-democratic theory, be inappropriate or encounter the other potential problems he identifies.

Thus, it can be argued that of Barendt's three lines of argument for freedom of expression, the third, citizen participation, is the most pressing, relating most closely to our fundamental democratic expectations and implying a unitary theory of public interest based upon citizenship. As it happens, it also chimes with the rhetoric, if not necessarily the policies, of Major and Blair Governments. Addressing inequalities of citizenship, or 'multiple deprivation' or 'social exclusion', therefore becomes a central and legitimate aim for media regulation.

Admittedly, in a society which is fundamentally inegalitarian, equality of citizenship may be viewed sceptically from the Left as a poor surrogate for substantive equality, though it may also have attractions in terms of proving more readily definable, certainly more likely to appear attainable within the capitalist system, and may serve as a salve for our collective, liberal conscience. In so far as the media are implicated in the delivery of this plurality of sources of information, difficult questions must be raised as to where the line is drawn between which parts of the media output are necessary prerequisites for citizenship and which (if any) are not. Before attempting to address this question, albeit tentatively, it is best first to clarify what exactly is meant by 'citizenship' and to question further its adoption in this context.

Though T. H. Marshall may be much criticised, his tripartite construction of citizenship, developed in the 1950s and early 1960s, remains a crucial landmark around which many discussions revolve and from which others depart. Barbalet (1988: 5) summarises Marshall's construct of citizenship as stating 'firstly, that citizenship is a status attached to full membership of a community, and secondly, that those who possess this status are equal with respect to the rights and duties associated with it'.

In essence, Marshall (1964: 78) identifies three 'elements' of citizenship. First, civil: 'the rights necessary for individual freedom – liberty of person, freedom of speech, thought and faith, the right to own property and to conclude valid contracts, and the right to justice'. Second, political: 'the right to participate in the exercise of political power, as a member of a body vested with political authority or as an elector of the members of such a body'. Third, social: 'the whole range from the right to a modicum of economic welfare and security to the right to share to the full in the social heritage and to live the life of a civilised being according to the standards prevailing in society' or, in Barbalet's terms, 'a right to the prevailing standard of life and the social heritage of the society' (Barbalet 1988: 6).

Interestingly, as Hogan points out, Marshall's approach to citizenship is 'institutionally grounded' and, we might note, historically contingent:

> The specification and elaboration of each of these bundles of citizen rights was a contingent function of the differentiation and development of distinctive institutions – the law courts, parliamentary democracy, and the welfare state – at different moments in the history of citizenship. (Hogan 1997: 45)

While the institutional structure and procedural values are clearly significant in this connection, this is not to the exclusion of clearly stated, substantive values. Thus, the attainment of Marshall's construct of citizenship appears to be closely associated with the full range of law jobs identified, after Llewellyn, by Harden and Lewis, and referred to in Chapter 1. Though not necessarily adopting Marshall's concept of citizenship, Harden and Lewis (1986) echo parts of it, noting that 'the expectations of citizenship are unlikely to remain static' (10), and associating the institutional framework with the underlying, value-laden precept of the rule of law (as a principle of institutional morality). They note also that 'Rule of law values . . . deny any ultimate division between the principles of citizenship and the requirements of effective government' (302).

Clearly, citizenship is central to the nature of democratic society and indeed, for Ranson and Stewart (1989), it is the unifying value for the public domain, though its precise definition will be subject to debate, and indeed historical capture and reinterpretation. Thus, it will be necessary to be clear as to precisely what is meant when the term is used in the context of debates regarding any contemporary phenomenon, such as the media.

Though presently unfashionable, if we return to Reith's tripartite definition of the BBC's function as the archetypal public-service broadcaster, we find a high degree of mesh between 'informing, educating and entertaining' and the needs of Marshall's civic, political and social aspects of citizenship. Certainly, there is a close parallel of civic and political citizenship goals in the media's 'educating and informing' functions, though the extent to which entertainment forms part of the social citizenship agenda may be more contestable. Clearly, there is the risk of this being considered grossly over-simplistic, with the definitions in themselves being too vague to be helpful; however, it is of some utility in indicating how the full range of the conventional public-service remit is relevant to citizenship.

What this suggests, and this proposition will be returned to, is that if something akin to this model of citizenship is an objective, something akin to the range of products provided by the public-service broadcasting model will have to be made equally available to all, if anything approaching equality of citizenship is to be achieved or maintained. The problem, of course, is that not all media deliver this range, with an increasing number of niche market providers specialising in entertainment. There may be some difficulty in determining whether social citizenship demands that we all have access to live coverage of our national team's soccer games as part of our cultural heritage, or whether the citizenship ideal is unabridged if we all have access only to highlights, while only those able or willing to pay extra for the facility may watch the games live. Less controversial, however, is the question whether citizenship demands that we all have free access to a whole range of editorial views in the run-up to a general election, or whether it is sufficient that we all have access to one or two 'impartial' accounts, with more politically affiliated views available to those who wish to and are able to purchase them. The latter, of course, is the current situation, with the heavily regulated BBC and ITV coverage in theory providing a degree of 'balance' which would not necessarily result from the market-driven, privately controlled press. The direct implication of this is a reassertion of the necessity for public-service media in fulfilling expectations of citizenship.

Nonetheless, there are, real, practical problems which must be addressed by those advocating citizenship as a central or organising concept in debates over the future regulation of the media. In general, these difficulties revolve around the question: 'How equal must access to the media be in pursuit of equality of citizenship?' Such problems have not, however, prevented commentators from advocating this approach, though without necessarily identifying clearly with a 'unitary' as opposed to 'common interest' concept of the public interest.

While acknowledging the existence of paternalistic, educative motives underlying the pursuit of public-service broadcasting, Blumler and Madge (1967: 48) identify two other premises on which claims for the media to serve citizenship objectives can be based. They refer to the majority of the public being 'spontaneously moved by a desire, however faint it may be at times, to discover more about their wider social and political environment' and – referring to our institutional political arrangements being based on a presupposition that the public are all equally qualified to participate in political processes – a resulting responsibility on the media 'to provide citizens with the information and understanding that they need to play an effective part in this operation of democratic checks and balances'. Again, the link between democracy, citizenship and the media is established.

Golding (1990: 85) proposes the concept of citizenship 'as a key element in the development of a more adequate analysis of the political role of communications institutions and processes'. He goes on to ask, 'To what degree and in what ways are people denied access to necessary information and imagery to allow full and equal participation in the social order?' (98), noting that 'communicative competence and action, and the resources required to exercise them, are requisites for citizenship' (99). He makes 'a claim for the resurrection of the concept of citizenship as a critical benchmark of enquiry in communication research' (100), to which might be added, 'and media regulation specifically'.

Golding makes this plea despite being fully aware of some inherent problems, towards which he himself directs attention. He talks of the 'information gap' whereby 'the educationally and socio-economically advantaged are able to enhance their advantages via communications media, whose distribution and consumption are such as to ensure that such social divisions widen' (96). The reproduction, or exaggeration of social hierarchy as a result of differential access to communications technology, to which the likes of Herman and McChesney (1997) and Schiller (1996) refer, is clearly a substantial obstacle to 'full and equal participation in the social order' (Golding 1990: 98). It appears that substantive inequalities in access to media may have to be addressed before something approaching equality of civic and political citizenship can be achieved. Clearly, such problems are much more likely to be exacerbated than resolved by the arrival of new technologies which are likely to heighten inequalities of access.

Still more fundamental, however, are concerns regarding the nature of what the media in fact does. Blumler and Gurevitch (1995: 98) note that 'a viable democracy presupposes an engaged citizenry' but if the media does not offer in practice meaningful information, education and entertainment, how can it contribute towards the attainment of citizenship ideals? Again, Golding is well aware of the problems identified here, stating that 'there can be no serious doubt that such sources as news media significantly and consistently provide *a partial and coherently weighted account* of many areas of social and political life' (85, emphasis added).

Of the various examples Golding cites in this connection, only one will be referred to here: that of Hall *et al.* (1978), where the authors consider the role played by the media in establishing or constructing the 'crisis' of street crime and police responses to it in the 1970s. Here, the authors identified 'a systematically structured *over-accessing* to the media of those in powerful and privileged institutional positions' (58, original emphasis).

The existence of structural relationships between the media and the powerful, and in particular a high degree of mutual interdependence, combines with the fact that most media are profit-oriented organisations, operating in a capitalist environment, to ensure that, in Blumler and Gurevitch's terms, 'the media can pursue democratic values only in ways that are compatible with the socio-political and economic environment in which they operate' (1995: 98). 'Instead of promoting a "marketplace of ideas", in which all viewpoints are given adequate play, media neutrality tends to privilege dominant, mainstream positions' (105). In the words of Hall *et al.*, 'The media . . . tend, faithfully and impartially, to reproduce symbolically the existing structure of power in society's institutional order' (1978: 58).

All of this might suggest some problems in advancing a concept of citizenship as an organising principle or focal point for media regulation, given the apparently symbiotic relationship between the institutions of the media and those of wider social power. However, it might also be taken to indicate the need for a clear, unitary theory of the public interest with which to challenge existing norms.

Inequalities in access to the media, reflecting broader social inequalities, combine with the structural relationship and interdependence between the media and the powerful to limit the potential for genuinely impartial news coverage, or reporting truly independent of the powerful ruling elite. In this light, the media can be seen as mediating, but also perpetuating, the power relationships between the rulers and the ruled. If this is the case, there appears to be a significant risk that reliance upon the media to enhance or further citizenship in any meaningful way may be no more than a pious hope. Radical critics might, of course, suggest that the nature of citizenship under capitalist liberal-democracies is such as to merely legitimise existing economic power relationships in any case, and that, as such, the pursuit of citizenship in this sense is in itself futile. Proponents of social democracy, however, may accept that existing economic inequalities do not deny the value in pursuing equality or less inequality in citizenship. The argument is that social exclusion is about not only economic disadvantage, but also related disadvantages across the range of citizenship criteria: multiple deprivation.

With that in mind, it is necessary to return to a consideration of whether the media can be expected to facilitate equality of citizenship. While the omens do not necessarily look hugely positive, and despite an apparently strongly entrenched position for the media, prospects for change and movement towards a more positive media influence on citizenship can be found. Though Blumler and Gurevitch (1995: 203) state that 'the political communication process now tends to strain against, rather than with the grain of citizenship', they also observe that 'Although political communication arrangements are systemically structured, they are not frozen in time but continually evolve'. The difficulty here is in identifying and taking control of the evolutionary mechanisms, in order to manipulate the structure towards, rather than away from, citizen-oriented objectives.

Two factors, amongst others, which have tended to induce change in political communication systems are identified by Blumler and Gurevitch (1995: 204) as developments in communications technology and 'relevant changes in the structure and culture of the surrounding social and political system'. Of the first of these, the increasing predominance of television through the 1950s and 1960s as the medium for political communication is the most obvious example, while in relation to the second type of factor, one example that Blumler and Gurevitch point towards is changing patterns of media regulation, including specifically as an illustration 'the break-up of public-service broadcasting monopolies in Western Europe' (205).

It therefore appears possible that, at a time in which technological change is occurring at a rapid pace and regulatory structures are in a state of flux, an opportunity presents itself for the communications media system as a whole to be redirected towards new goals. In this sense, the stage is left vacant for the arrival of a new conceptual focal point which pushes the media towards democracy-serving outcomes and acts as a coherent objective for the activities of regulators and the regulatory structure, though it will, admittedly, be pushing against the dominant non-interventionist spirit of the age.

Like Golding (1990), Collins and Murroni (1996) make a case for citizenship serving as this key organising concept. Though the present author has indicated elsewhere (Feintuck 1997c) reservations regarding Collins and Murroni's structural recommendations for the practical implementation of this policy, the principle itself seems worthy of the most careful consideration.

Starting from a premise that 'freedom of access to the information necessary to full participation in economic, political and social life is a central element of citizens' entitlements in modern societies' (1996: 76), Collins and Murroni consider the application of USOs as applied to date in Britain primarily in relation to telecommunications and other privatised utilities. The potential for the extension of USO-type arrangements to the broader media field will be considered in later chapters, but it should be noted here that their application depends upon the definition of a baseline level of service which is deemed adequate to avoid social exclusion, and the precise level of which will be highly debatable. Just as having access to a public pay-phone is not the same as having a phone in one's own home, access to the Internet via a community resource in, say, a village hall, or to satellite television in a pub or club, are not the same as having on-tap access which brings the potential to develop experience and expertise and maximise the benefits on offer.

Collins and Murroni (1996: 78) go on to discuss what they call 'cultural rights' as an aspect of the citizenship agenda. A sense of collective identity can be furthered via the media and, far from resulting in homogeneity, can produce genuine diversity, for example in the Welsh-language productions of the BBC and S4C, and in Scots Gaelic via the Gaelic Programme Fund initiative. These are, however, only examples of a wider phenomenon identified as 'community service obligations' which may be imposed upon public-service (whether the BBC or commercial, licensed) broadcasters. In general, British public-service broadcasters have been required to produce a universally accessible service, free at the point of use, which fulfils requirements imposed via the BBC Charter or licence conditions of producing a range of programmes. Collins and Murroni conclude that 'The community service obligation of broadcasting can thus be defined as viewers' and listeners' entitlement to access to a range of information, entertainment and educational programmes at affordable cost' (79). Of course, such public-service requirements are not imposed presently upon subscription or pay-per-view services, and digitalisation promises a huge growth in such niche services.

In presenting their analysis of the challenges currently facing media regulation, Collins and Murroni draw upon the findings of the IPPR's Commission on Social Justice, which established four objectives which it was believed should influence government policy:

1. 'security' – policies aimed at prevention, or failing that relief, of poverty;
2. 'opportunity' – policies designed 'to increase autonomy and life chances';
3. 'democracy' – 'policies designed to ensure diffusion of power within government and between government and people'; and
4. 'fairness' – 'policies designed to reduce unjustified inequality' (or 'social exclusion').

The Commission sought to apply these as 'Benchmarks through which policy makers as well as the public can judge policy options' (Collins and Murroni 1996: 14). These mesh closely with a notion of citizenship, and, in the present context, it should be noted that in particular the last three of these may also serve equally well as criteria against which the effectiveness of the activities of media regulators may be measured: outcomes of regulation can be assessed against these standards.

To date, regulation has been reactive, focusing on form within the sectoral and cross-media marketplaces and largely consisting of *ex post facto* reaction to changing technological circumstances. Now and in the future, positive regulation is required to ensure the widespread circulation of and access to a range of information and cultural products, and this must be confirmed positively as the key regulatory objective. Something akin to

USOs may need to be imposed, but, in terms of regulatory practice, integrated regulation of the cross-media market, including control of technological gateways, focused on outcomes is necessary if this objective is to be achieved.

If such regulation is to be meaningful, it must be possible to assess outcomes against known and identified criteria, and it seems reasonable in this respect to adopt the kind of citizenship-oriented principles identified by the Commission on Social Justice in the way that Collins and Murroni suggest. Collins and Murroni (1996: 13) identify the key statement in the Commission on Social Justice's work as being that 'the foundation of a free society is the equal worth of all citizens', and this can supply an overarching objective for areas of social policy, including media regulation, which can be rendered more specific by breaking it down according, say, to the benchmarks provided by the Commission on Social Justice. The key question to be asked of any media regulation policy or structure then becomes, 'Does this policy/structure further equality of citizenship so defined?'

The limitations of the concept of equality of citizenship have already been acknowledged, in terms of failing to challenge, and perhaps even tacitly legitimising, substantive economic inequalities. In addition, there is no doubting the gravity of the problems which must be addressed by those recommending plurality of the media as a route to enhanced citizenship; the issues raised and acknowledged by the likes of Golding, Blumler and Gurevitch, and Hall et al., must be taken on board. It is perhaps worth restating, however the glimmer of hope provided by Blumler and Gurevitch's analysis of the factors that are catalytic in changing the nature of political communications systems, which include technological development and changes in regulatory structures. The current conjunction of these events presents an opportunity to seize the agenda, and, via a more sharply focused regulatory process, seek in the name of citizenship to maximise whatever plurality and diversity can exist.

The citizenship agenda incorporates choice maximisation, as pursued by Lewis (1996), though arguably strengthens the case by placing choice alongside other democratic expectations such as accountability and equity, rather than risking unduly privileging choice at the expense of these other crucial democratic expectations. Under this agenda, plurality of the media is pursued not as an end in itself, but as a means of furthering effective choice, as a prerequisite of meaningful citizenship. As a potential quasi-constitutional principle for Britain, it appears to capture the spirit of the interventions seen elsewhere by constitutional courts when seeking to ensure media plurality and diversity. It appears to reconfirm the interdependence of the media and the public sphere, railing against the threat of privatisation of communication identified by Schiller (1996), and privileges the public resource aspect of the media over competing, commercial, perspectives. It appears ultimately to justify, in pursuit of a clear concept of 'the public interest', the restriction of corporate property rights in the media.

While vague claims of public interest or justifications for intervention (or lack of it) are open to reinterpretation or capture,

> A regulatory system overtly designed to give effect to "furtherance of equality of citizenship" (or the avoidance of social exclusion) as the public interest . . . would be less susceptible to abuse or being ignored, and could usefully provide a starting point for the kind of rational policy-making process which Hitchens (1995) has identified as necessary. (Feintuck 1997c: 4)

The remainder of this book examines in more detail some of the different regulatory structures and policies for media regulation applied to date, both in Britain and elsewhere. In addition to principles, structures and especially institutional features such as accountability and transparency must be considered. Arguably though, the central reason underlying the failure of regulatory institutions to date, and for the difficulties they are likely to face in a future that is uncertain in terms of technological development, is the absence of a clear, organising principle for the regulatory endeavour. As discussed above, tensions between competing rationales for media regulation have not been articulated or resolved, but rather have been absorbed, ignored or preferred one over the other on a pragmatic, ad hoc basis. Pursuit of a developed concept of citizenship appears to offer a constant and meaningful objective in itself, and a standard against which policies can be judged.

PART TWO

Regulatory Practice in Britain

CHAPTER 4

Regulating Media Ownership and Control

– 4.1 OWNERSHIP IN PERSPECTIVE –

Though the focus now turns away from the conceptual basis for regulation of the media to consider instead some examples of regulation in practice, the theoretical foundations explored in the previous chapters provide the basis for analysis of the regulatory practices under consideration here.

Though behavioural regulation is not always easily classified, regulation of the media essentially falls fairly easily into two categories: regulation of content, and regulation of ownership or control of media enterprises, which approximate to Hoffmann-Riem's classifications of imperative and structural regulation (Hoffmann-Riem 1992a). The first considers what may be broadcast or printed and may consist of positive programming requirements, such as under the ITC licence requirements for a range of programmes applied to public-service commercial television broadcasters in Britain; or it may consist of negative requirements, limiting what can be broadcast, for example on grounds of taste and decency. The second category, regulation of ownership or control, which will be the primary focal point here, may in turn be subdivided into directly structural controls (for example, prescribing the growth of an organisation in one media sector beyond a certain limit, based on numbers of companies or market share in terms of turnover or audience share) and behavioural controls related to structure (for example, specifying activities or actions that would be subject to sanction, perhaps as an abuse of a position of power). Competition law, whether of general application or media-specific, may be focused either on form, which has predominantly triggered intervention in the UK, or effects (essentially the consequences of abuse of a dominant position), which underlies the EU approach to the subject, though the Competition Bill presented to Parliament in October 1997 will have the effect of bringing UK competition law into line with the EU approach in the future.

A further distinction, which is signficant in Britain, must be drawn between statutory, state-imposed regimes of regulation, such as those applicable to broadcasting, and the essentially self-regulatory processes employed in relation to much of the advertising industry by the ASA, or in relation to the newspaper industry by the PCC; self-regulation will be addressed directly in Chapter 5. In relation to Britain in particular, attention must be drawn to the existence of, and reliance upon, self-denying ordinances applicable in different contexts to government, regulators, the courts and the media. These are arguably the result of the absence of clear principles for regulatory intervention, and perhaps symptomatic of the absence of developed and articulated principles underpinning constitutional arrangements.

In this chapter, three predominantly structural examples of current regulatory practice that relate to ownership or control of media are considered. The first of these is newspaper takeovers and mergers, the area of media ownership regulation with the longest history in Britain. This will highlight significant questions of regulatory discretion, raising in turn questions of accountability to be returned to in Chapter 5. The next area to be examined is the application of media-specific competition law in the form of the Broadcasting Act 1996. An analysis will be made of the structural measures aimed at controlling cross-media ownership, and particular emphasis will be placed on understanding the changes made to the framework established by the Broadcasting Act 1990. The final subject scrutinised in this chapter also arises out of the 1996 Act, but can be viewed essentially as an attempt by the state to respond to a specific technological development: the imminent introduction of digital terrestrial television.

These examples illustrate the issues raised for regulators by ongoing changes in both market structure and technology, and in particular highlight the problems arising out of the absence of a clear, principled approach to the regulatory endeavour. Though based broadly upon pluralism of ownership and competition law principles as outlined in Chapters 2 and 3, it appears that lack of conceptual clarity, and a resulting lack of clear objectives risk undermining this regulatory activity, at least in relation to its aim of ensuring a diverse media output, the underlying public interest justification upon which regulatory intervention is largely based. The latter two examples considered in this chapter also reveal the increasing EU influence over media regulation in Britain.

The examples considered here, however, also raise broader questions relating to the place of regulatory structures within the constitutional scheme. The role of the courts in relation to regulatory activity will be raised here, and returned to both in Chapter 5 and, on a comparative basis, in Chapter 6, while the relationship between national and international regulatory regimes, considered in both this chapter and the next, raises the question of whether the nation state is any longer the appropriate level at which to regulate an increasingly global media economy.

Carried over from Chapter 3, and of particular significance in the context of the structural regulatory mechanisms considered here, is the idea that diversity in media output, via diversity in ownership, is consistently presented as an objective of regulation, yet it appears necessary to view this not as an end in itself, but as a mechanism for serving the needs of citizenship. Given this surrogacy arrangement and the absence of any necessary connection between pluralism of ownership and diversity in output, it is perhaps appropriate to consider and analyse structural regulation in terms of the extent to which it serves successfully as a surrogate for imperative, content-focused regulation which might be expected to pursue more directly the objective of diversity of output.

– 4.2 Newspaper Takeovers and Mergers –

Though the press must be viewed in the increasingly cross-media context, justification for considering this sector in isolation for the moment is twofold. First, that the press is the oldest of the media and, having struggled in its early history against state control and censorship, is the most resistant to regulation. Second, that in terms of the informative and critical aspect of media power, the press continues to claim that it fulfils these functions in greater depth than the broadcast media.

In the modern era, 'Traditionally, economic arrangements for the Press have involved a minimum of intervention by the state. To own a newspaper has been regarded as the commercial manifestation of the liberty to speak' (Gibbons 1991: 97), while in the Western European tradition, the majority of broadcast media have until very recently been regulated against public-service standards. As such, the press retains certain sectoral distinctions, notwithstanding the current context of technology convergence and trends towards cross-media and international conglomeration.

In Chapter 1, the high degree of concentration of ownership now present in the British newspaper market was noted. As Seymour-Ure (1996: 43) demonstrates, a position where the three largest press companies controlled an already significant 52 per cent of circulation of national daily and Sunday titles in 1947 was transformed to a situation where the three largest concerns in 1994 controlled 76 per cent of national circulation, with a similar trend of concentration taking place within the local/regional press market via the development of chains of titles (see Seymour-Ure 1996: Chapter 3; Curran and Seaton 1997: Chapter 7). The fact that 70 per cent of newspaper circulation is now of a Conservative orientation is a result, states Hutton (1995: 40), 'produced not by competition in the market but by manipulation of the ownership rules by Conservative press tycoons'. In light of these trends, it is perhaps surprising to find that a regulatory regime exists at all, and to find that the question asked by the 1947 Royal Commission – 'whether such concentration as exists is on balance disadvantageous to the free expression of opinion or the accurate presentation of news' (Negrine 1994: 62) – has remained an apparently important concern for government (see for example DNH 1995a) and commentators alike.

Though the issue of concentration in press ownership may appear particularly acute in Britain, it can also be observed elsewhere. As Bagdikian (1992: 17) notes, in the huge US market 'a handful of corporations [have gained] control of most daily newspapers', with fourteen companies controlling half or more of the daily newspaper business in 1992, whereas the same share was controlled by some twenty companies only seven years earlier. Considering Western Europe, however, Humphreys (1996: 96) concludes in effect that while press concentration has its own dynamic, 'oligopolistic competition is the rule and that Britain provides the most striking example of this phenomenon.'

In the context of an increasingly global media and economy, heightening concentration in the press market is not surprisingly an international issue, with Rupert Murdoch – in Schiller's terms 'the Australian-English-American media mogul' (Schiller 1996: 112) – being only one example of the trend towards controlling press concerns alongside other media interests on a worldwide basis (see Tunstall and Palmer 1991). Thus, it seems proper to consider the regulation of press ownership as part of a broader, international media market and, given the widespread availability of newspapers via the Internet, to acknowledge the new, convergent, technological context in which the press operates. That said, although British cross-media ownership regulation under the Broadcasting Acts of 1990 and 1996 and proposed EU measures seek to take the broader view, by attempting to integrate newspaper ownership alongside the holding of broadcasting licences in establishing overall thresholds for regulation of cross-media ownership, a more long-standing regime exists which continues to purport to regulate press ownership as a separate sector.

The Fair Trading Act 1973 (FTA) includes specific measures controlling the takeover and merger of both national and local newspapers, which go beyond general takeover and merger provisions. Under the terms of the FTA, newspaper acquisitions are subjected to scrutiny where a proprietor's newspapers, including the paper to be taken over, total an average daily circulation of 500,000 or more; proprietorship, either personal or through company structures, being defined in terms of holding a controlling interest. To be lawful, mergers crossing this threshold require the consent of the Secretary of State, which may be either conditional or unconditional. The Secretary of State in some cases will refer the matter for consideration by the Monopolies and Mergers Commission (MMC), but in a number of exceptions to the general rule *may* and, in the case of a newspaper which is not to be continued as a separate title, *must*, decide the matter without reference to the MMC. The other situations which the Secretary of State is not obliged to refer to the MMC are 'where the newspaper is not economic as a going concern and he is satisfied that the case is one of urgency if it is to continue as a separate newspaper', 'where the newspaper being transferred has an average circulation of 25,000 or less per day of circulation' and 'where the MMC has failed to make its report within the appointed time-limit' (Whish 1993: 673).

Thus, the FTA provisions consist of a mixture of specified thresholds and practices, and regulatory discretion exercised by the Secretary of State. The presence of the MMC in the process appears to offer reassurance against fears of politically motivated action by the Secretary of State, especially given that the MMC is required to take into account 'the public interest'. Unfortunately, the statutory definition of 'the public interest' in this context is so vague as to be virtually meaningless, requiring the consideration of 'all matters which appear in the circumstances to be relevant and, in particular the need for accurate presentation of news and free expression of opinion' (s58(1) FTA).

However, the reality does not necessarily match the superficial appearance of these provisions. As Whish (1993: 675–8) demonstrates, in practice the degree of discretion vested in the Secretary of State is much more wide-ranging than at first might appear to be the case. In addition to the ability to impose conditions on newspaper takeovers and mergers, the Secretary of State also has the power to appoint members of a panel of additional MMC members who may be utilised in newspaper references. It is also the case that a large number of takeovers and mergers will fall within the exceptions to the provisions, which allow the Secretary of State the discretion not to make a reference to the MMC, and, even where a reference is made, the Secretary of State is not bound to follow the conclusions reached.

Ainsworth and Weston, writing in 1995, concluded that 'Extensive reliance on [the] exceptions (most recently in *The Guardian's* acquisition of *The Observer* and the acquisition of *The Independent* by a consortium led by Mirror Group) has meant that in practice the majority of important newspaper acquisitions have escaped MMC scrutiny' (Ainsworth and Weston 1995: 3). Curran and Seaton (1997: 294) report some 120 newspaper takeovers between 1965 and 1993, but the fact that the MMC dealt with only twenty-nine references regarding newspaper acquisitions between 1965 and 1994, and of those twenty-three were cleared, leads Ainsworth and Weston (1995: 5) to question whether the practical effect of the FTA system justifies 'the administrative burden, expense and delay that it creates', and indeed 'whether there is really any justification for continuing to treat newspaper mergers under different procedural rules than other types of merger'.

All in all, the Secretary of State enjoys wide-ranging discretion, and, given the 'fierce political argument' that Whish (1993: 677) notes in relation to some newspaper takeovers (especially the acquisition by News International of *The Times* in 1980 and *Today* in 1987, and repeated take-over proposals relating to *The Observer*, particularly its purchase by Lonrho in 1981), is quite reasonably, subject to suspicions of pursuing party political interests and, vulnerability to 'both political pressure and the manipulation of the companies' economic strengths' (Gibbons 1991: 99). It would certainly be problematic for a Secretary of State to face cabinet colleagues with a decision which allowed jobs to be lost as a result of a newspaper closure rather than let it be taken over, even if the takeover resulted in greater concentration of ownership. Given the relatively weak economic position of many newspapers, this is a reality which must be faced on a regular basis.

In Chapter 2, the drastic reduction in numbers of Left-leaning British newspapers in the post-war era was noted, alongside changes in ownership patterns (Humphreys 1996 Chapter 3; Negrine 1994: Chapter 3). Clearly, concentration of ownership, to the extent that ownership impacts upon editorial freedom, can inhibit the political diversity of the press, though this remains an essentially contingent relationship. The precise relationship between newspaper takeovers, closures, political orientation and general market forces and trends in 'product loyalty' cannot be identified with certainty, but it is obvious that, to the extent that newspapers help form public opinion or at least establish part of the climate in which public opinion is formed, the control of newspapers is a highly contentious party political issue. The failure by the Secretary of State to stop acquisitions by Rupert Murdoch's group of titles (spanning the popular, quality and middle-ground markets) during the Thatcher years may not be without significance, (as was noted in Chapter 2) and the mere continuation of a number of titles does not in itself, guarantee pluralism in terms of editorial line (see Gibbons 1992). Robertson and Nicol (1992: 506) describe as 'understandable' the MMC's reluctance to enter into investigations into the political allegiances of newspaper proprietors, but believe that the public-interest criteria established by the FTA to guide the MMC's investigations do require 'an assessment of the consequences of the transaction on the availability to the public of a reasonable variety of editorial opinion'.

With all this in mind, it seems democratically necessary (if not perhaps politically convenient for those in government) for discretion in relation to newspaper acquisitions to be properly 'confined, structured and checked' (Davis 1971) and perhaps taken out of the sphere of government influence. Whish (1993: 678) seeks to confine the discretionary element, stating that 'there would be much to be said for removing the element of political discretion in this area by making all newspaper mergers referable to the MMC, subject to a *de minimis* exception', though it would probably be necessary in such circumstances to consider also making MMC findings binding. Both Robertson and Nicol (1992: 505) and Gibbons (1991: 99) in effect propose a restructuring of discretion, requiring the imposition on those proposing newspaper acquisitions of a requirement to demonstrate that the proposed takeover or merger would not operate against the public interest, or even a burden of proving to the MMC that the acquisition would positively serve the public interest.

Another option might be to hand over such matters to the judiciary, as part of either a general or specialist jurisdiction. The potential costs and benefits of judicialising this system would have to be weighed carefully in order to assess whether any of the problems of cost and delay identified by Ainsworth and Weston (1995) in relation to the present system would simply be reproduced or even heightened. In addition, any such proposal would depend for its effectiveness upon the British judiciary being able and willing to adjudicate on politically contentious issues, an area in which judges are, at least overtly, usually wary of treading.

Whish (1993: 679) states that 'The provisions of the FTA 1973 for controlling other mergers are very different from those governing newspapers', and that in other areas of mergers and takeovers 'The system of control is benign and is essentially predisposed in favour of mergers'. The evidence presented here should, however, be enough to convince that in practice there is little difference between the predisposition of general merger controls and those specific to newspaper takeovers. The high degree of concentration of ownership and lack of pluralism in the British press has certainly not been unduly restricted by the press-specific FTA provisions. On the whole, Ainsworth and Weston's conclusion that, in reality, the regime for the regulation of newspaper acquisitions rests largely upon the discretion of the Secretary of State, and that the game as presently played is not worth the candle, is almost certainly correct.

The Labour Government's Competition Bill, brought before Parliament in October 1997, fails to amend the process relating to newspaper acquisitions, and also declines to address the specific issue of predatory pricing that were raised by competitors in relation to the pricing policy of *The Times*. It is unclear whether the proposed replacement of the MMC with a 'Competition Commission' will have more than symbolic significance.

The Government's failure to take this opportunity to address competition issues in the newspaper market is disappointing as, in so far as ownership or control of newspapers is a political issue, whether in the party or broader, democratic sense, it is reasonable for the state to make special provision to protect perceived public interests in a pluralistic press. At present, however, within the permissive, discretionary structure of the FTA provisions and the nebulous construct of the public interest applied, the statutory measures on newspaper acquisitions, in so far as they have any effect, operate simply to leave the power of determination essentially within the hands of the government of the day; a prime example of ritualistic regulation masking raw political power.

- 4.3 Licensing Commercial Television and Regulating Cross-media Holdings -

The focus here will be on two aspects of British competition measures specific to the media, concentrating on the interrelated issues of how licences to broadcast commercial, terrestrial, analogue television have been and will be allocated, and how restrictions have been imposed on cross-media holdings. The primary focus will be on the impact of the provisions of the Broadcasting Acts of 1990 and 1996, their intention, the procedures and principles adopted and the outcomes. Though these measures must be viewed alongside general competition provisions and also, in relation to cross-media regulation, measures specific to newspapers and radio, they represent the primary mechanism via which British governments have sought to regulate the television market. As will become apparent, a significant issue here, noted in Chapter 3, is how markets, and hence market shares, are to be measured. Questions of 'market definition' and the difficulties in establishing 'media exchange rates' for calculating cross-media market share are highlighted in attempts to regulate and limit cross-media holdings.

As long ago as 1975, Lewis considered the allocation of franchises for Channel 3 by the (then) IBA. Though Lewis was writing in an era of still limited frequencies, he observed a system with little legal control and few other institutional restraints on the wide-ranging discretion held by the IBA. He found little informed public discussion of the issue, no open hearings prior to franchise allocation, that the criteria applied by the IBA were crude and not published, and that the reasons given by the IBA (when any reasons were given) were inadequate.

In 1981, Elliott conjured up the image of 'chasing the receding bus' to illustrate what he perceived as weaknesses in the approach taken in the 1980 Broadcasting Act. In the post-Annan Committee era, and with the technological revolution having now come over the horizon and clearly fast approaching, Elliott observed that the 1980 Act had simply *assumed* the desirability of government regulation of broadcasting (still substantially relying on the fast disappearing conditions of limited airwaves), and had sought to maintain the BBC/ITV duopoly, ensuring that even with the coming of Channel 4 a significant degree of government control would be retained by virtue of powers of appointment to Channel 4's management. Like Lewis six years earlier, he noted the absence of adequate institutional controls over franchise allocation procedures, and no requirement to give meaningful reasons for decisions. The IBA was assumed to be the repository of 'the public interest' in such matters, but the concept remained hopelessly ill-defined. The thrust of Elliott's piece is that the 1980 Act not only failed to respond adequately to change which was already occurring, but, perhaps more significantly, failed to provide a framework for regulation in an era of more rapid and fundamental change which was already threatening to leave the existing regulatory structures behind.

As Barendt (1993: 13) notes, the Government's apparent intention when introducing the Broadcasting Act 1990 was 'to apply a lighter touch to programme control' in relation to commercial television broadcasters, as well as reforming the licence allocation procedure relating to them. In reality, however, the procedures followed by the ITC under the Act were scarcely less controversial than those of the IBA which it replaced, containing what Hoffmann-Riem (1996: 108) refers to as 'inherent contradictions', while, as Barendt (1993: 13) notes, in practice the Act 'imposed as many new restraints on broadcasters' freedom as it lifted'.

Though its introduction was driven largely by the all-pervasive market-oriented spirit of the age which informed so much of Thatcherism, the regime established ten years later by the 1990 Act appeared to offer some improvements on what went before. Admittedly, it could still be viewed as reactive rather than forward-looking, a fact to which both its failure to regulate the rise to total dominance of BSkyB in British DTH satellite broadcasting, and the need for a further major act only six years later, bear elegant testimony. Harlow and Rawlings state (1997: 274) the new franchising procedure for the allocation of licences marked a shift in terminology from 'contract' to 'licence' and suggested, therefore, a more public law-oriented approach to broadcasting which might offer some potential benefits in terms of establishing criteria for decision-making, requiring reasons for decisions and thereby increasing transparency and accountability. The extent to which these potential benefits have accrued in practice is highly debatable and must be weighed against the Act's effect, described by Hutton (1995: 33) in terms of destabilising the entire ITV system.

The licence allocation system resulting from the 1990 Act took account of two criteria: a financial sustainability test and a programme quality threshold. Assuming that bidders met both criteria, franchises would normally be awarded by the ITC to the highest bidder, though the ITC retained a power under section 17 to accept a lower bid in place of a higher one 'where there are exceptional circumstances which make it appropriate for them to award the licence to another applicant'. Thus, the 1990 Act introduced a hybrid system of franchising, embodying aspects of both price bidding and public interest, the latter in this case being defined in terms of the problematic concept of programme 'quality' (Seymour-Ure 1996: 109). As Prosser (1994) observed, the fact that only half of the licence awards made in the first round of Channel 3 franchising under this new regime were to the highest bidder suggests that 'exceptional circumstances' must have been exceptionally common! Though Harlow and Rawlings (1997: 277) suggest that in giving preference to other factors than simply the price bid, this outcome 'underscores the continuing relevance of "public interest"', it is unclear exactly what the term was taken to mean by the ITC, and Harlow and Rawlings' other conclusion, 'that rather more discretion might have been exercised than had been envisaged in Parliament' (ibid.), is perhaps more telling.

Outcomes of ITC licence allocation procedures under the 1990 Act have been challenged directly in the courts by losing bidders on two notable occasions. In 1992, following the first set of regional licence awards under the new regime, Television South West (TSW) sought to challenge the loss of its licence (R. v. ITC, ex parte TSW Broadcasting, The Independent, 27 March 1992; see Jones 1992), while more recently a losing bidder in the contest for the fifth channel licence also sought judicial review of the decision (R. v ITC ex parte Virgin Television Ltd, [1996] EMLR 318; see Marsden 1996).

Both cases, however, illustrate a marked reluctance on the part of the courts – in the TSW case the House of Lords – to interfere in relation to the substance of the decisions taken by the ITC. This should not be unexpected, and indeed, as Prosser (1997: 262) indicates, the courts are 'sensibly avoiding second-guessing the substantive decisions'. That said, the TSW judgement appeared to impose a requirement on the ITC to provide more in the way of reasons for its decisions on licence allocation; in particular, in the circumstances of TSW, a holder of an existing franchise which believed itself to be the highest bidder for the new franchise. Such a move is clearly to be welcomed in terms of furthering rationality, transparency and accountability. Despite this judgement, however, a degree of lack of transparency in the ITC's procedures was revealed again five years later in the Virgin case.

While both Virgin and UKTV passed the financial sustainability test, the ITC determined that neither crossed the programme quality threshold test established by section 16(1)(a). Neither was therefore eligible for the licence award, and Channel Five Broadcasting (Channel 5) was awarded the licence in the face of one remaining application, whose cash bid was much lower. In addition to (unsuccessfully) raising questions over procedures adopted by the ITC in allowing Channel 5 to amend the details of its bid to ensure that it passed the financial sustainability test, Virgin sought to challenge the basis of the Commission's decision relating to its programming plans.

In particular, it sought to draw attention to inconsistencies between the advice provided to the Commission in papers produced by its staff advisers, and the Commission's conclusions on programming. However, Marsden (1996) notes, in relation to Virgin's unsuccessful challenge, that 'the courts have shown no propensity to challenge the assembled expertise of the ITC in determining qualitative standards in programming' and that, given that the argument presented on this point by Virgin was found to be 'both impermissible and hopeless', he concludes that 'the likelihood of a successful future challenge to the quality threshold appears minimal'. Marsden questions, however, whether the regulatory role in relation to programming quality currently resting with the ITC may be about to be diminished, given its more limited role in relation to DTT, just as the role of the IBA was limited in 1984 in relation to programming requirements for cable television services which were placed under the cable authority's jurisdiction (Veljanovski 1987).

Prosser (1997: Chapter 9) appears to consider the outcome of the 1992 *TSW* case to be a marked improvement on what went before. It has to be emphasised, however, that he rightly also points out that in reality, 'in both the allocation of Channel 3 licences and the more recent allocation of those for Channel 5 the outcome was determined more by discretionary decisions on quality matters than by bidding in the market-place' (266). As such, it is reasonable to expect a high degree of transparency and reasoning in such cases, and whether the decision in TSW is adequate in this respect is very questionable, in that it is limited to the situation of a highest bidder in possession of an existing licence, and is not necessarily of wider application. It can be argued that the principle of fully reasoned decisions needs to established on a general basis; not just in relation to existing franchisees, but also in relation to new applicants for licences both in terrestrial, analogue television and in similar allocation processes in relation to multiplexes in the brave new world of DTT where essentially the same issues arise. In the absence of adequate guarantees of openness in such decision-making processes, it is impossible to be sure what, if any, model of the public interest has been utilised when the relevant authority reaches a decision.

Though raising interesting and important issues in itself, the allocation of broadcasting licences via hybrid franchising procedures must be viewed against the background of limits on those seeking licences who also hold interests in other media. The 1995 White Paper (DNH 1995a), which preceded the 1996 Act, emphasised three objectives for the regulation of cross-media ownership or control:

1. the promotion of diversity in media material, and the expression of a range of views;
2. the maintenance of a strong media industry, 'for the economic benefit of the country'; and
3. ensuring the proper operation of markets, including access for new entrants to markets, and the prevention of cross-media subsidies or predatory pricing. (DNH 1995a: para. 6.19)

The White Paper (DNH 1995a: para. 6.25) proposed that in relation to the television sector and cross-media holdings including television broadcasting, the ITC will be expected to balance these three conflicting public interest criteria. While these are all perfectly legitimate objectives, there remains significant doubt as to whether they are sufficiently clear as to allow the existing regulators to achieve them, and in practice this suggests that wide-ranging discretion, subject still to inadequate institutional safeguards, will remain with the ITC.

It should be noted that the British Government moved ahead with the 1996 Act despite the possibility of an EU Directive on the same subject being brought forward. In practice, the European measure appears to be on a slow track, and has been opposed equally by the former Conservative and present Labour administrations which claim that media ownership provisions should be subject to the principle of subsidiarity, as a matter which is best addressed at the national level. The problems of establishing common ownership regulations across Europe, even aiming only at harmonisation, suggest that these would be likely to be only at a lowest-common-denominator level, and may by themselves prove ineffective, replicating the kind of difficulties identified by Humphreys in the federal context of Germany. Beyond this point, it might in any case be questionable whether EU competence extends to questions of ownership, as opposed to the kind of technical issues addressed in the Advanced Television Standards Directives (1995/47) and the December 1997 Green Paper (European Commission 1997) on technological convergence, both of which are focused on internal market issues of the compatability of technology across the EU (see Chapter 6).

The complexity of the British provisions, assuming that other countries present similar difficulties, certainly appears to render trans-European regulation unlikely. In part, this complexity derives from difficulties in identifying market shares and appropriate thresholds for intervention or prohibition. Market definition is a perennial problem for regulators seeking to ensure competition. It is an essential prerequisite for determining intervention thresholds, whether established by reference to a percentage market share (in terms of turnover or advertising revenue, say), the existence of a dominant position, or by reference to market reach or audience share or degree of influence in relation to the media whether individually or as a whole.

In Britain, the position is peculiarly complicated as a result of the application of different thresholds, based on different factors, established by different pieces of legislation. In general, British competition authorities tend to show an interest when a threshold of 25 per cent of a market is controlled by one player or group. In the case of newspapers, however, the provisions of the FTA, as noted earlier, allow for intervention when a takeover involves circulation in excess of 500,000, equating to less than 5 per cent of the market. Huge difficulties are encountered even in relation to measuring market share in a single market, such as radio, where different bases for measuring market share may produce very different outcomes. For example, 'Capital Radio's impact is twelve times higher measured by its share of time spent consuming the media than if measured by revenues' (Congdon et al. 1995: 9). Such complexities are heightened in relation to attempts to measure cross-media market shares, and clarity is not helped by the net result of measures such as those contained in the new Schedule 2, which Gibbons (1996) rightly states 'combines audience share with various fixed limits on ownership'.

It should be apparent that, although the EU measures to date establish common technical standards across the Member States, this does not mean that all competition law provisions are common. For example, at present there remains a marked contrast between on the one hand, the emphasis of EU Articles 85 and 86 which focus on the prohibition of distortion of competition and abuse of a dominant position, and on the other, existing British measures which use market share, a structural concern, as the trigger mechanism, though the Competition Bill 1997 appears to incorporate the basic principles of EU competition law into British law.

In addition to general competition provisions, however, the EU continues to make moves towards a directive on media ownership. The first steps were taken in 1992 (see Hitchens 1994; Feintuck 1995) but progress has been exceedingly slow, with a further paper expected in 1998. In its 1996 form, the proposed directive would have established a 30 per cent upper limit on holdings in any one media sector (newspapers, radio or television), combined with an upper limit of 10 per cent total media market share. Though acknowledging that these limits are not particularly objectionable in themselves, Doyle (1997) raises a number of practical problems in relation to both market definition and the difficulties of applying a unified formula to the very different existing patterns of ownership across the range of Member States.

The 1997 proposals for the Directive, however, as Doyle (1997) indicates, reflect a move away from an emphasis on 'pluralism' (apparently implying both ownership and output) in earlier proposals, where the legal competence of EU bodies to act might be in question, to a focus specifically on ownership in the context of the EU's internal market agenda. In addition, and as an apparent attempt to bring recalcitrant Member States (especially Germany and the UK) on board, increased flexibility in relation to the proposed ownership limits for Member States is suggested. While increasing the likelihood of consensus, this is unlikely to improve the effectiveness of the measure or to produce meaningful harmonisation. Indeed, Doyle goes so far as to suggest that the change of name of the proposed directive, from 'Media Pluralism' to 'Media Ownership', and the increased degree of flexibility for individual Member States are symptomatic of a change of emphasis which means that 'the Directive is no longer about guaranteeing an equal right to pluralism (as represented by diversity of ownership) for all EU citizens, irrespective of which European markets they live in'.

Collins and Murroni (1996: 68) suggest a tiered or stepped approach to media ownership in combination with other proposed measures, for example guaranteeing journalistic independence by way of behavioural control over media owners. They present a specific proposal to restrict holdings across four sectors (national newspapers, regional newspapers, television and radio) stepped down from 40 per cent to 15 per cent, depending on whether a player or group has interests in one, two, three or all four sectors. While the kind of proposal presented by Collins and Murroni has many superficial attractions, not the least of which is apparent simplicity and clarity, in practice it contains implicit assumptions regarding a 'media exchange rate' and appears to understate the difficulty in establishing market share even within one sector. While the tiered or stepped approach to setting limits on ownership within and across media sectors is in principle an attractive one, it remains questionable whether the minimum level of diversity it would ensure across the media as a whole is adequate, and in the modern context such a measure must be expanded to factor in control of key aspects of the technological infrastructure, which appears at least as significant as control of production companies.

That said, the benefits of clarity and simplicity are not to be underestimated, especially when faced with the prospect of the nightmarish complexity of a journey through Schedule 2! While the broad public-interest principles included in the 1995 White Paper might be criticised on grounds of lack of detail, the same cannot be said of the cross-media measures contained in the labyrinthine Schedule 2 to the 1996 Act. In the spirit of this book, it is intended to provide the traveller only with information regarding some of the more important landmarks to be found in Schedule 2 rather than a comprehensive description of all its many and varied features; Gibbons (1996) provides an excellent, comprehensive commentary on the Schedule 2 provisions and their effects, and the DCMS (1998c) offers a useful summary.

The most straightforward aspect of the measures is the absolute limits on ownership. In relation to commercial (i.e., other than BBC) television, paragraph 11 of Schedule 2 establishes that if a person (natural or legal) controls more than a 15 per cent share of the total audience time, they may not hold two or more licences for Channel 3 and/or Channel 5, or have more than a 20 per cent interest in two or more such licences, or provide a foreign satellite service and hold (or hold a 20 per cent interest in) such a licence. Paragraph 4 of the Schedule disallows both the holding of a national Channel 3 licence together with a Channel 5 licence, and the holding of geographically overlapping regional licences. Paragraph 5 also imposes an absolute limit of three on the holding of multiplex licences for DTT, which will be considered shortly. In relation to radio, it should be noted that the Schedule does not allow the holding of more than one national licence for a radio service, whether analogue or digital.

Paragraph 11 contains the new limits on cross-media holdings which include newspapers and licensed television or radio services. It must be emphasised, however, that these restrictions do not require the break-up of any pre-existing cross-media groups, and refer only to future acquisitions. Essentially, this is a liberalising set of measures, as Gibbons (1996) notes, removing many of the former upper limits on cross-ownership. Under the new rules, however, the owner of a national newspaper with a market share of 20 per cent or more is not permitted to hold a licence for either Channel 3 or Channel 5, or a radio licence, ruling out both News Corporation and Mirror Group from an expansion into regional commercial television. The owner of a local newspaper with a local share of more than 20 per cent may not hold a regional Channel 3 licence for the same area.

As might be expected, however, the complexity of the media market does not permit its regulation to be carried out entirely by rules. Rather, a wide-ranging discretion is granted (by para. 9) to 'the relevant authority' (ITC or RA) to prevent the granting of a licence for a broadcast service to a body corporate which is (or is connected with) the proprietor of a newspaper 'if the relevant authority determine that in all the circumstances the holding of the licence by that body corporate could be expected to operate against the public interest'.

The Schedule goes on (in para. 13) to establish the criteria to be applied as indicative of the public interest. These include:

a) the desirability of promoting –
    i) plurality of ownership in the broadcasting and newspaper industries, and
    ii) diversity in the sources of information available to the public and in the opinions expressed on television or radio or in newspapers,
b) any economic benefits . . .
c) the effect of the holding of the licence by that body on the proper operation of the market within the broadcasting and newspaper industries or any section of them. (para. 13, Sch. 2, Broadcasting Act 1996)

The tension and conflict between these competing public-interest claims is obvious, as noted in Chapter 3. The regulators will have to balance potential economic benefits against the values of pluralism and diversity and the effects on competition. This leaves the regulators with an unenviable task, akin to comparing apples with oranges and, in the British context we cannot be sure that any such decision will be taken via a transparent process, or even necessarily that adequate reasons will be required or given to permit checks on the rationality of such decision-making. Thus, the absence of a meaningful construct of 'public interest' permits, or even encourages, inconsistency in regulation and also hands to regulators significant and largely unchecked, discretionary power.

Clearly, the regulation of cross-media holdings is not one that can be confined to national borders in an increasingly international media context, though whether or not British measures mesh with, or run counter to, the principles of potential EC provisions will become clear only when (or if) the Commission eventually produces a directive on media pluralism and ownership. Questions of EC competence to legislate in this area aside, previous delays in finalising such a measure and opposition from certain Member States including the UK, suggest that it may still be some considerable time before such a measure emerges.

In practice it is difficult to predict the medium-term outcomes that will result from the introduction under the 1996 Act of the combination of set limits on ownership or control, audience share criteria and the exercise of discretion by the regulatory authorities introduced by the 1996 Act. Certainly, a minimum level of diversity of ownership will be ensured, though whether this will result in the maintenance or enhancement of meaningful diversity in programming or meaningful competition is doubtful. To some extent, the answer to this question may well depend on whether or not it is assumed that existing arrangements amount to meaningful diversity. If it is assumed that present arrangements do not maximise the diversity of media output available to all citizens, Barendt's observation can usefully be restated: 'Conventional competition regulation preventing, for example, new combinations without disturbing existing patterns of ownership may not be enough to achieve this goal' (Barendt 1993: 123).

As the present author wrote shortly after the passage of the 1996 Act,

> In so far as the previous regime has already allowed 63% of national newspaper circulation to be controlled by only two groups, Rupert Murdoch's News Corporation and Mirror Group, and has allowed Murdoch also to take the lead in British satellite broadcasting . . . the omens are not good. It should be expected that the best outcome now likely, from the point of view of diversity, would approximate to the present situation of oligopoly, with worse outcomes being a real possibility. (Feintuck 1997b: 209)

It can be argued that, though focused on cross-media ownership, the measures fail to provide an integrated response to technological convergence and revised ownership patterns. Indeed, Hitchens (1995a) points towards a general mismatch between the regulatory forms adopted and the regulatory objectives, deriving, she suggests, from an incrementalist approach to media regulation at a time of technological revolution; in this sense, Elliot's bus still appears to be accelerating away. In particular, treating control of DTT multiplexes separately from other media interests appears to fail to acknowledge that such crucial gateways form an important new media sector in their own right, and the potential influence over the television market to be exerted by those who control multiplexes would tend to suggest that they should be included in the assessment of the size of cross-media empires. Just as the 1990 Act failed to include non-domestic satellite television in its establishment of limits on cross-media holdings, so the failure to integrate multiplexes for DTT into the calculation of cross-media holdings under the 1996 measures may allow powerful groups or individuals to shape the new market.

– 4.4 Regulating Digital Terrestrial Television –

The measures contained in the Broadcasting Act 1996, aimed at regulating holdings in conventional broadcasting and cross-media holdings including broadcasting, reflect the fast-changing market environment in which media regulation now takes place. The measures to be addressed now, arising out of the introduction of DTT, also reflect market issues, but are driven to a large extent by technological development.

The arrival in spring 1997 of Channel 5, Britain's latest and last national analogue television channel, was overshadowed by the promise of DTT in 1998. While everyone is reasonably familiar with the basic mechanics of transmission and reception in relation to traditional, analogue television, for the uninitiated, perhaps daunted by talk of 'conditional access systems', 'multiplexes' and the like in relation to DTT, a little background might be helpful by way of introduction to the relevant technological issues.

DTT promises to bring a huge increase in the number of television channels available, while at the same time introducing better picture quality, improved stereo sound and wide-screen display. This will be achieved by replacing traditional transmission of analogue signals with digital transmission via binary codes which will be unscrambled at the receiver's set through digital decoding equipment. The new technology allows the content of a number of different television programmes to be transmitted simultaneously on a single frequency (via 'digital compression'), with capacity built in to allow for channels or programmes requiring especially high-resolution images to be delivered with enhanced picture quality while other services may be transmitted at a lower quality. In addition to increasing the number of channels, digital compression also frees up potentially valuable parts of the spectrum for sale, perhaps to the telecommunications industry (Feintuck 1997b). Blocks of the digital spectrum – 'multiplexes' sufficient to carry a wide range of channels, have now been allocated by the Independent Television Commission (ITC 1997) to licensed multiplex providers (see Feintuck 1997c).

Television viewers will continue to receive the DTT signal via their conventional aerial, but initially will need to buy a decoder (conditional access system – CAS) at an estimated cost of between £200 and £400, though it is expected that, subsequently, television sets with in-built decoding equipment will appear on the market. Conventional analogue transmitters will be switched off in due course, though certain services will remain not subject to direct payment by the viewer, while others will be encrypted and charged for on a subscription or pay-per-view basis in much the same way as satellite and cable television is presently (Feintuck 1997b).

Arguably, the key issue for those concerned with media regulation is that, if not adequately regulated, the provider of the decoding equipment could exercise substantial influence over television programming, being in control of not only the allocation of channels to broadcasters but also the organisation of the electronic programme guide (EPG), a navigation system through which viewers will locate the programmes they wish to receive. In effect, those controlling key 'gateways' within the new broadcasting market, will wield enormous power, if not adequately regulated. The risk is that neither programme producers, nor conventional broadcasting corporations, or indeed the viewer will be able to exert much influence if the range of options ultimately delivered is managed unresponsively by those controlling the decoding technology and EPGs. The problem is paralleled in the air transport market where, if the international computerised reservation system (CRS) were to be controlled by one major airline, say British Airways (BA), there would be a natural tendency for BA to produce a system which prioritised its flights and tickets over those of its competitors in the information provided via the CRS to travel agents and thence travellers. In this field, EU legislation (Regulation 2299/89, as amended by Regulation 3089/93) has sought to ensure equality of treatment between the CRS controller airline and its competitors (see Goh 1997).

If a situation arises where such gateways in the DTT distribution network fall into the hands of a player with a significant stake also in programme production or distribution, the pursuit by other parties, whether producers or distributors, of commercial or non-commercial goals which run counter to the corporate interests of the gateway controller will become exceedingly difficult. Vertically integrated corporate empires which include control of production, distribution and reception, and which may influence viewing habits also by promotion via the press (Sadler 1991), will enjoy to the full the synergistic, and ultimately monopolistic strengths noted by Herman and McChesney (1997).

Carrying over from the policy of the previous administration, there is no doubt that for the duration of the 1997 Labour Government's term, DTT will be flavour of the month. Though the Government's consultation paper issued in February 1998 (DCMS 1998a) discusses the economic impact of the introduction of DTT and states that DTT will be part of a television market, it is clear that the Government views DTT as the primary delivery platform in the future. That said, it should be noted, however, that although DTT is the current focus of much attention, there is also potential for the further development of satellite broadcasting, though competing for the British market with the well-established BSkyB is likely to be considered an unattractive proposition. Of possibly still greater long-term significance, though as yet little used in Britain and dependant on a massive investment in the cable infrastructure, could be reception of television via high-capacity fibre-optic cable which could integrate familiar television programming with video on demand, telecommunications and information technology services.

This then is the technological background to the digital revolution to be regulated under the provisions of the Broadcasting Act 1996. Though sections 40–72 of the 1996 Act also make parallel provisions for the regulation of digital terrestrial radio, the focus here is on the primary broadcast medium, television.

Part I of the Act is focused on the licensing of multiplex services for DTT. Sections 1–39 establish the statutory framework for the allocation of frequencies for multiplexes and for their regulation, inevitably not a straightforward task, especially during the transitional phase of switch-over from analogue to digital transmission. The Act anticipates that multiplex providers will deliver packages of a variety of services, intended to appeal to a wide audience, though themed multiplexes are also a possibility. In addition, section 28 ensures provision of capacity via multiplexes for existing analogue service providers (the BBC and independent broadcasters licensed for Channels 3, 4 and 5) whose digital broadcast version of programmes, 'qualifying services' under section 2(2), will remain free at the point of reception.

The allocation and enforcement of multiplex licences are dealt with in sections 3–17, with the Act providing for the Secretary of State to determine multiplex frequencies which are then to be allocated by the ITC. Sections 3–5 establish general licence conditions, while section 12 adds supplementary, specific conditions and section 10 allows the ITC to impose financial conditions upon the grant of a licence, essentially mirroring those in the 1990 Act relating to the financial security of the licence holder for conventional, terrestrial television. Included in the specific conditions of section 12, at subsection (1)(g), is a requirement imposing standards as to the technical quality and reliability of the multiplex service, in pursuit of the objectives established in the EU Advanced Television Standards Directive (95/47).

Section 8 establishes criteria which the ITC must take into account when considering applications for available licences from would-be multiplex service providers. The criteria include the extent of geographical coverage for the proposed service, the timetable for bringing the service on-stream, the financial viability of the proposal, 'the capacity of the digital programme services proposed to be included in the service to appeal to a variety of tastes and interests', and that 'the applicant has acted in a manner calculated to ensure fair and effective competition in the provision of such services'. Thus, these general conditions appear to demand a guarantee of minimum standards of diversity in programming and the avoidance of anti-competitive practices by those controlling the provision of digital services.

While these criteria are in some respects clearer than the equivalent terms in the 1990 Act relating to the ITC's allocation of franchises for commercial terrestrial licences, and incorporate a similar financial viability test, it is worthy of note that the new provisions do not seem to establish a 'quality threshold' as demanding as that which must be crossed by those seeking regional ITV licences. Although the ITC retains a general brief of ensuring 'quality' in programming under the terms of section 2 of the 1990 Act, there is nothing in the 1996 Act specifically establishing such a requirement in relation to digitally broadcast services. It should be noted also that the rather vague terms of section 8(2)(f), seeking to avoid anti-competitive practices by those seeking multiplex licences, must be viewed alongside the regulatory function of Oftel in relation to CASs, which will be considered later.

Section 8 is most noteworthy, though, for its establishment of an overarching principle which the ITC is seemingly obliged to apply when allocating multiplex licences. The Commission must consider whether the grant of a licence 'would be calculated to promote the development of digital television broadcasting in the United Kingdom otherwise than by satellite'. This makes explicit that the Government's policy at the time the Act was passed was the rapid development of DTT as the primary means of delivery, a policy unchanged by the arrival of the Labour Government in 1997. Section 28 seeks to further this policy by establishing a privileged position for existing broadcasters of analogue terrestrial television (BBC, regional ITV companies and Channels 4 and 5) which will have multiplex capacity reserved for them, presumably in an attempt to ensure the early develop-ment of a digital service carrying a range of 'quality' programming. Sections 19 and 31 introduce specific provisions for the protection of Welsh and Scots Gaelic language services in DTT.

By virtue of section 16, multiplex licences will initially be granted for a period of twelve years and, if granted within six years of the commencement of the Act, will be renewable for a further twelve-year period. Renewal in these circumstances can be denied by the ITC only where a licence holder has failed to comply with licence conditions or will not be able to meet any supplementary conditions which the Commission may impose, or if the Commission is not satisfied that the licence holder would comply with such requirements were the licence to be renewed. Section 17 empowers the ITC to impose sanctions for breach of multiplex licence conditions, ranging from the imposition of financial penalties through to a reduction of the licence period, and ultimately revocation of the licence.

Separate to the provisions relating to multiplex licences are those for the licensing of digital programme services (i.e., the programme provider as opposed to the multiplex licensee) in sections 18–23. These are to be subject to the same conditions, for example relating to taste and decency, monitored by the ITC in relation to conventional licensed television broadcasters under the 1990 Act. Licences will, however, be issued 'essentially, on demand' (Gibbons 1996), subject only to general requirements as to the applicant being a fit and proper person to hold such a license; terms which are not necessarily uncontentious in themselves (see Hitchens 1995b).

Section 33 addresses the medium-term decision to switch off analogue transmission, requiring the Secretary of State to keep under review the development of DTT services, the expectation being that simultaneous transmission of analogue signals ('simulcasting') will continue until such time as the vast majority of viewers are receiving DTT. Estimates as to this period vary but are commonly in the region of 10–15 years (see DCMS 1998a).

Conspicuous by their absence from the primary legislation on broadcasting are detailed measures concerning arguably the key regulatory issue arising out of DTT, namely the control of CASs or receiver decoder equipment. This, states Gibbons (1996), commenting on section 12, reflects the government's wish not to intervene in market activity which will itself, the government believes, result in time in the emergence of an industry standard. As has already been indicated, whoever controls the CASs, potentially exercises significant control over what the viewer may watch. It allows the controller, in its ability to organise the EPG and allocate channels, to discriminate between broadcasters. In addition, many concerns have been voiced regarding the problems of compatibility between equipment supplied by different manufacturers, and the potential for a destructive war of formats such as that experienced in the early days of home video-cassette recorders. In practice, though, it might be thought that some of these concerns would be lessened if the development and marketing of CAS equipment were to be undertaken by a major multiplex provider, or an established player in pay-television such as BSkyB, given that it would then be hard to imagine any other potential competitor attempting to launch alternative decoder equipment. However, while such a situation might avoid a potentially destructive battle, the consumer will need some reassurance that such a dominant degree of control over both the distribution system and technological gateway would not lead to the abuse of this power. Clearly, any such abuse could impact adversely on citizens' ability to access a diverse range of broadcast material though, in the current consumerist climate, the best comfort to be expected is perhaps summed up in the observation by Herbert Ungerer of the EU's Directorate General IV (Competition) quoted by Marsden (1997b) that 'Consumer benefit will result from increased possibilities of supply only if markets are liberalised and gates are kept open'. While the comment as to liberalisation may be more closely connected with the EU's economic agenda than with the kind of citizenship interests discussed in Chapter 3, on this occasion the interests of citizen as citizen and citizen as consumer appear to coincide so far as the maintenance of free movement through gateways is concerned.

Though the EU has produced general statements on standardisation, interconnection and interoperability of telecommunications, information technology and other communications equipment, many of the issues specific to CASs are now addressed directly by the Advanced Television Standards Directive (95/47). Article 4(c) establishes a requirement that:

> Member States shall take all the necessary measures to ensure that the operators of conditional access services, irrespective of the means of transmission, who produce and market access services to digital television services . . . offer to all broadcasters, on a fair, reasonable and non-discriminatory basis, technical services enabling the broadcasters' digitally-transmitted services to be received by viewers authorized by means of decoders administered by the service operators, and comply with Community competition law, in particular if a dominant position appears. (Art. 4(c), Advanced Television Standards Directive 95/47)

The UK Government has now introduced, by secondary legislation, measures (Advanced Television Services Regulations 1996, SI 1996/3151) which implement the Directive, Regulation 11 which largely reproduces the terminology of Article 4(c). In force from the same date as the Regulations (7 January 1997) is a Class Licence (under section 7 of the Telecommunications Act 1984) introduced by the Secretary of State, to authorise the running of CASs.

Britain's telecommunications regulator, Oftel, is to play a significant role in this area, in terms of both licensing the CASs and establishing guidelines for the CAS sector. In this respect, Oftel (1997c) has identified four key objectives:

1. ensuring that control of conditional access technology is not used to distort, restrict or prevent competition in television and connected services, i.e., is not used anti-competitively;
2. ensuring that control of conditional access technology does not lead to consumer choice being artificially constrained in relation to both consumer equipment and the range of services available;
3. facilitating the ability of consumers to switch between delivery mechanisms; and,
4. facilitating consumer choice by ensuring ease of access to relevant information.

Oftel indicates that its guidelines, within the framework established by the Regulations and the Class Licence, 'are part of a systematic effort to ensure consistency of approach to the regulation of communications networks, whether they are wire or fibre-based or wireless, or broadcast or hybrids of these' (Oftel 1997c).

The active involvement of Oftel, hitherto primarily the regulator of telecommunications, in relation to the development of CASs for DTT, is to be welcomed. It is an acknowledgement of the convergence of media and communications technology and may point the way towards a future in which a unified regulatory regime is put in place. In the meantime, however, the measurement of audience or circulation share as an indicator of strength of cross-media holdings remains inadequate if it fails to integrate into this calculation the crucial factor of control of technological gateways. Disappointingly, while paragraph 5 of Schedule 2 to the 1996 Act establishes a maximum of three multiplex licences which may be held together, it does not factor this holding into the overall limits on cross-media ownership.

There is no doubt that the CASs and EPGs required for the viewer to receive DTT form new pinch-points in the commercial television market, with control of these gateways permitting the possibility of domination of the market by one player. BSkyB, is already virtually the monopoly player in British satellite television, and is part of Rupert Murdoch's News Corporation group that controls over 35 per cent of the British national press. This group also looks likely to be first in the field with DTT decoders and, as a probable key supplier of major programming to DTT (through exclusive control of major sporting events and new films), has the potential to develop rapidly a monopoly power over this new market.

The imminence of the arrival of DTT and its importance in the minds of significant media players, were emphasised in early 1997 when applications were made for the first available multiplex licences. Competing with an application from Digital Television Network (DTN), wholly owned by CableTel (Britain's largest cable television company), was a consortium called British Digital Broadcasting (BDB), incorporating three of the biggest players in British commercial broadcasting: BSkyB, Carlton Communications and Granada Television. With the active cooperation of the BBC, BDB made an application based on proposals to provide fifteen new channels. If this application had been granted as it stood, it would have allowed Rupert Murdoch, the key figure behind both BSkyB (Britain's major satellite broadcasting company) and News Corporation (whose publications account for over one-third of the British national newspaper market), to exercise a further significant influence over the media via control of multiplexes and the associated CASs.

In June 1997, despite acknowledging the qualities of a competing bid from DTN, the ITC awarded control (ITC 1997) of the three commercial multiplexes for DTT to the BDB consortium. However, influenced in part no doubt by advice from Oftel (Oftel 1997a and b), the ITC was prepared to accept the BDB bid only if BSkyB were to sell its one-third equity holding to the other consortium members, themselves both already major media players.

Despite BSkyB's withdrawal from the consortium, Don Cruickshank, Oftel's Director General, continued to express concern regarding BSkyB's likely position of dominance in relation to programme supply to the new channels, especially in the key areas of sport coverage and movie premieres. He noted that even with BSkyB excluded from holding a share in multiplex licences, 'the participation of BSkyB . . . as a long-term supplier of certain pay TV services, in particular sports programming, raised substantial competition concerns in the pay TV network and conditional access markets' (Oftel 1997d). This reflects the situation described by Herman and McChesney (1997: 68) in the USA, where media giants like Disney and Time Warner which increasingly provide their own products, notably films, on a privileged basis to their own channels can effectively shut out competitors from the market.

On the day after the announcement of the ITC's decision, it was observed that 'The BDB affair has exposed the regulatory turf war between Mr Cruickshank's Oftel and the ITC, making it even more imperative for the Government to produce a new, more robust regulatory system for the new media technologies' (*The Guardian* 25 June 1997). A degree of tension between regulators sharing jurisdiction is inevitable, and perhaps even helpful in the short term if it facilitates the articulation of clear regulatory standards. However, it is by no means certain that this will in fact be the outcome and, in the longer term, it might be expected to result primarily in uncertainty and may impede the identification and attainment of regulatory goals. It may also lead to resentment amongst those who feel that they have suffered at the hands of an uncertain regulatory regime.

The losing bidder for the multiplexes, DTN, was reported (*Financial Times; The Guardian* both 25 June 1997) to be considering an application for judicial review in relation to the licence award. However, the precedents on challenges to ITC licence awards by TSW and Virgin, considered earlier in this chapter, suggest that such a step would be related more to publicity than anything else, given the courts' track record of reluctance in over-turning ITC licence allocation decisions. Evidence in this field suggests that the British courts cannot necessarily be relied upon to ensure rationality or even transparency in the exercise of power such as the award of licences to broadcasters. It can be argued that British courts, basing their actions to a large extent upon the limited concept of 'Wednesbury reasonableness' and a near-exclusive focus on procedure, do not apply the same, rigorous standards of review as do, for example, their US counterparts (see Harden and Lewis 1986). In Harlow and Rawlings' terms (1997: 280), the British version might properly be viewed as not even a 'light touch', but a 'soft touch'.

This example demonstrates the fact that the kind of reactive and marginal reform of the British media regulation regime brought about in recent years has failed to resolve underlying tensions between competing regulatory approaches and philosophies. Indeed, in confirming attempts to allow the coexistence of competing and potentially conflicting rationales and without subjecting decision-making to adequate scrutiny, it indicates a degree of complacency and myopia which is likely to prove dangerous in the context of the ongoing media revolution.

– 4.5 Same as it Ever Was? –

A certain lack of clarity is evident in relation to the vision of the role of the state as embodied in the media regulation practices just discussed. Measures designed to bring about a particular model of competition are applied, though based on somewhat arbitrary fixed limits and differing approaches and in the absence of a clear definition of the media market. The regulatory machine has been reformed, in response to the changing market and technological environment, but without the development or statement of clear objectives appropriate to new circumstances. Indeed, the previous and present governments' unswerving adherence to the rapid development of DTT, as opposed to cable or DTH satellite, as the primary delivery platform suggests that they have failed to challenge the views of DTT's proponents and exponents, who Marsden (1997b: 3) states have presented it as 'a paradigmatic, determinist "revolutionary" policy choice'. The absence of anything approaching a serious media policy or fundamental review of practices is clearly illustrated.

Though the changes to the statutory position brought about by the 1996 Act may be condemned as simply reactive – a response to the changing media market, they face the still more serious charge of failing to iron out underlying defects in the system. In particular, the lack of clarity in regulatory objectives remains, and is likely to be resolved pragmatically by the outcome of the 'regulatory turf war' between the ITC and Oftel, rather than as a result of informed, public debate.

The failure of the 1996 Act to integrate control of DTT multiplexes and CASs into calculations of broader market share is worrying and short-sighted. No aspect of the media market can be treated in isolation in such a fast-changing environment; thirty years ago it was apparent to Blumler and

Madge (1967) that 'It is essential that [the] modern communication process should be examined as a whole and not by studying certain parts in isolation'. Just as the exclusion from the relevant provisions of the 1990 Act for non-domestic satellite broadcasters allowed Murdoch's BSkyB to extend its overall empire, to define the shape of the British DTH satellite broadcasting market, and also to influence the shape of broadcasting as a whole, so failures in the regulation of DTT may have consequences not limited to that particular media sector. The implications of the spread of the Carlton and Granada empires into DTT, though not necessarily problematic in themselves, must be assessed in conjunction with their other substantial holdings in regional Channel 3 rather than in isolation.

In summary, the regulatory patterns established in relation to conventional television and DTT are highly reactive in nature, with government policy and legislation not steered in the direction of clear objectives, but rather blown by the gusty winds of change. An acknowledgement that pluralism in ownership is not an end in itself but merely instrumental in the furtherance of citizenship objectives might provide a stronger anchor for regulation in the tidal wave of change. In addition, the application of an unambiguously citizenship-oriented approach may also help in the interpretation of both broadly stated assertions of public interest justifications for regulation (for example, as stated in DNH 1995a), and the complex, technical provisions contained in Schedule 2 to the Act.

The difference in approach to regulating the broadcast and printed media has already been referred to in Chapter 3, and will be returned to in Chapter 5. However, it is worth noting here that in an era of technological convergence, where both television news-type services and newspaper material are available via the Internet, such differences become increasingly difficult to justify. In addition, the increasingly international nature of broadcasting and of press ownership may make the policing of broadcasting content, such as that carried out by the ITC and BSC, increasingly unfeasible.

This does not necessarily constitute a case for a move to lowest-common-denominator regulation, which presumably in this case would equate to the kind of regulation, or lack of it, achieved by the PCC in relation to the press (see Chapter 5). Neither should it be seen as an argument towards moving in the direction of more appointed boards, such as the ITC or BSC, drawn from the conventional ranks of 'the great and the good'. It probably draws us in the direction taken by Collins and Murroni (1996) of a single communications regulator, best able to take an overview of the media market but, crucially, structured in such a way as to ensure transparency and rationality in the exercise of its discretion. Though the question will be returned to, it is worth noting here that Oftel, the new arrival on the media regulation scene, is relatively enthusiastic regarding the rationalisation of regulation towards a single regulator model (see Graham (forthcoming)), but on a basis which excludes regulation of content, an exclusion which, given the underlying objective of regulation, would seem to risk undermining the utility of any such move.

Powers such as those exercised by the ITC and BSC, or the powers of appointment and influence exercised by the Government in relation to the appointments to the BBC's Board of Governors and to a lesser extent Channel 4 (discussed in Chapter 5), must be exercised in the sunshine of public scrutiny. Thus, in addition to substantive reforms being indicated in relation to ensuring the presence and pursuit of rational objectives for the regulatory endeavour, a new range of procedural safeguards must also be considered, especially given the absence in Britain of clear constitutional principles, and weaknesses in the judicial system in respect of elaborating principles of general application.

In essence, it might seem that the regulatory system does little more than legitimise the outcome of market tendencies within the media, being left with more symbolic than substantive significance. Though tinkering at the margins, the existing system continues to allow high degrees of concentration within and across different sectors of the media, and demonstrates no likelihood of establishing and/or moving towards clear public policy objectives. The regulatory system is essentially reactive, and in respect of ownership patterns largely fails to establish an alternative agenda to that which results from the exercise of market forces, and therefore offers flimsy protection to citizenship values. As was hinted at in earlier chapters, it may be that a conceptual leap must be made in which it is acknowledged that the essential democratic role played by the media demands that a move be made away from a simple model of ownership, towards a model approaching 'stewardship', in which those who control the media (especially essential facilities such as technological gateways) are placed under duties, actively enforced by regulators, to serve not only their individual or corporate interests, but also those of all present, and future generations of citizens. This theme be returned to in Chapter 7.

Despite two opportunities in recent years, in the form of major pieces of legislation relating to the media and the coming to power of a new government in 1997, Britain appears to be likely to continue to struggle on into the twenty-first century with a system of media regulation scarcely worthy of the name, comprisig of inconsistent and ineffective measures which fail to fulfil democratic expectations. Central to these is the expectation of accountability in the exercise of power, the subject of the next chapter.

CHAPTER 5

Structural Design and Accountability in Regulation

– 5.1 ASPECTS OF ACCOUNTABILITY –

Previous chapters have considered values, objectives and some of the mechanisms utilised in regulating the media, and noted in general the democratic requirement that power, whether public or private, should not be unlimited. They have not, however, in general focused on the limitations placed upon those who exercise regulatory power. In this chapter, the focus is shifted from the predominantly structural regulation of media markets, to the activities of the media and those who regulate them, from the perspective of accountability.

Liberal-democratic expectations such as freedom of expression and property rights may appear generally to have militated against strong regulation of the media in such a way as to defeat competing democratic claims for pluralism, diversity and equality of access to the media. That said, regulators have undoubtedly exercised, and no doubt will in the future continue to exercise, wide-ranging discretionary powers over the democratically significant media, and the examples considered in Chapter 4 appear to indicate that such powers are not always utilised in pursuit of clearly identified objectives.

Harlow and Rawlings (1997: 272) note how the kind of franchise allocation process first introduced into broadcasting under the 1990 Act tends to maximise agency discretion. With the discretion available to regulatory agencies in mind, it is to be expected that regulators should be accountable in the exercise of these powers. This chapter considers the extent to which those who regulate the media in Britain are adequately subjected to mechanisms which serve this end via the three processes, now familiar to many British public lawyers, of, after Davis (1971), confining, structuring and checking their discretion.

In essence, Davis's tripartite agenda requires discretion to be:

1. 'confined', to that realm where discretion is preferable to rules, in terms of the benefits it may offer;

2. 'structured', in such a way as to maximise its potential benefits, while minimising the risk of arbitrariness, by use of a system of guiding principles indicative of the manner in which it will be exercised; and

3. 'checked', via both internal review procedures and external scrutiny by independent bodies such as the courts.

Thus, argues Davis, discretion must be 'cut back' where it is not beneficial, necessary or therefore advisable, while wherever discretion is appropriate it must be structured via either a process of 'internal rule-making', in the form of the development of publicly available codes of practice or the like, or the imposition of guidelines from outside; and it must be subject to scrutiny within the institutional hierarchy of the body exercising the power in addition to offering the potential for external, authoritative, independent review by the likes of courts or tribunals. Though there remain potential difficulties in Davis's agenda, particularly in establishing the optimal point for the exercise of discretion, the extent to which Davis's criteria are met can nonetheless be utilised as a key indicator of the degree of accountability existing in the practice of media regulation.

It should be noted that 'accountability' is used in this chapter to refer to two related but distinct ideas. The first means a requirement to give an account of one's actions, either directly to the public or via public authorities, which will often feed into, but is not necessarily connected to, the second, which means to be accountable in the sense of being liable to sanction if found to have acted in breach of some requirement or expectation attaching to the exercise of power. The latter, liability to legal sanction, is the traditional public lawyer's version of accountability, and in particular focuses on the potential for the courts to impose sanctions upon bodies found to have been in breach of established standards. The former is, however, arguably more important, as it requires the body to provide sufficient information to render it subject to meaningful scrutiny, and relates more to democratic legitimacy than the narrower basis of legality. The provision of such information may in itself be sufficient to establish accountability without the need for formal legal action. Given the expense and time involved in legal challenge, the absence of any strong duty to give reasons in British public law, and real doubts regarding the ability of conventional adversarial processes to resolve satisfactorily the kind of complex, polycentric disputes often associated with media regulation issues, it becomes clear why accountability via the courts should be considered something of a last resort.

It is against this framework that regulatory bodies will be assessed in this chapter and, sadly, will be found wanting in certain respects. To a substantial degree, the failure of British regulators to meet these expectations is accounted for by an absence of both constitutional principles of general application and developed, articulated principles specific to the endeavour of media regulation; thus, their discretion remains unstructured. In addition, the absence of clear constitutional principles leaves British courts, when compared with their overseas counterparts, in a relatively weak position from which to seek to intervene and control the exercise of these powers (see Chapter 6).

The role of the Secretary of State in choosing to intervene (or not) in relation to newspaper takeovers and mergers, was considered in the previous chapter, and the absence of requirements of transparency in decision-making was established. In this chapter, consideration will be given to the discretionary powers of government, both formal and informal, to intervene in the activities of broadcasters, and also the impact of restructuring in the form of trends towards separating regulation from broadcasting (IBA to ITC) and towards 'disaggregating' the BBC. Also to be considered are the quasi-judicial discretionary powers of those bodies charged with resolving complaints regarding the media, including the newly formed, statutory BSC, and also the self-regulatory PCC. Finally, consideration will be given to the regulation of what Herman and McChesney (1997) and Schiller (1996) identify as the underlying financial heart of the media – advertising – considering the different bases for regulation embodied in the statutory ITC in its regulation of broadcast advertising and the self-regulatory ASA which controls the rest of the advertising industry.

It is necessary here also to consider more generally the structure of the regulatory machinery as a whole. It should already be apparent that generally speaking, these bodies are, continuing to regulate the media on a sectoral basis, an approach increasingly challenged by the trends towards cross-media ownership and technological convergence. Though there have been ad hoc acknowledgements of these developments, such as the introduction of measures specific to cross-media ownership in the Broadcasting Acts of 1990 and 1996, and in particular the role assigned to Oftel in relation to DTT and CAS arrangements, the regulatory scene is still predominantly filled with single-sector regulators operating media-specific policies, in an environment of ever more convergent media. This conventional approach is increasingly questionable, and consideration must be given to the development of a single regulator along the lines of the 'Ofcomms' suggested by Collins and Murroni (1996). Their approach appears to offer potential benefits, despite the substantial difficulties already noted, especially in terms of market definition and 'media exchange rates', and also the risk of regulatory 'capture' by the powerful corporate interests supposedly subject to regulation (Feintuck 1997c).

In addition to technological convergence and the increasing presence of cross-media conglomerates, a third trend, that of globalisation, must also be

LIVERPOOL JOHN MOORES UNIVERSITY
LEARNING SERVICES

considered when examining the structure of regulation. The development of a Global Information Infrastructure (GII – manifested in the form of the Internet) proceeds apace, and Schiller (1996: 113) quotes with approval a *New York Times* column stating that 'satellite technology has largely made national borders irrelevant'; and this, true as it is, poses a new order of problems for national bodies intent on regulation. To question whether, in an era of trans-frontier communications, national attempts at regulation are largely futile, is essentially to provide the answer in the question. Yet in a world still based upon the foundation stone of the nation state, in theory at least, it is inevitable that regulation will still be attempted at a national level and moves towards international regulation will meet with resistance. Inevitably in such a situation, the existence of concurrent national and international legal regimes will pose some 'nice' questions, raising further obstacles to the likelihood of the courts offering an effective accountability mechanism in relation to those who regulate.

It is, however, important to re-emphasise that regulatory actors are not, and should not be, subject to accountability via the courts alone. Indeed, it can be argued that the courts might most appropriately be viewed only as a safety net or backstop in relation to the accountability of media and other regulators. It is preferable that accountability should be achieved primarily via the structuring and internal checking of discretion, though with a necessarily high degree of transparency imported into decision-making in order to facilitate scrutiny. The availability of background information underlying decisions, and meaningful reasons being given for decisions, are important prerequisites of effective accountability. In the absence of adequate transparency, it is difficult to subject decision-makers to meaningful scrutiny and to be sure that they are accountable in either sense of the word.

In the absence to date of either freedom of information legislation or overarching principles of administrative procedure, in Britain the norm in bodies carrying out governmental functions has traditionally been one of secrecy, with access to information the exception. Moves towards granting access to government-held information under the last Conservative administration, related to John Major's Citizen's Charter initiative, can essentially be viewed as tokenism (Birkinshaw 1994), while it remains to be seen whether the new Labour Government's proposals to introduce a freedom of information act will be sufficiently hard-hitting to achieve all that might be hoped for in this respect.

As Birkinshaw (1996: 24) demonstrates, 'Information is inherently a feature of power. So too is its control, use and regulation', and exclusive control of information, whether by government, or, as Schiller (1996) argues persuasively, private corporations, is in fundamental opposition to democratic ideals. Certainly, access to information is a crucial aspect of accountability, but it must be viewed alongside structural design in making an overall assessment of the accountability of a regulatory organisation. The other key issue to auditing accountability is the identification of clear objectives for the regulator, in the absence of which it is difficult to hold the regulator to account for any substantive failures to achieve institutional goals. As was identified in the first part of this book, the absence of established and clearly expressed goals has been one of the fundamental weaknesses of the media regulation system to date, and represents a significant obstacle to meaningful accountability.

- 5.2   FORMAL POWER AND INFORMAL INFLUENCE -

It is clear that, in Britain and elsewhere, national governments will exert much power and influence over the general environment in which the media operate. Government may also play a significant role in establishing the agenda for future media development, though in recent times there is a strong appearance of the running being made by the corporate masters of technology, rather than proactive decision-making by democratically elected government. In particular, the regulatory framework for satellite broadcasting, and the acceptance by both the previous Conservative and present Labour administrations of DTT, as opposed to satellite or cable, as the predominant platform for the future delivery of television, appears to have been driven more by the development of the relevant technology by its corporate proponents than by any detailed consideration in democratic fora of the full range of alternatives. Democratic fundamentals lead us to expect, however, that such decision-making powers will be exercised within a framework of principles embodied in the constitution, pre-eminent amongst the democratic expectations being that of accountability.

It might be expected that, consistent with their duties of party political impartiality, public-service broadcasters would be insulated from government interference in relation to their output. While the BBC is notionally independent, it clearly has close relationships with government, not least because of government powers of appointment to its board of governors, which will be considered shortly. The main commercial television broadcasters (to date at least), the ITV regional companies and ITN, though operating in a commercial environment, are subject to public service requirements via the franchise agreements through the ITC. Even here, questions can be raised about the degree to which the ITC may be influenced in its judgements by government pressure, and about its composition of government appointees. Thus, the structural position of broadcasters *vis-à-vis* government seems to have important potentialities for the degree of independence from influence, and, not surprisingly in Britain, has developed incrementally and without radical review. In terms of its innovative structure, however, Channel 4 represents a relatively modern attempt to create a public-service-oriented television channel, and its structure and position are not without interest.

Though responsibility for the fourth channel was allocated to the then IBA under the Broadcasting Act 1980, it was not to be managed on a franchise basis like ITV regional companies, but rather was subjected to what Negrine (1994: 98) describes as 'imaginative regulatory and funding mechanisms'. Though a public-service broadcaster as generally conceived, Channel 4 is subjected to very different requirements as to range of programming from those applied to Channel 3 regional companies.

In Negrine's terms (1994: 97), in the climate of the late 1970s and early 1980s the watchwords of traditional British public-service broadcasting – 'balance', 'impartiality' and 'objectivity' – were 'too crude to cope with the complexity of contemporary life in Britain' and 'failed to reflect the political spectrum in its entirety', tending to 'exclude or denigrate all those who strayed outside the centre of the political stage'. Seymour-Ure (1996: 108) sees Channel 4 as providing a partial response to 'a persuasive case that the [BBC/ITV] duopoly was structurally and financially biased towards the common denominators of society and culture, even if not the lowest common denominators'.

Though still required to put out minimum total hours in respect of news, current affairs, education programmes, etc., Channel 4 has a particular brief, overseen now by the ITC, not to aim at the same mass audiences as ITV and BBC1, but to serve 'minority' interests or 'tastes and interests not generally catered for by Channel 3' (Peak and Fisher (eds) 1996: 166). Amongst other aspects of Channel 4 that distinguish it from other public-service broadcasters in Britain are the fact that it does not produce its own programmes but instead buys them from independent producers, acting in effect as a televisual publisher; and the fact that it was funded at the outset by a levy on the advertising revenue of regional, commercial ITV companies which sold, and retained the revenue from, advertising on Channel 4.

However, as Channel 4 established itself, both in terms of programming and, consequentially, as a locus for niche advertising, the financial safety net provided by the levy on other commercial broadcasters became less necessary and justifiable. Under the funding formula provided by the Broadcasting Act 1990, which allowed money to flow in either direction, Channel 4 was allowed to sell its own advertising, but still with a safety net, to be provided by the Channel 3 companies. The formula, however, ultimately resulted in the highly successful Channel 4 effectively subsidising the ITV companies to the sum of £74 million in 1995 (Peak and Fisher (eds) 1996: 166); money which, as Seymour-Ure (1996: 109) notes, could otherwise have been spent on commissioning programmes.

As a result of its innovative funding basis and unusually specific public-service brief, Channel 4 is somewhat distanced from conventional British arrangements for public-service broadcasting and is accountable against different criteria; it remains, therefore, an exception to the general pattern. Noted earlier, in relation to the Secretary of State's powers over newspaper acquisitions, was the fact that in practice, legal mechanisms of accountability via statutory measures, may in reality merely serve to disguise thinly what amounts to poorly confined and structured ministerial discretion. In other media-related areas, wide-ranging government discretion can also be seen, sometimes deriving from statutory grants of power, sometimes based upon the government's ability to apply pressure associated with its general position of influence and more specifically its power of patronage.

An example of government discretion deriving from direct statutory grant arose in the context of the ban on broadcasting the spoken words of those associated with certain proscribed organisations, most notably Sinn Féin and the Ulster Defence Association, in the late 1980s and early 1990s. Robertson and Nicol (1992: 27) describe the ban as 'a plain infringement on the right to receive and impart information', a summary which requires only the additional observation that in Britain, as opposed to the USA for example, positive rights to freedom of expression do not exist in law.

The ban was based, in relation to ITV companies, upon powers granted by section 10 of the Broadcasting Act 1990 (previously section 29, Broadcasting Act 1981) and, in relation to the BBC, on conditions contained in the Licence Agreement which supplements the BBC's Charter. The statutory provisions permit the Home Secretary to order the ITC to 'refrain from broadcasting any matter or classes of matter', offering the clear potential for prior restraint of broadcasters, with the only avenue of redress being to challenge the minister's exercise of discretion by way of judicial review.

When judicial review was sought (R. v Secretary of State for the Home Department, ex parte Brind [1991] 1 All ER 720), it became clear that the grant of discretion to the Home Secretary by statute meant that to succeed, a challenge would have to demonstrate that the minister had acted 'unreasonably'. In practice, this standard of review allows enormous latitude to those vested with discretion, on occasion requiring challengers to demonstrate in effect that the decision-maker had taken leave of their senses. In practice, of course, the 'ban' was demonstrably ludicrous from the time that Channel 4 took the decision to dub actors' voices over pictures of spokespersons for the proscribed organisations, but the 'soft' standard of review meant that legal accountability in relation to the discretionary power was virtually meaningless, a problem compounded by the fact that, in the situation of either a party of government with a strong majority, or cross-party support, accountability through Parliament is also rendered largely impotent.

While the section 10 powers are obviously significant, still more wide-ranging powers of government intervention in relation to broadcasting also exist. The BBC's Licence Agreement permits the Government, in the case of a perceived emergency, and where it is considered expedient to do so, 'to take possession of the BBC in the name and on behalf of Her Majesty'. Originally included as part of the Government's response to the General Strike of 1926, it has never been applied to its full effect, though Robertson and Nicol (1992: 26) note that it was used during the Falklands War to permit the Government to use BBC transmitters to transmit propaganda broadcasts into Argentina.

It is possible that the incorporation of the ECHR into UK domestic law will provide the basis for a principled challenge to some such powers, though, as is the case in relation to privacy, it is uncertain precisely what impact incorporation of the Convention will have when interpreted and applied by British judges. However, in any event, the use of statutory powers is only one mechanism, and not necessarily the preferred one, by which British governments seek to impose their will upon broadcasters. The degree of potential influence that can be achieved via the use of less formal or direct interventions must also be noted.

The power of patronage might be difficult to measure but should never be underestimated, and the Government enjoys extensive powers of appointment which remain a significant tool for exerting leverage over broadcasters. The BBC's governors are appointed notionally by the monarch, but in practice by the Prime Minister of the day. The BSC established under the Broadcasting Act 1996 consists of a Chair and up to fifteen Members, all appointed by the Secretary of State at the DCMS, who also appoints the Chair and Members of the ITC and the RA. Since Channel 4's coming of age as a public corporation in 1993 (see Negrine 1994: 99), its members have been appointed by the ITC who of course, in turn, are government appointees.

The Government's power of appointment also extends far beyond broadcasting into other aspects of the media. For example, the post of President of the BBFC remains in the Home Secretary's gift, and Andreas Whittam-Smith's appointment to the post in December 1997 followed a reported row between the Home Office and the BBFC's former head over policy relaxations in relation to sexually explicit and violent material; the

same issue that a year earlier had led to high-profile divisions
BBFC and local authorities over Cronenberg's *Crash*. Wheth
Smith, founder and former editor of *The Independent*, proves
pliant in relation to the government's generally conservat
remains to be seen, but it is unlikely that the Home Secre
appoint to such a position a person who was believed to have strongly
opposing views to those of the Government of the day. Certainly, as Curran
and Seaton (1997: 217) note, under the previous, Conservative administration the Nolan Committee on Standards in Public Life found strong
evidence as to party political bias in public appointments.

While such appointments are clearly matters of public record and
knowledge, and subject to scrutiny via Parliament and the media, they
remain a sphere of strong government patronage. Robertson and Nicol
(1992: 28) relate this patronage to the apparently compliant response by the
BBC in 1985 to government pressure not to screen the controversial *Real
Lives* documentary concerning terrorism in Northern Ireland, when, they
state, the BBC 'cravenly banned the scheduled programme after Mrs
Thatcher had condemned it, unseen, as likely to encourage support for
terrorists'. Seymour-Ure (1996: 69) notes that the Thatcher Governments,
to a much greater extent than any previous government, 'seemed ready to
treat the BBC and IBA governors as political placemen and women', and he
gives examples of their willingness to 'interfere directly with programmes',
'accuse producers and interviewers of deliberate bias' and to 'impugn
broadcasters' patriotism' (see also Negrine 1994: Chapter 6).

Though such incidents may come to light relatively infrequently, they
acquire a high media profile when they do. However, given the very nature
of such 'pressure', it is difficult to be clear as to the precise extent to which
governments successfully exert influence over broadcasters. What is obvious, however, is that a very real potential exists for the exercise of
influence in a hidden and unaccountable manner, especially when, for
example in the run-up to licence or Charter renewals or reviews of the
licence fee, public-service broadcasters are most heavily dependant upon
active government support.

– 5.3 RESTRUCTURING PUBLIC-SERVICE BROADCASTING AND REGULATION –

Seymour-Ure (1996: 69) describes 'what many broadcasters and Thatcher
opponents perceived as the Prime Minister's remorseless hostility to most of
the public-service broadcasting ethos', and how the Government agenda for
public-service broadcasting in the 1980s eventually became the introduction

of what he calls 'The standard Thatcher solutions' of deregulation and competition. Certainly, these 'solutions' are familiar across the whole of the then public-sector with market, or more properly 'quasi-market' (Le Grand 1991), principles being introduced into education (Feintuck 1994) and healthcare (Longley 1993), the deregulation of public transport, and the wholesale privatisation of the electricity, gas, telephone and water utilities during the Thatcher years (see generally Graham and Prosser (eds) 1988). Backed by legislative attacks on trade union and local government power, these measures were central features of the Thatcherite agenda of what Gamble (1994) refers to as establishing the legitimacy only of the market and the strong central state.

Implicitly acknowledging the existence of a distinctive public-service orientation for conventional broadcasting, Thatcher had determined that investment in cable technology should not be carried out by the public sector, given that its emphasis at that stage appeared to be as a medium for entertainment, rather than the full range of services associated with public-service broadcasting. Only limited private funds were put into the costly, risky and long-term project of developing a cable infrastructure and thus, even by the late 1980s, the 'benign duopoly' (Seymour-Ure 1996: 68) of BBC and the ITV companies still faced relatively little competition from cable or satellite broadcasters, and continued to carry with them a large amount of public goodwill; the public-service broadcasters therefore possessed a fair degree of legitimacy, rendering them less vulnerable to attack than their counterparts in other areas of the public sector. Though not enough to fend off the Thatcherite onslaught entirely, public support for public-service values was enough to ensure that the reform of broadcasting, and its regulation, took what appears, at first sight at least, a less radical course than that of other public services. In essence, the introduction in the Broadcasting Act 1990 of the competitive auction (discussed in Chapter 4), hybridising cash auction and programme quality principles, represents the embodiment of the conflicts within Cabinet (Seymour-Ure 1996: 69) as to how to apply Thatcherism to the broadcasters.

In addition to this new mechanism for allocating broadcasting licences, the 1990 Act is also noteworthy for the establishment of the ITC, taking over the regulatory aspects of the IBA's functions and separating these functions from direct responsibilities for programming. Implicit in criticisms of the performance of the IBA (Lewis 1975), and especially the lack of transparency in its operation, were concerns over potential conflicts of interest between the IBA's joint roles as broadcaster and regulator of the commercial television industry. As Gibbons (1991: 146) notes, despite the structure of allocating regional licences to private, commercial broadcasters, the IBA had exercised 'ultimate control over the programmes that were disseminated because they retained responsibility as the broadcasting authority' and under section 3(2) of the Broadcasting Act 1981 the IBA had retained the ultimate power to intervene directly to maintain or provide the service if a programme provider failed to comply with its directions. Gibbons goes on, however, to draw attention to the concerns expressed, amongst others, by the Annan Committee (1977) over an apparent reluctance on the part of the IBA to use its powers to force resolutions where difficulties arose in individual ITV companies.

The separation of broadcasting from regulatory functions brought about by the 1990 Act meant, states Gibbons (1991: 147), that 'Under the new regime, the ITC and Radio Authority will not have such a stake in maintaining services and protecting companies'. Writing in 1991, it was unclear to Gibbons whether the kind of consensual and essentially corporatist relationship between the IBA and the ITV companies would be replaced by a more conflictual and adversarial relationship between the companies and the ITC. Gibbons went on, however, to speculate perceptively about whether the new regime would lead to a more robust regulatory approach, and in particular whether procedural requirements attaching to the imposition of sanctions by the ITC would lead to a greater articulation of reasons and justifications for intervention. Gibbons (1991: 148) also noted the potential for the increased 'juridification', or resort to legal rules and legal redress mechanisms, in relation to broadcasting regulation under the 1990 Act structure.

As Curran and Seaton (1997: 330) note, 'Although deprived of direct control over schedules, the new regulatory agency [ITC] was given an arsenal of new powers, including the right to shorten franchises and to fine', and 'Public warnings issued to under-performing television companies indicated moreover its willingness to use these powers'. However, while the 1990 Act gave the ITC a new role in relation to policing the operation of commercial television broadcasting in Britain, separating the regulatory function from programming responsibilities, the position and functions of the BBC were arguably more problematic for the market-oriented reformers.

Though by the 1980s the BBC shared the public-service field with the ITV companies and Channel 4, it was still arguably the primary repository of public-service values, enjoying a worldwide reputation for its quality and range of programming, and it was still, notably, an advertising-free zone. As with much of the traditional public sector, and other potential or actual alternative power centres where opposition could find a base, the BBC was a natural target for Thatcherite 'reform', especially in its capacity as a significant influence on public opinion. Curran and Seaton (1997: 216–35) give a splendid description of how 'The BBC ducked and weaved in every way it could' (219) to avoid the Thatcherite onslaught, and how it ultimately emerged, if battered, not broken.

Like the range and type of services it provided, the relationship between governors, managers and programme makers at the BBC had grown incrementally since the Corporation's inception in the 1920s. Though its independence was supposedly assured by virtue of its renewable Charter, and through its Licence Agreement, the potential for political influence in the case of individual, controversial programmes has already been noted. Thatcher's agenda, however, seemed to go beyond this as she sought to impose the values of her brand of Conservatism upon the BBC in the form of 'New Managerialism' and especially the introduction of an internal market.

A phenomenon which can be identified in the reform of various public services in the 1980s, most notably the NHS (Longley 1993), the introduction of internal markets is said to encourage efficiency, especially cost-efficiency, via the disaggregation of large organisations and the development of independent cost centres free to purchase from a range of suppliers. In the introduction of such market-centred concepts into an organisation such as the BBC or NHS, however, important and difficult questions arise, not least of which is who – managers or practitioners (programme makers) – will wield the entrepreneurial power.

As Curran and Seaton chart, the outcome of this struggle was pre-determined in the case of the BBC by the appointment of Marmaduke Hussey as Chair of the Governors and later John Birt as Director General. The appointment by the Thatcher Governments of individuals who were without question 'one of us', and who would actively manage the Corporation, was furthered by the introduction of a series of teams of management consultants who, as they note, 'tend, on the whole, to accentuate the role of managers'. In what Curran and Seaton describe as 'a radical shift in power within the BBC', a 'programme-led hierarchy' was replaced by 'a management-led structure' (1997: 223).

Although the BBC had not been selected for privatisation, a consequence perhaps of the still widespread sense of public support for it that the old public utilities and local government services on the whole lacked, it was still to be subjected to the rigours of the market in the form of 'Producers' Choice'. Under this initiative, producers would be expected to buy in services as cheaply as they could from within the budget allocated to them. However, Curran and Seaton (1997: 226) note 'That the real purpose of the exercise was to shut departments was made clear by the simple diktat that, while producers were encouraged to look outside the BBC for services, production departments were prohibited from trying to sell their services beyond the Corporation'. The process of continuous revolution at the BBC was furthered by a huge increase in staff turnover, and the increased use of short-term contracts and freelance workers.

However, the BBC continued to produce quality programmes throughout the 1990s, though highly regarded and creative programme makers as diverse as David Attenborough, Mark Tully and Dennis Potter may have considered this to be despite, rather than because of, any of the Birt reforms (Curran and Seaton 1997: 230). Though the Major Government proved somewhat less antagonistic towards the BBC than Thatcher's, in the final analysis the BBC's survival appears to have depended on the fact that it continued to hold a good, if not predominant, share of the audience throughout the 1990s, having previously adjusted its position to form something of an alliance with ITV in terms of public-service values and programming (Seymour-Ure 1996: 159). Despite the increasing presence of alternative sources and styles of broadcasting, the BBC's range and quality of programming, and its continuing worldwide presence combine to maintain its legitimacy, and render it difficult for any government to abandon it in something approximating to its historical, licence fee-funded, form.

While full privatisation of the BBC seems to have been fended off for the foreseeable future, there remains a real argument over whether in reality the ongoing lack of transparency in its management renders it, in any case, public in name only. Though remaining, at least formally, a public body – in its World Service television operation, in the marketing of its programmes to other broadcasters and in the start-up in 1997 of a twenty-four-hour news service in preparation for the advent of DTT – the BBC has shown itself to be increasingly aware of the commercial realities of the 1990s. Whether in the longer term the BBC will be forced down either a core service option (in which it largely functions to fill gaps in an otherwise commercially driven broadcasting market), or a wider service option (in which the BBC could diversify indefinitely, though retain a public-service remit which, alone, would be funded publicly) remains unclear (Foster 1992; Blumler 1992: 4). Foster correctly identifies the risk of the first course as being a loss of legitimacy as, with shrinking, niche audiences, the justification for public funding withers away. The second option, on the other hand, would appear to pave the way for privatisation, though presumably on a disaggregated basis in order to promote competition.

The internal markets introducted in both the BBC and NHS appear to have produced similar effects. The decentralisation of management to numerous new cost centres appears to result in a burgeoning of activity, at the devolved level, for accountants, lawyers and bureaucrats in general, arguably more than offsetting any financial benefits resulting from decentralisation. In addition, as Hutton notes in relation to the reforms of the BBC:

> The internal market brings important cultural change in the organisation. Audit becomes the *raison d'être* rather than programme making. The relations of trust and co-operation upon which any great corporation is built are broken down by the new reliance on formal monitoring mechanisms. The relentless downwards pressure on costs forces managers to lower wages and employment conditions. It becomes harder to build any culture of commitment to the organisation. The initial cost savings are offset by the collapse in the corporate ethic. (Hutton 1995: 222)

However, unlike the NHS where even the far from radical Labour Government of 1997 is committed to reforming the worst excesses of the atomised, internal market, some of those that might be expected to be natural critics of 'Birtism' do not necessarily wish to reverse the disaggregation process, and indeed may even be supporters of it. Collins and Murroni, closely associated with the left-of-centre IPPR, state that the Birt reforms, though painful, have strengthened the BBC (Collins and Murroni 1996: 146). They propose that the move away from the traditional, vertically integrated, structure should now be completed by 'the creation of arm's-length entities each of which would trade with other elements of the BBC and with service providers, clients and partners outside the BBC' (147). They identify four potential 'distinct, semi-autonomous entities' (scheduling and channel control, programme production, transmission and engineering, and 'commercial exploitation') which would have 'line management responsibility to minimize the paperwork and bureaucracy that have dogged the introduction of internal markets under producer choice'. The result, they state would be that 'The BBC would then more closely approximate to the federal business model of Unilever and ICI . . . than to the vertically integrated one of traditional nationalised industries'.

However, by way of contrast with management priorities in organisations concerned solely with the commercial production and marketing of commodities, the task of mangers of public services is more complex and involves enabling 'the reflective participation of citizens but also the government of collective action in the public interest' (Ranson and Stewart 1989: 19). It is therefore necessary to distinguish between public-and-private sector management, for 'The management task in the private domain is a singular (unilinear) task serving individual wants. In the public domain, managers have a multilinear task to serve an unlimited variety of individual needs and create collective welfare' (*ibid.*)

While few would argue today for a return to the more problematic aspects of the traditional British model of nationalised industries, in particular the all-pervasive lack of transparency and accountability in their management, it can be forcefully argued that there is little obvious benefit that would accrue from further disaggregation of the BBC. In itself, the model proposed by Collins and Murroni would do nothing to align the BBC better with public-service, as opposed to commercial, rationales; it would not lead to a clearer articulation of public-service values and objectives. Equally, though it might enhance internal economic efficiency and bring the BBC more into line with the commercial *Zeitgeist*, it would not in itself lead to greater transparency or public accountability.

In absorbing and accepting the value-for-money imperatives of economy, efficiency and effectiveness so central to the New Public Management agenda of the 1980s and 1990s, proposals such as those of Collins and Murroni may lead to a loss of sight of the need to reassess the fundamental public-service basis for the BBC's existence, and to reposition the Corporation in the new, highly competitive media market. If the opportunity for the assertion of modern public-service values is not taken now, the BBC will indeed be highly vulnerable to attack from 'New Thatcherites', within whatever political party, as the new media market becomes established.

What is crucial at the present time is the reinvestment of the BBC with legitimacy; a new mandate for a new media era. Part of that is the identification of the public-interest and public-service values, but another part is ensuring that the Corporation meets expectations of accountability. Keane (1991: 57) notes that 'The programming decisions of public-service bureaucracies are not subject to continuing and detailed justifications', and the fact that the BBC has maintained public support throughout the challenges of the 1980s and 1990s must be despite, rather than because of, the accountability mechanisms in place. However, it may also be accounted for in part, perversely, by attempts by a Conservative Government, increasingly viewed popularly as illegitimate, to undermine the BBC via public attack and private attempts to influence.

To be fair, Collins and Murroni (1996: 151–7) do address this issue in addition to recommending the further development of the internal market structure. They propose that the role of the BBC's governors should be reformed, so as to emphasise the Corporation's public-service remit, via the application of two principles: that it is the governors' role is to represent the public, and that the public should have formal and informal influence over the governors in their 'representative' role. In effect, they propose a role as 'non-executive directors' for the Corporation, with their regulatory role confined to representing the interests of 'stakeholders' (152) and the monitoring of the general direction of the BBC, under a Board of Management and the Director General, against performance indicators established on a three-yearly basis.

The governors would in turn be accountable to the general public both informally, via release into the public domain of audience responses and of minutes revealing reasons for decisions, and formally, via non-binding guidance given by 'Citizens' Juries' and through public appointments processes for BBC Governors, ensuring representation of the regions and special-interest groups. Collins and Murroni (1996: 155) propose that the shortlisting and selection criteria, and reasons underlying eventual selections, should be made public, and carried out by a cross-party Commons Select Committee rather than by the relevant government minister. Curran and Seaton (1997: 348) consider taking this a stage further, seeking to make *all* appointments to membership of broadcasting authorities via the Select Committee, and, proposing that the BBC should be put on a statutory footing, replacing its present Royal Charter basis, so as to increase the BBC's security and independence, end the periodic uncertainty in the run-up to Charter renewal, and, reduce the wide-ranging potential for government influence.

There does appear to be significant potential in the proposals for increased democratisation of the BBC, and there certainly appears to be a strong case for greater separation of government, regulators and broadcasters within public-service broadcasting arrangements. The discretion of both government and regulators must be properly confined, and adequately structured and checked. Across the board, those claiming to be acting in pursuit of the public interest in broadcasting must be transparent in their workings, and subject to adequate internal and external checking mechanisms. Compliance with this agenda, and the consequent increase in accountability, will lead to enhanced legitimacy. However, in an era in which quality and range of programming may not prove enough to protect it from the commercial imperative, it remains necessary to address directly some of the issues raised in Part One in order to justify more clearly the both rationale for public-service broadcasting and its regulation.

– 5.4 COMPLAINTS AND 'STANDARDS' IN BROADCASTING –

The redress of grievances, or felt wrongs, is one of the essential 'Law Jobs' identified in Chapter 1. One forum in which grievances may be addressed is the law courts. However, as Birkinshaw (1994) establishes, extra-judicial grievance redress is arguably of at least as great a significance in the modern day. As he rightly notes, 'a public lawyer's interest in the process of accountability and complaint resolution is not diminished simply because there is an absence of a judge or counsel, prerogative orders or writs. The pursuit of effective procedures for accountability and resolution of grievances is what counts' (24).

In this section, the resolution of complaints regarding media behaviour and output will be considered, and its importance, despite there being scarcely a courtroom in sight, demonstrated. The dispute resolution processes discussed here form a potentially important part of the structures of accountability (in both its senses) relevant to the media, and whether this potential is in practice fulfilled will be the central question to be addressed.

As will be discussed shortly, complaints regarding the press are addressed largely through self-regulatory mechanisms. However, it should come as no surprise, given the pattern identified earlier of greater regulation of broadcast media, to find that complaints over broadcasting, in relation to both broadcasters' practices and the content of their programmes, are dealt with not by loose, self-regulatory mechanisms, but by bodies created by statute and with members appointed by government.

The Broadcasting Act 1996 established a new body, the Broadcasting Standards Commission (BSC), with responsibility for monitoring the output of licensed commercial broadcasters and dealing with complaints. The BSC results from the merger of the former Broadcasting Standards Council (established informally in 1988 but put onto a statutory footing by the 1990 Act) and Broadcasting Complaints Commission. The Broadcasting Standards Council had been the body responsible for controlling standards in output, especially in relation to taste and decency, while the Broadcasting Complaints Commission, like the non-statutory, self-regulatory PCC in relation to the press, had a primary role of dealing with complaints regarding media behaviour, 'fairness' in coverage, and especially intrusion and invasion of privacy. It was thought, not unreasonably, that there was a degree of public confusion over this division of responsibilities, which the merger in the form of the new BSC is intended to resolve.

The fact that the BSC, with up to fifteen members which are appointed by the Secretary of State, will, like its predecessor, be required by statute to draw up and oversee a code of practice relating to broadcasting standards, confirms the high degree of statute-based intervention in this area, which is in addition to the formal and informal powers of government and the statutory powers of the ITC over licensed services. As Robertson and Nicol (1992: Chapter 15) indicate in their consideration of the arrangements before the 1996 Act, the existence of a statutory framework did not deny the existence of wide-ranging discretion vested in the regulatory authorities, and it might be concluded that despite the union of their functions in the BSC, little has changed in this respect.

Despite such statutory measures, it must also be noted that a significant degree of self-regulation, or even self-censorship, also takes place in relation to programme content, especially within the BBC, where, though subject to rulings by the BSC, matters of questionable content are in effect resolved by referral up the institutional hierarchy. Robertson and Nicol (1992: 627) demonstrate how, in practice, the BBC applies its own Programme Rules to what will be broadcast, and how it pursues a strongly paternalistic model of self-censorship, for example severely restricting the broadcasting of 'four-letter words' in popular soaps, or in crowd noise at football matches, while taking a far more liberal approach in this respect to less populist, more high-brow, radio channels 3 and 4 and in 'serious' television drama.

It should be remembered that such self-censorship operates in addition to the limits imposed by the requirements of the Family Viewing Policy, or watershed policy, developed by the old Broadcasting Standards Council and incorporated in the ITC Code and by annexe to the BBC Licence Agreement. In an attempt to resolve 'the dilemma of balancing the rights of adult viewers against the social dangers that adult viewing may harm children and those who are "psychologically frail"' (Robertson and Nicol 1992: 612), restrictions on violent and sexually explicit material are gradually lessened after 9p.m. as, in theory, the number of children (and presumably the 'psychologically frail') watching television declines. In addition to such restrictions, the ITC Programme Code also requires warnings to be broadcast immediately before the screening of potentially 'disturbing' programmes, or those containing violent or sexually explicit material or 'strong language', and the BBC also adheres to this requirement.

This panoply of codes and practices of censorship, whether deriving from statutory authority (and imposed via licence agreements) or self-imposed, in addition to common and criminal law restrictions relating to obscenity and blasphemy, and the statutory control of videos via the BBFC (under the Video Recordings Act 1984), does not, however, avoid the operation of discretion in this area by broadcasters and regulators alike. Certainly, important self-denying ordinances still exist, especially for the BBC, and though to break them would have important potential consequences in relation to public opinion and support, ultimately they remain flexible enough to allow a high degree of paternalistic discretion to operate, as demonstrated by the dual standards applied to populist and 'high-brow' programming. The statutory and licence/Charter provisions provide adequate scope for broadcasters to choose between a conservative or progressive/challenging approach to programme content; however, it seems that the BBC generally takes a strongly self-denying approach, sometimes seeming not even to track, but rather to stay some way behind, changing standards of social acceptability.

It is not possible to quantify the extent to which government influence and pressure plays a part in this, whether directly or via appointments to the

BBC and the broadcasting regulators, though it is reasonable to expect that it is significant, especially at times when Licences or the Charter are up for renewal. Again, the argument must be that such discretion has to be adequately 'confined, structured and checked' and, where control over programme content is in question, must be exercised transparently.

The powers to be exercised by the BSC appear in essence identical to those previously exercised by its predecessors. Following a complaint, the Broadcasting Complaints Commission had the power to require the broad-caster to publish the adjudication (usually it is broadcast on the same channel as the programme subject to the complaint at a similar time to the original broadcast) but it could not require an apology or correction, nor require the provision of financial compensation. Its determinations were largely based on paper submissions, though it had the power to hold hearings in private, where the proceedings were treated as confidential and cross-examination was permitted only rarely (Birkinshaw 1994: 176).

The Broadcasting Complaints Commission and its successor, the BSC, consist largely of lay members unconnected with broadcasting, appointed by the Government. While this lay dominance may indicate a high degree of independence from the broadcasters (though not necessarily from the Government), it is also possible to suggest, as Robertson and Nicol (1992: 547) do, that this accounts for why 'some of the adjudications appear out of touch with the realities of broadcasting and may explain why the [BCC] in its [first] ten years of operation . . . made such an insignificant contribution to developing ethical guidelines for broadcasters'.

In relation to the high-profile issue of 'unwarranted infringement of privacy' (section 107(1)(b) Broadcasting Act 1996), the BSC takes on the brief formerly dealt with by the BCC, but comparisons can readily be made with the PCC's role in relation to the press under its code. The problem here is likely to be one of consistency, given the value-laden discretion which the word 'unwarranted' grants to the BSC. As Robertson and Nicol (1992: 553) commented in relation to the BCC, 'Each case will turn on its own facts and involve a judgement on the importance, not only of the allegation made in the programme, but of whether the invasion of privacy has been really necessary to provide evidence to support that allegation'. Inconsistency in this respect, whether within the broadcasting sector or across different media, appears undesirable since it runs the risk of breaching the fundamental tenet that like cases should be treated alike.

In the context of the debate following Princess Diana's death, the BSC announced in November 1997 a new Code on Fairness and Privacy which was said to tighten controls on broadcasters in relation to privacy. The revised Code states that broadcasters 'should not intrude unnecessarily on private behaviour', though it does not seek to define a private place; and it states that secret recordings of conversations must be justified by reference to 'an overriding public interest', though again without defining this concept (*The Guardian*; *The Independent*; *The Times* all 25 November 1997).

The question, in essence, seems to be reduced to not so much the seriousness of the invasion of privacy, but its necessity in the gathering of an important public-interest news story. The competing claims of media freedom and individual rights of privacy, both fundamental liberal-democratic expectations, are in clear opposition here, though the principles on which such decisions are based, vital if any degree of confidence and consistency is to be imported into the process, have not been developed and articulated.

The BSC also acquired the functions of the Broadcasting Standards Council, which, in addition to dealing with complaints from the public relating to standards in broadcasting (violence, sex, taste and decency, bad language, coverage of disasters, and issues of race and gender) also had a role in researching public attitudes and trends in broadcasting. If it decided to investigate a complaint, the Broadcasting Standards Council held a hearing, generally in private, and invited those responsible for the programme in dispute to make representations. It could require the broadcaster in question to publish its findings in terms virtually identical to those relevant to the BCC, 'in such a manner and within such period as it may direct'. Whether the occasional transmission of findings, or publication in the *Radio Times* or *TV Times* or even at the broadcaster's expense in a national newspaper, is an adequate sanction, is debatable.

Clearly, question marks existed in relation to both the Broadcasting Standards Council and the Broadcasting Complaints Commission, and – in the absence of any significant conceptual clarification, greater procedural transparency or harder-hitting sanctions – these have been transferred wholesale into the new BSC. In respect of all three aspects of our agenda – the extent of discretion, its effective structuring, and the existence of checks upon it – question marks remain.

In addition to the BSC, the ITC will continue to play an important active regulatory role in relation to both broadcast advertising and the control of adherence to programme content requirements under the licence. Most significantly in this respect, it plays a part in dealing with complaints through interpreting the BSC's guidance and applying it to independent programmers, enforcing requirements via its ability to impose sanctions through licensing powers, and regulating advertising on commercial television. The RA fulfils similar functions in relation to commercial radio broadcasting while the BBC, though free of the issues raised by advertising and not subject to the same legal requirements by virtue of its Charter as opposed to statutory basis, seeks to apply via its own internal mechanisms essentially the same principles and standards as are applied to commercial broadcasting.

One final issue needs to be addressed in relation to complaints of unfair treatment at the hands of the media namely, that of a so-called 'right to reply'. As Humphreys (1996: 57–9) indicates, various jurisdictions (though not Britain) incorporate statutory rights to reply into their mechanisms for regulation of the media. Addressing this question as part of a consideration of 'access to the broadcast media', Barendt (1993: 163) notes that the publication of Broadcasting Standards Council or Broadcasting Complaints Commission (now BSC) adjudications does not equate with the ability granted to a complainant in other jurisdictions to frame their own answer. Indeed, Barendt has significant doubts as to the extent to which this provision fulfils the requirement of Article 23 of the 1989 EC Directive (89/552) that requires 'a right to reply or equivalent remedy' should be available in all Member States. It seems reasonable to reflect that any attempts to harmonise the commercial activity of broadcasting within the EU requires the harmonisation of complaints mechanisms and remedies such as rights of reply, though whether this will result in harmonisation at a meaningfully high standard or lowest common denominator is unclear.

Likely difficulties in harmonising standards are also demonstrated in relation to regulation on grounds of taste and decency, where cultural expectations vary widely across Europe. Even within Britain, however, commentators invariably point towards the lack of clarity that exists in relation to the overlapping codes covering taste and decency produced by the BSC, ITC and BBC; and Robertson and Nicol (1992: Chapter 15) suggest strongly that one single code should replace them. The row between the Home Office and BBFC that preceded the arrival of Andreas Whittam-Smith as the BBFC's new President also raised the problems of inconsistency between the standards applied by the BBFC in licensing videos, and the standards applied in the criminal law relating to obscenity (*The Guardian* 19 December 1997). There is little doubt that lurking behind the various ill-defined standards applied by the range of bodies is a more fundamental lack of clarity regarding the essential purpose the act of censorship, and in particular who is to be protected and from what. Difficult questions involving individual and group claims as to rights to view, and rights not to be offended, must be resolved before clarity can be achieved.

The various bodies that deal with complaints regarding broadcasting can each be assessed against two criteria: the extent to which they provide effective redress for individual complaints and the accountability of those who regulate. In so far as these bodies may perform a public function, their exercise of discretion may be expected to conform with constitutional expectations of accountability, in relation to both the substance of their decisions and the procedures they adopt. Though the statutory foundation of those who deal with broadcasting complaints undoubtedly renders them susceptible to judicial review, the unwillingness of the courts to intervene is clear, especially where matters of party political fairness are involved (*R. v BCC, ex parte Owen* [1985] 2 All ER 522). Though this may be problematic, given the courts' potentially significant role in acting as an ultimate check on the exercise of discretionary power, judicial reluctance to become embroiled in controversies in which clear rationales and principles do not exist is probably understandable. That said, if the judiciary are not prepared or not constitutionally empowered to develop such principles, it is all the more important that the political institutions consider carefully and articulate clearly the basis on which media regulators exercise power, the mechanisms they are to employ and the ends they are intended to achieve. In the absence of such conceptual clarity, it will be impossible to ensure that discretion exercised in the handling of complaints regarding broadcasting is adequately 'confined, structured and checked'.

Significant questions arise in relation to the ability of bodies such as the BSC to provide meaningful redress of grievances, as well as in relation to the manner in which they exercise their discretionary powers. Barendt (1993: 113) in particular notes the difficulties created not only for individual members of the public seeking grievance redress, but also for producers and broadcasters who will have to predict the reactions of a range of different regulatory bodies to any proposed programme.

There is a real sense in which the processes currently in existence represent little more than symbolic reassurance that something will be done about standards of conduct in the media. However, the evidence seems to suggest that they fulfil little useful purpose for either the media or the general public, or for providing consistency, clarity or effective grievance redress. To the extent that they are perceived to be ineffective, even their symbolic value may be undermined.

– 5.5 SELF-REGULATION –

Provided that those who regulate do so effectively, with regard to clear substantive and procedural principles, and are adequately accountable, it can be argued that the question of who it is that regulates is of little concern. Self-regulation, in Graham's terms (1994: 190) amounting to the delegation of the public policy task of regulation to private actors, is often used in relation to the 'professions', occupations such as medics and lawyers, where a public-interest element and ethical standards attach to the occupation or activity. In addition to considering self-regulatory regimes in terms of effectiveness measured against the achievement of identified objectives (no easy task in itself in this context), it is vital also, given the public-interest element in their work, to consider the degree to which self-regulatory bodies are accountable to both those they regulate and the general public. In respect of both of these criteria for assessment, the performance of the Press Complaints Commission (PCC) has been subject to severe criticism.

Though the PCC is the highest-profile example of self-regulatory processes in British media regulation, advertising, on which the media are heavily dependant, is also largely subject to self-regulation. The exception to the generally self-regulatory approach to advertising is broadcasting, where the ITC plays a statutory role in regulating advertising by licensed broadcasting.

When considering advertising, the persuasive power of the media is seen at its most obvious. That it is believed that the media can persuade is evidenced by the vast sums of money spent on advertising by both private enterprises and government alike in pursuit of public support for their products. Except for broadcast advertisements and the general background of law such as defamation, obscenity and blasphemy, the advertising industry in Britain is regulated entirely by the Advertising Standards Authority (ASA). Commentators tend to be far less vicious in their criticisms of the role of the ASA compared with that of the PCC, yet precisely the same questions must be asked: does the ASA effectively protect the public interest in relation to advertising and is it adequately accountable in its operation?

Identified elsewhere (Feintuck 1997c) have been the risks of regulatory capture when agencies may become so closely associated with their subject of regulation that it becomes impossible to discern a divergence of interests; at such corporatist moments, the public interest, supposed to be protected by the regulator, may readily be compromised. Such risks may reasonably be expected to be heightened in a self-regulatory situation, where the regulators are drawn from and answerable to the industry concerned. Thus, transparency, always a prerequisite of accountability, may be of particular significance in relation to self-regulatory agencies, given their close relationship with the industry under regulation.

Against the criteria of effectiveness and accountability, the self-regulatory mechanisms employed in the form of the PCC and the ASA will now each be considered briefly in turn.

– 5.5.1 PRIVACY AND THE PCC –

The PCC's Code of Practice covers a range of subjects including accuracy and fairness in reporting, chequebook journalism, reporting and race, and disclosure of sources. However, the PCC's role has generally been subject to particular scrutiny and criticism in relation to its policing of complaints regarding privacy and media intrusion.

Recently in Britain, the question of privacy and media intrusion has, most frequently been raised in the context of the activities of journalists and photographers inquiring into the lives of both public personalities and those individuals temporarily caught up in some current news story. The long lenses of the paparazzi and the use of surveillance devices, together with tactics approaching mass picketing by 'the media scrum' of the homes and workplaces of those in the news have played a significant role in the battle for circulation, especially though not exclusively within the tabloid market.

Writing in early 1998, it is difficult to avoid considering these issues in the context of the controversy regarding the relationship between the media and the Princess of Wales, whose death in 1997 and initial accusations of the press having played a part in the events leading up to her fatal accident provoked a massive, if not always well-focused or well-informed, debate of these issues. Almost inevitably in a Britain confused, though somewhat obsessed, regarding the place of the monarchy and especially present members of the royal family, stories regarding Prince Charles, the late Princess Diana, and the Duchess of York have tended to raise the question of privacy in its most vivid, if not necessarily enlightening, colour.

Seymour-Ure (1996: 259) identifies a range of key episodes, from the so-called 'Squidgy tape' (in 1990, the publication of an apparently affectionate telephone conversation between Princess Diana and a friend), to the 'toe-sucking episode' (in 1992, the publication of photographs of the Duchess of York with her financial advisor at a pool-side in St Tropez), through to the 'Camillagate tape' (in 1993, a tape of apparently pillow-talk phonecalls between Prince Charles and Camilla Parker-Bowles) and the 'gym photos' (in 1993, the publication of photographs taken of the Princess Diana while working out in her Chelsea gym). Of course, this list is far from comprehensive, and in particular does not include the 'photo-fest' covering the relationship between Princess Diana and Dodi Fayed in the weeks running up to their fatal accident in Paris. The extent to which these publications reflect the degree or nature of the public interest in the royal family, or alternatively the power of the media to create an interest, is uncertain, as is the case also in relation to the media's coverage following Princess Diana's death.

It is easy to have sympathy with the individual temporarily caught up in some high-profile news story whose house or workplace becomes besieged by reporters and camera crew, or with an individual whose private life is given high-profile scrutiny or treatment by the media in the interests of selling copy or increasing viewing figures. What might be more doubtful is the degree to which those normally in the public eye should be entitled to defend their privacy when they believe that the media have intruded unfairly into their private lives. An immediate problem is apparent, namely of identifying where the line is drawn between the public activities of an individual, in which the public arguably have a legitimate interest and about which they have an entitlement to be informed, and an area of private life from which the individual can legitimately expect to exclude the public and the media.

Gibbons (1991: 132) rightly raises the issue of the ability of an individual to restrict availability of information about themselves, an aspect of individual liberty, set against appeals on the part of the media to a claim of public interest in the story or information concerned. He identifies also the difficulty in distinguishing between a story involving genuine public interest, and something in which the public may be interested, which may or may not coincide. The problem is that of finding a meaningful way of distinguishing between unwarranted intrusions into individuals' private lives, which should arguably be unlawful, and those situations where investigative journalists may carry out activities with a legitimate claim of acting in the public interest.

It is important to remember the general legal position, which the Government's 1995 White Paper expresses thus:

> The position of the press in the United Kingdom is . . . in no way special: editors and journalists are subject to the general law in the same way as any private citizen. They face no special constraints, and, with a few minor exceptions, have no special privileges. (DNH 1995b: para. 2.4)

As Robertson and Nicol (1992: 40) summarise it, 'The publication of intimate details of private lives without the slightest public-interest justification cannot be the subject of legal action unless they have stemmed from a breach of confidence or some other legal wrong. There is no substantive protection for privacy in British law', though existing and proposed data protection measures may be relevant in specific cases (Birkinshaw 1996: Chapter 6). Truth is an effective defence to libel actions, so that in the absence of an action for breach of confidence, or copyright, or trespass, a person who claims to have suffered an invasion of privacy at the hands of the press will have no avenue of legal redress; and, in any event, given the substantial restrictions on availability of legal aid, the PCC becomes in effect a surrogate libel court.

As Humphreys (1996) demonstrates, Britain is unusual, though not unique, in failing to have either a criminal or civil law of privacy or even provision of a right to reply. A very different approach can be seen in

France, where the strong statist tradition has resulted in privacy laws, arguably so severe as to inhibit effective investigative journalism (Humphreys 1996: 58). Again, this contrasts markedly with Britain, though cultural differences in attitudes between Britain and France, especially as regards sex and marital (in)fidelity, may be at least as significant. What the French example does arguably illustrate is the fact that excessive respect for privacy may inhibit the investigation of matters of legitimate public concern, and may prevent the publication of material in contravention of claims to freedom of expression. As ever, the issue is one of competing claims, both of which fall within the general group of expectations immanent within liberal-democratic theory.

An alternative to legislation is the establishment of effective self-regulatory mechanisms combined with elements of external scrutiny. Humphreys (1996: 58) uses the example of the Swedish Press Council which, in conjunction with the ombudsman, appears to offer an effective way of holding the press accountable to the public despite the absence of a Privacy Act as such. It is worth remembering, though, that the political and social culture of Sweden is essentially 'group oriented corporatist' (Humphreys: 13–4) in nature, contrasting markedly with Britain, and that strong traditions of freedom of information may limit the need for piecemeal uncovering of scandal by the media.

When faced with questions of privacy and media intrusion – competing claims, one of which must be privileged and protected at the expense of the other – it is apparent that different jurisdictions have adopted different solutions based on any combination of criminal, civil or self-regulatory mechanisms, and deriving from the cultural, political and constitutional norms prevalent in that country. What then is the British response?

Typically, what is found is an incoherent muddle, lacking in clear objectives and principles, and arguably with those who police the issues having 'rubber teeth' (Curran and Seaton 1997: 368) as opposed to the sharper version on which watchdogs usually rely. While the problems of invasion of privacy are potentially common to all investigative media, separate systems have developed in relation to the broadcasting and newspaper industries, the former (as discussed previously) predictably given the tradition of heavier regulation of broadcasting, subject to regulation with a statutory basis.

In relation to the print media, however, the PCC – an example of what Seymour-Ure (1996: 257) describes as 'collective self-regulation' – was born in 1991 of its predecessor, the Press Council (established 1953), which had been so discredited as to become little more than a joke. From 1963 the Council had begun to incorporate lay members and a lay Chair, and by the mid-1970s had a 50 per cent lay membership and a lay Chair. By 1989 the Council was dealing with a case-load of almost 1,500 complaints per annum, and though newspapers were generally prepared to publish Press Council findings against them, a certain lack of authority was indicated by the absence of stronger sanctions, combined with lack of certainty over what standards were to be expected and arguments over the formality (or informality) of procedures adopted. Alleged abuses by the press, especially in terms of invasions of privacy – in particular the high-profile 'royal' cases, but also others involving for example the family of 'Yorkshire Ripper' Peter Sutcliffe – contributed to the development of an apparent widespread public concern, manifested in political threats to establish statutory control if the press failed to regulate itself adequately. This echoed the arguments which had first led to the establishment of the Press Council, again under threat of legislation.

The Calcutt Report appeared in 1990 (Calcutt 1990; see Munro 1991), recommending the replacement of a Press Council with a Press Complaints Commission, which would have eighteen months to demonstrate that effective self-regulation was possible or else face the introduction of statutory control. Wishing to be seen to be taking a stronger line, the press industry's response was to establish the PCC which was funded by an industry levy and with a majority of lay members. It established a sixteen-clause Code of Practice in an attempt to define standards. Though the majority of complaints it dealt with related to alleged 'inaccuracy' in reporting, the highest-profile cases remained those concerning to invasions of privacy.

When Calcutt reviewed press self-regulation for a second time (Calcutt 1993), he concluded that the self-regulatory regime, to which the PCC was central, had not been effective and lacked independence from the newspaper industry. The 1993 Review recommended the introduction of a statutory complaints tribunal with wide-ranging powers. It also recommended the creation of specific criminal offences relating to physical intrusion and that consideration should be given to civil remedies for infringement of privacy. In essence, as Collins and Murroni (1996: 111) report, Calcutt's conclusions were that 'press self-regulation did not work sufficiently well to justify the continuing absence of a tort of infringement of privacy'.

The findings of the Calcutt review were subsequently considered by the National Heritage Select Committee, which controversially recommended the continuation of a voluntary, self-regulatory body along the lines of the PCC but with an ombudsman being created by statute to deal with cases where the complainant remained dissatisfied after consideration by the PCC. The Select Committee also recommended the introduction of a Protection of Privacy Bill, containing both criminal and civil elements, a recommendations which has been followed in attempts to introduce Private Members' Bills. It was in response to the Select Committee's recommendations that the Government published its proposals in May 1995 (DNH 1995b)

While a government minister famously suggested that the press was 'drinking in the last-chance saloon', the response of the Government to the recommendations of Calcutt and the Select Committee was (to continue the metaphor) merely to extend the drinking hours. In essence, the Government's position as represented in the 1995 White Paper was to reject the Select Committee's proposals, finding insufficient grounds for a statutory press tribunal or ombudsman and insurmountable problems in the way of the introduction of criminal provisions and/or a statutory right to privacy enforceable in civil law. Ultimately, the Government proposed to continue with only slight amendments to the self-regulatory regime.

The 1995 White Paper properly located the debate on privacy in the context of the freedom of expression provisions of Article 10 of the ECHR. It also acknowledged, however, the ability granted to signatories to qualify the right by reference to the protection of the rights of others, including the right to respect for private and family life guaranteed by Article 8. In relation to proposals for criminal sanctions for invasion of privacy, the Government found definitional problems and thereby sidestepped a detailed consideration of arguments relating to public interest and privacy. In relation to civil offences, the majority of respondents to consultation had believed that existing laws did not adequately protect privacy, and supporters of a civil remedy largely located their support within the context of principle and international commitments such as the ECHR. The potential threat posed by any new legislation to investigative journalism was considered only in passing, though in conjunction with the already tough regime relating to defamation in Britain and the absence to date of freedom-of-information measures, the potential for further stifling public knowledge of the activities of those in public life must clearly be an important issue. Ultimately, the Government recognised that a balance would need to be struck in any legislation, between freedom of expression and privacy, and acknowledged the need for a public-interest defence. The White Paper also considered the problem of access to civil remedies for those of limited means, given the limitations of the legal aid system.

However, it is arguably the case that the Government's responses rested on an adherence to a broad political conviction in favour of self-regulation, rather than on careful consideration of the underlying issues. In other areas, for example the self-regulatory structure for City institutions under the Financial Services Act 1984, the Conservative administrations from 1979 onwards demonstrated a clear preference for self-regulation and market forces rather than overt intervention by the state. The White Paper clearly states that, *in principle*, self-regulation of the newspaper industry is to be preferred to statutory control (DNH 1995b: paras 2.5 and 4.13).

The Government placed great emphasis on the freedom of the press, stating a belief that the imposition of any statutory control of press activities in relation to privacy would lead to accusations of government regulation of content, and therefore censorship. Certainly, there is some agreement with this approach from the 'last of the old-style press barons', Lord Rothermere, Chair of Associated Newspapers, who states, 'I don't like the idea of a privacy law: self-regulation must really apply in a free country' (*The Guardian*, 1 December 1997).

In addition to voicing such ideological predispositions, the 1995 White Paper also emphasised what the Government viewed as significant improvements to the self-regulatory machinery introduced since the appointment of former Conservative Government Minister Lord Wakeham as Chair of the PCC earlier that year. The appointment of a Privacy Commissioner (one of the PCC's lay members) with special responsibility for investigating complaints and passing them to the PCC for consideration under the Code of Practice, the increased representation of lay members generally, the willingness of Lord Wakeham to accept third-party complaints and indeed to initiate inquiries, and the increasing incorporation of the Code of Practice into editors' and journalists' contracts of employment were all offered by the Government as evidence of progress being made by the PCC. Despite this, the Government did acknowledge the need for further improvements to the self-regulatory model, in particular the establishment by the newspaper industry of a compensation fund for those whose privacy is infringed in contravention of the Code of Practice.

In summary, the Government determined that there would not be a press tribunal or ombudsman established by statute, that it was impossible to establish a statutory right to privacy, and, that the best available option was therefore, the improvement of existing self-regulatory arrangements. Despite attacks on these conclusions from many backbench MPs, the media were able to report the government's proposals as being, not surprisingly, welcomed by both the press and the PCC, with, ultimately, control of editors and journalists remaining substantially with their newspapers' owners/publishers.

The concluding paragraph of the Government's response states that the future of the (self-)regulation of the press hangs on the industry carrying out such regulation effectively:

> Only if it is prepared to take such action will it satisfy the demands of Parliament and the public for a more effective system of independent regulation of the press offering real prevention, or redress for those harmed by unwarranted actions by the press. (DNH 1996b: 6.4)

While the Government therefore ruled out immediate statutory intervention in relation to the press, there is an implicit threat in this last paragraph. However, in light of the approach demonstrated in the rest of the White Paper, the press could be relatively confident that, as part of its general approach to regulation, the Conservative Government was unlikely to call last orders at 'the last-chance saloon'.

That said, evidence of a pattern of piecemeal reform, so familiar from other aspects of media regulation, can also be seen in relation to media intrusion. In creating a statutory tort of harassment and two new criminal offences, the Protection from Harassment Act 1997, had as one of its targets the activities of the 'media scrum', though its effects are likely to remain at the margins of the question of intrusion of privacy and it does nothing to resolve the conceptual framework in which the conflict between claims of privacy and public interest takes place (see Lawson-Cruttenden and Addison 1997).

There is little sign that the Labour Government will differ dramatically from the standpoint of its predecessor in relation to the press and privacy. Though the new Lord Chancellor, Lord Irvine of Lairg, made warlike noises in his first interview after appointment (The Observer 27 July 1997), statutory moves remain less likely than the development of a privacy law on an ad hoc, case-by-case basis, by the judiciary, following the Government's proposed incorporation of the ECHR into UK domestic law. The ECHR provisions may make a difference in terms of clarifying the issues, or they may not. The fact that it appears to be the Government's intention that the provisions should be likely to give rise to causes of action only in relation to the activities of public bodies, suggests not, and, in any event, the way in which the Convention's broadly drawn Articles will be interpreted by British judges remains uncertain.

A clear opportunity to make a statement on the question of privacy arose only four months after the election of the new Government, with the controversy surrounding the press's role in the life and death of Diana, Princess of Wales. However, probably wisely, the Government chose not to enter into the highly charged atmosphere of the period by making any dramatic proposals or gestures in this respect. Rather, it was left to the PCC to reflect upon its own and the press's actions.

The reaction of the PCC's Code Committee, consisting of newspaper editors, was to propose specific reforms to the Code, which outlawed the use of photographs taken on private property and strengthened the protection from harassment of minors, especially the Princes William and Harry (see The Independent and The Times both 18 September 1997). In particular, the proposals include an attempt 'To define private life in terms, for instance, of people's health, home life, family relationships and personal correspondence into which the Press should not intrude without overriding public interest' (*The Times* 26 September 1997). Lord Wakeham, the PCC's Chair, was reported as stating that 'Motorbike chases, stalking and hounding are unacceptable – and editors who carry pictures obtained by them will be subject to the severest censure by the PCC', though the same report concluded that 'Nevertheless reporters on the tabloids were confident [. . .] that the "public interest" test would allow them to continue to "doorstep" the subjects of a big story' (*The Independent* 26 September 1997).

It may still be a little extreme to say, as Stephen Glover did in *The Independent on Sunday* (14 September 1997), that 'The idea that public and not-so-public figures have no right to privacy is fundamental to tabloid philosophy, and has spread even to the broadsheets', but his conclusion that the self-denying ordinances announced by the press in the aftermath of Princess Diana's death would be adhered to only briefly, is probably reasonable.

In fact, when they eventually emerged to take effect from 1 January 1998, the revisions to the PCC Code were clearly not as draconian as Lord Wakeham's earlier statement might have suggested; the reported fact that 'Editors broadly welcomed the proposals' (*The Guardian* 19 December 1997) is perhaps indicative of this. Though the revised Code does seek to stop the 'persistent pursuit' of newsworthy individuals, the revisions do not go as far as demanding an 'overriding public interest', as the new BSC code does in certain circumstances and as it had been thought that the PCC revisions would. Rather, the PCC Code retains the public-interest defence to claims of invasions of privacy, adding only that it must be proven to be 'exceptional' in cases involving children. The Code remains somewhat vague and subject to interpretation regarding those places where privacy can 'reasonably' be expected.

Clearly, constitutional norms are of some significance in laying the foundation upon which privacy laws are based. In Britain, the absence of a principled, public law tradition means that emphasis is placed on private law remedies, available in effect only to the wealthy, such as actions for defamation. By way of contrast, in the USA, in the spirit of openness and freedom of expression embodied in the Constitution, and more recently in Freedom of Information and Sunshine legislation, the 1964 Supreme Court judgement in the libel case of *New York Times v Sullivan* ((1964) 401 US 265) supported press freedom, narrowing the scope for defamation and permitting the publication of any stories relating to public officials, even erroneous statements, unless it is demonstrated that the publication of falsehoods was knowing or reckless.

Whether either jurisdiction has the balance right is debatable. While the British system arguably fails to offer adequate safeguards for individuals caught up in the news, the American position might appear to disregard or ignore the existence of a private realm for public figures. It distinguishes between those in public office and those not, but may seem to fail to acknowledge adequately that even public officials may be entitled to a degree of privacy.

As Collins and Murroni (1996: 113) correctly state, 'Rights are seldom absolute. Both the right to privacy, if right it be, and the right to freedom of expression and information are limited by consideration of proportionality, public interest and the claims of countervailing rights'. They propose a statutory offence of infringement of privacy, to be policed in part by their proposed all-purpose, unified communications regulator who is to be subject to judicial review. Definitional problems aside, this seems attractive as it provides for review by a body identifiably separate from the interest group being supervised.

Both Collins and Murroni (1996) and Curran and Seaton (1997) are sceptical, however, regarding any new regulatory body were it to consist entirely of government appointees, along the lines of the BSC in broadcasting. Indeed, Curran and Seaton's conclusion is that the way out of this bind is to create a self-regulatory system that actually works. They draw a comparison with the advertising industry, where they say 'there is consensual support for it and the self-regulating agency has sanctions' (Curran and Seaton 1997: 369). As Robertson and Nicol (1992: 547) suggest, independence from the industry being regulated can lead to regulators losing touch with the realities of the industry, and so, in an attempt to ensure both independence from the press and a degree of industry support via continued links with the industry, Curran and Seaton (1997: 369) propose that a revised Press Commission which consists equally of representatives of the general public (not just 'the great and the good') and of the press (and not just editors) should be able to adjudicate and enforce their judgements as a result of legally binding contracts with newspapers. They acknowledge the potential need for such a measure to be underwritten by statute if publishers will not otherwise agree to be bound by such arrangements.

In relation to reluctance to address head on the issue of privacy, a high degree of continuity exists, with governments of both political persuasions unwilling to grasp the nettle and intervene to impose meaningful regulation on the popular press. As was the case in the decision to exclude non-domestic satellite provisions from the ambit of the 1990 provisions, it is likely that governments remain aware that it is not in their interests to make enemies of those who wield considerable media power. The risk, however, is that short-term party political interests are allowed to transcend more wide-ranging, and long-term, public-interest values in both privacy and a free, diverse and active media.

There is no doubt that defining the extent and nature of privacy rights is an unenviable task, and no government is going to wish to be associated with a measure that could be equated with censorship of the media. However, if a self-regulatory regime is to continue, it must be credible and effective. It must, whether with or without statutory backing, develop its own principles and be seen to have the ability to enforce hard-hitting sanctions. Continued reliance on the PCC as presently constituted, and despite reforms, appears to lack all credibility; and it appears to do more to protect the interests of non-interventionist government and the commercial judgement of newspaper editors and proprietors than it does the general public interest.

The proposals of Collins and Murroni (1996) and Curran and Seaton (1997) hold some promise, in terms of marking a shift away from a situation where the primary purpose of the PCC might be viewed not so much as protecting the public, but as protecting the press from the potential for statutory control. That said, knotty problems regarding definition of privacy rights remain to be untangled, and it seems unlikely that all will be resolved by the application of broad principles such as those in the ECHR. Inevitably, the difficult task of interpreting such provisions and applying them in the British context will, especially in the absence of statutory measures, fall to the judiciary, leaving a high degree of uncertainty as to the precise contours and extent of any future privacy law. Whether this situation is preferable to the development of a genuinely effective system of self-regulation, is a debate that must be had.

– 5.5.2 THE ADVERTISING STANDARDS AUTHORITY –

Television advertising is controlled by law, both by domestic measures (in Britain policed by the ITC) and, not surprisingly in light of the potential for spill-over transmission across national boundaries, by European provisions. Both the Council of Europe's Convention on Transfrontier Television, and the EU's Broadcasting Directive 1989 (89/552) seek to harmonise minimum standards, requiring the clear demarcation of advertising from programming and limiting the percentage of broadcast time given over to advertising and the frequency of commercial breaks, though Article 19 of the Directive permits Member States to impose stricter limits than those established in the Directive. (Barendt 1993: Chapter 9; Skouris 1994)

While television advertising is therefore closely regulated by national and international law, the rest of the British advertising industry – in print, cinema and on hoardings – is run almost entirely on a self-regulatory basis under the aegis of the ASA. This is not to say, however, that the ASA operates entirely in a legal vacuum, as advertisers are subject to general, background law obscenity, blasphemy, defamation, etc., and to advertising-specific law relating to misleading advertisements etc.; and the ASA is subject, despite not being a statutory body, to the supervisory jurisdiction of the courts via judicial review procedures.

The ASA is, in effect, an umbrella group for the various trade associations in the advertising industry, which aims to enforce the requirement of the British Code of Advertising Practice which seeks to put flesh on the Authority's skeletal position that advertising should be 'legal, decent, honest and truthful'. The ASA's Committee of Advertising Practice (CAP), which draws up and revises the relevant Codes of Practice, consists of members of the advertising industry; but its governing Council, which has the power to approve or override CAP decisions (Graham 1994: 197), has at least half of its membership made up of persons unconnected with the advertising industry (Munro 1997: 12). In addition to handling complaints regarding specific advertisements, the ASA routinely monitors the advertising industry's output, including prepublication scrutiny, and reports the findings of its investigations in a monthly 'Case Report'. Graham (1994: 200) identifies the release of decisions and reasons into the public domain as an important legitimating factor.

Where a breach of the Code is found, the sanctions applied by the ASA, appear at first sight far from draconian, but seem to be effective. The ASA will require an advertiser to amend or withdraw an advertisement found to be in breach of the code, and any advertiser who fails to comply with such a requirement will find it impossible to place advertisements in publications or sites controlled by those in the trade who are ASA members.

It is at this stage that the self-regulation of the advertising industry appears to diverge from the PCC's self-regulatory activities in relation to the press. The key to success of the ASA scheme is that it is actively enforced by those in the advertising trade, while a large sector of the press appear to be far from content to support the attempts of the PCC to impose and enforce standards. The fact that a broadly consensual approach appears to exist at this level in the fiercely competitive advertising industry does not mean, however, that disputes regarding the ASA's exercise of power do not arise.

The efficacy of the ASA regime can obviously be questioned in individual cases. For example, the Benetton poster campaigns in pursuit of the sale of knitwear, clearly intended to shock, emphasised the bind in which the ASA can find itself, as did the controversy over the Conservative Party's 'Demon Eyes' posters featuring Tony Blair in the 1997 General

Election campaign. Should the ASA allow a 'shocking' advertisement to run and allow the public to be shocked, or should it ban the advertisement and provide the affronted advertiser with the media publicity attendant upon such a ban? It is a no-win situation for any regulator of the advertising industry, and it is not necessarily fair to base criticism of the ASA on such examples. Some body, whether self-regulatory or statutory will inevitably have to employ discretion over such determinations if any control over advertising is to be exercised. The important question is not so much who regulates, but rather the extent to which whoever exercises power in the supposed public interest is accountable for their actions. Accountability in the exercise of discretionary power can be facilitated by the confining, structuring and checking of discretion, and in particular through transparency in the exercise of powers and through liability to sanction, including scrutiny in the courts.

Following the decision in *R. v. ASA, ex parte The Insurance Services plc* (1990 2 Admin LR 77), it is now well established that as a consequence of fulfilling a function which, if the ASA did not exist, would have to be fulfilled by a body established by the government, the ASA is subject to the procedural and, in so far as they exist, substantive requirements enforced by the courts via judicial review. Thus, the ASA must act in good faith and follow fair procedures in reaching its decisions, and must not act illegally or irrationally (as defined in case law). In general, however, as Lidbetter (1994: 115) notes in connection with a review of both the ASA and ITC, the courts appear 'to treat the substantive decision of a body which they regard as having expertise in a given area with deference', the indication being that courts will be very reluctant to overturn decisions of the ASA on substantive grounds and on the whole are likely to confine their scrutiny to the decision-making process.

This difficulty in persuading a court to overturn the decision of an 'expert' body such as the ASA is a double-edged sword. Clearly, on the one hand, such a body is likely to have greater knowledge and experience of the substantive issues in question than judges, and may use more appropriate mechanisms than adversarial courtroom process. On the other hand, however, too great a degree of judicial deference to decision-makers may put off prospective challengers to decisions and allow discretion to remain unchecked. The risk is of having decision-makers potentially abusing discretion without adequate checks, though judges intervening on substantive grounds without clear, substantive principles to guide them is at least equally problematic.

This situation throws up some nice problems for academic lawyers, but should not be allowed to hide an important underlying truth relating to the self-regulatory function carried out by the ASA in the advertising industry. The fact is that the system of self-regulation enforced by the ASA is generally, by way of stark contrast with the PCC, considered by commentators to be successful.

Like the press, the advertising industry would seem to be an obvious target for statutory control if a government ultimately determined that standards were persistently falling below acceptable levels. In the case of the overtly commercial advertising industry, it would be more difficult for the industry to justify itself on claims of freedom of expression (whether in terms of arguments from truth, self-fulfilment or citizen participation), given that its fundamental and undeniable *raison d'être* is to sell products, as opposed to the more high-minded justifications offered for their existence and claims of freedom by newspapers. Ignoring, for the moment, the fact that newspapers are essentially commercial enterprises, and in themselves constitute a product to be sold, newspaper editors can at least (some more plausibly than others) resort to freedom of expression arguments to defend themselves from the threat of statutory control. The same argument also provides a useful way out for politicians fearful of intervening in 'the freedom of the press' for concerns over the public opinion-forming power that the press might wield against them.

Without either the freedom of expression argument or the leverage over government available with which to defend itself against the possibility of the imposition of statutory regulation, the advertising industry is more vulnerable, and in essence just has to make self-regulation work. The advertising industry's collective will in favour of self-enforcement of regulation is therefore fully mobilised. By way of contrast, the newspaper industry, and in particular the tabloid sector, with the shield of the claim of freedom of expression available to them, appears to feel more able, in pursuit of scandal and therefore circulation, to flout attempts by the PCC to establish standards of conduct, safe in the knowledge that any government will be reluctant to intervene.

In considering the role of the ASA and its supervision via judicial review, Lidbetter (1994: 115) posits two alternative rationales for the advertising industry's preference for self-regulation. On the one hand are the benefits of 'flexibility and informality which may offer an opportunity to avoid some practical and constitutional difficulties that limit the utility of controls imposed by law'; while on the other is the possibility that 'self-regulation is merely a means of industry avoiding the imposition of a statutory backed set of regulations which could go further than the controls imposed by self-regulation'. Both of these justifications are essentially pragmatic, and a preference for one over the other might ultimately depend on whether one is a lawyer or an advertising executive! That said, it is clear that there is no evidence that self-regulation inherently runs counter to public interest, or democratic or constitutional expectations. Consideration of the ASA alongside the PCC suggests that self-regulation, provided that it fulfils basic requirements of accountability, is not in itself problematic, but rather that it is the context in which self-regulation operates that ultimately determines whether it can provide appropriate and effective regulation.

– 5.6 THE WAY AHEAD OR THE ROAD TO NOWHERE? –

If it is accepted that regulation of the media is necessary, or even desirable, it must also be acknowledged that it is impossible to insulate the media entirely from political pressures. At the highest level, the media form part of the context in which politics operates, and it is therefore inevitable that a two-way process of influence will occur between politicians and the media. That said, there is a massive difference between the media operating in the realm of politics and the media being subject to party political pressure as part of the media regulation regime.

The exercise of discretion in regulatory activity is probably both inevitable and in places necessary, but if the ultimate justification for intervention in the activities of the media and in the operation of media markets is that of furthering democratic goals, them it must be expected that those who regulate via the exercise of discretion operate within the matrix of fundamental democratic precepts, central to which is accountability. At the start of this chapter reference was made to Davis's tripartite agenda for maximising the benefits of discretion while minimising the risks of it turning into arbitrariness. In light of the matters considered since then, it is now possible to draw some conclusions as to the extent to which the discretion of media regulators is adequately confined, structured and checked as defined by Davis. Unfortunately, it has to be concluded that clear failures can be identified in relation to all three aspects of the control of discretion.

It can be argued that discretion is not adequately confined to that realm where it is necessary and appropriate, given the apparently over-wide discretion vested in the Secretary of State over newspaper acquisitions, and the wide-ranging discretionary power of appointment to regulatory bodies vested in government. The structuring of discretion, by reference to organising principles, is markedly lacking throughout, with a distinct absence of clear rationales and objectives for intervention permitting pragmatic and opportunistic regulation in response to short-term political objectives. Absent here is not only a coherent system of principles specific to the media regulation regime, but also more generally, though equally significantly, the failure of the public law system to impose upon the regulatory system a set of clear and meaningful standards deriving from constitutional norms. In Britain, with judges wary to challenge 'expert' decision-makers, little attempt is made to develop, articulate and impose democratic principles such as a meaningful concept of the public interest, for fear of being perceived to be interfering with the merits of decisions. To take note of such judicial defensiveness is not to criticise the judges as such, but rather to comment upon the lack of judicial creativity which results from the absence of a strong and buoyant position for judges within a constitutional system which fails to articulate and protect clear democratic principles. Whether the incorporation of the ECHR will assist in this respect, by providing a foundation for greater judicial activism, or whether the potential impact of the Convention's terms will be undermined by the tradition of judicial deference and defensiveness remains to be seen. By way of contrast, Wacks identifies a clear tendency in the US courts 'to adopt a purposive construction of the First Amendment; to ask, in other words, what forms of speech or publication warrant protection by virtue of their contribution to the operation of political democracy' (Wacks 1995: 36).

Consequent on the position of British judges, and the absence of alternative, meaningful mechanisms to challenge the activities of either the media or their regulators, is the failure to check adequately the discretion which regulators exercise. The limited supervisory role of the courts, primarily supervising procedural aspects of discretion and willing to strike down only the most egregious of abuses on substantive grounds, limits the capacity for external checks on discretion; while the absence of constitutional or statutory measures requiring the basics of good administration leaves regulators free to ignore the necessity of internal institutional mechanisms for checking discretion.

Thus, the exercise of discretion by those regulating the media is on the whole woefully unaccountable. Both the formal powers of government, such as broadcasting bans and referrals on newspaper takeovers and mergers, and the informal powers of patronage and pressure are, given the relatively marginal influence of the courts, subject only to the flimsy devices of Parliamentary accountability. Though courts have started to develop a requirement for administrators to give reasons for decisions, the fact that the Channel 5 licence allocation procedure led to a judicial review action revisiting much of the ground previously covered in the TSW case suggests that it is not yet the situation that the ITC's procedures are invested with sufficient transparency to ensure that losers perceive the process as legitimate.

Consideration of the reform of the BBC and the degree to which change was driven by the political ideology of the government of the day provides an object lesson in the extent to which the public-service broadcasting system is vulnerable to party political influence. Though the BBC has not yet been subject to formal privatisation, there is a sense in which that formal step is not necessary. All the evidence suggests that in reality the BBC is already in private hands; that is to say, that the BBC can be subject to government influence and is governed opaquely, in the absence of the degree of transparency and therefore accountability that should be associated with a public corporation. The reform of the BBC, in terms of disaggregation both already achieved and proposed, adjusts the Corporation to a more market-oriented modus operandi, but does nothing to further or protect the public service values supposedly at the heart of the BBC's activities, and clearly demonstrates an economics-based approach, reflecting, according to Hutton (1995: 223) the universalising of the culture of audit, rather than a broader, public policy-driven agenda. As in other areas, this democratically crucial aspect of the media has already proved vulnerable to capture by proponents of market forces, and this is substantially due to the failure to develop clear public-interest criteria with which to defend it. The lesson has to be learnt that, as we continue to live under the all-pervasive Thatcherite legacy, positive steps must be taken to defend those activities that are valued, if they are not in due course to be subjected to the effects of market forces.

If pluralism in the media is considered a valuable democratic asset, then it is worthy of effective defence, on that ground, and not because of incidental market benefits which may accrue. The dominance of market-oriented values in current political debate, is, however, virtually unchallenged, however, and in this sense initiatives from the EU are hardly likely to help. The central objective of the EU in this area is the establishment and maintenance of a single market in which goods and services may move freely. Though at times moves to further this agenda may have a contingent effect of increasing or preserving pluralism in media ownership and/or output, pluralism remains in essence a hostage to fortune. In practice, any move to harmonisation of regulatory mechanisms is likely to be at a lowest-common-denominator level, with the onus on individual states to act beyond this, provided that such steps do not run counter to the single-market agenda. The confusing problems of concurrent legal regimes – such as was the case in relation to challenges to attempts by the UK Government to stop the 'Red Hot Dutch' broadcasts of sexually explicit material into Britain (Coleman and McMurtrie 1995) – and of overlapping jurisdiction will not go away, though in so far as they might force national regulators and courts to develop and articulate clear objectives for their activities and interventions, they are to be welcomed. It is quite clear, however, that even multiple avenues of legal challenge provide no guarantee of effective protection from, or redress for, perceived wrongs at the hands of the media, as Lord Spencer (brother of the late Princess Diana) and his ex-wife found in January 1998, when refused leave by the European Commission on Human Rights to challenge before the Court the British Government's failure to protect their privacy.

All is not negative, however, and this chapter and others have identified potential improvements. Recommendations on opening up appointments procedures to the BBC and regulatory bodies are to be welcomed, and the merger to form the BSC must be treated positively in its role of clarifying the regulatory regime, though further steps must be taken to reduce, or at least render transparent, the numerous loci of censorship of broadcast content referred to in this chapter.

Commentators also appear to view the inception and development of Channel 4, as something of a reinvention of the public-service tradition in the modern context. Channel 4 is considered to be a commercial broadcaster which successfully performs public-service functions. Though dependant on advertising revenue, it has a specific brief to cater for niche markets. In this it has been hugely successful, and it has also produced positive spin-offs in terms of the British film industry and the independent television production sector. To some extent, it is more independent of and insulated from government influence than the BBC, and is regulated by the ITC against a specific, rather than general, public-interest brief. In all of these senses, Channel 4 can be considered a public service broadcasting success story.

The other interesting lesson to be drawn from this chapter is the fact that the question of who regulates does not appear to be as important as how regulation is carried out. Contrasting the performances of the ASA and the PCC indicates that self-regulation can be perceived to work in the media environment, though the precise context appears crucial. As Page has written,

> So long as the conditions of effective self-regulation are satisfied, viz. the individuals whose conduct is the object of control belong to an organization which is sufficiently motivated to regulate their conduct and which has effective sanctions at its disposal for this purpose, there is no reason from the point of view of efficiency why self-regulation should not be adopted as an alternative to direct governmental regulation or regulation by agency. (Page 1987: 322)

The motivation, collective self-interest, must outweigh the individual interests of those regulated, as is manifestly the case with the advertising industry but not in the newspaper trade, where in some sectors circulation appears to matter above all else. Though by no means the only indicator of the efficacy of a regulatory regime, the sanctions, must be effective. Typically, in self-regulatory professions such as medicine or the law, the self-regulatory body has strong sanctions available to it, including ultimately the striking off or withdrawal of licence to practice. The PCC has no such strong sanctions available and, indeed, lacks even an equivalent to the ASA's ability, following an adverse finding, to exclude an offending advertiser from placing any future advertisement in its members' publications.

Graham (1994: 197) rightly points towards the significance of internal structures and accountability mechanisms in establishing accountability, and therefore legitimacy, in self-regulatory regimes. At the same time, note should be taken of Munro's observation (1997: 13), borne out by the findings of this and the previous chapter, that a government-appointed regulator would not necessarily be any more independent or accountable than a self-regulatory body. Thus, it is not necessary to prescribe particular structures for regulation, but to reaffirm the necessity for transparency and accountability, whatever form is adopted for different aspects of media regulation. The Labour Government's allocation of responsibility for interest rates to the semi-autonomous Bank of England, and the proposal to set up an independent Food Safety Agency that is separated from both the food industry and the Ministry of Agriculture, Fisheries and Food and which has a clear public-interest brief, are moves to be watched with interest, but at first might appear encouraging precedents which could be applied to the sphere of media regulation. Whatever reforms, if any, are introduced to the regulation of the mixed-economy of the media, however, it must be right that 'As far as possible, censorious and bureaucratic forms of regulation should be avoided. Public intervention in the market should be open, accountable and positively enabling' (Keane 1991: 154).

Certainly, any moves towards greater transparency, such as those advocated by Collins and Murroni in relation to appointments, are to be welcomed, and it may well be that the proposed Freedom of Information Act (Home Office 1997b) will bring specific benefits in relation to the scrutiny of regulatory activity. It is fair to conclude, however, that any such improvements are likely to be relatively marginal unless clear objectives are established, both for specific aspects of media regulation and for the regulatory regime as a whole. The incoherence of the jurisprudence relating to the difficult issue of privacy and the media, applied by both the PCC and, as Wacks (1995) indicates, the courts, may well, as Munro (1997: 8) suggests, demonstrate something about the lack of workability of existing conceptions of 'privacy' and 'public interest'.

In the context of media convergence, differences in approach and standards applied by different sector-specific regulators such as the BSC and PCC can no longer be acceptable, if they ever were. If there is to be any hope of regulating the new hybrid media such as the Internet, a consistent, and principled approach must be adopted. However, it is important that the brief of any new single regulator must encompass regulation of output and specifically diversity of content, since it is this objective which surrogate forms of regulation (structural and behavioural) are intended to serve.

A statement as to the regulatory rationales and a clear vision of the desired outcomes are necessary before regulatory intervention takes place or is even contemplated. At present, in the absence of such objectives the regulatory machine rolls on, but its progress, in democratic terms on the road to nowhere, is determined not by public-interest criteria, but by the proponents of the market who appear to have seized the steering wheel. As Curran and Seaton (1997: 362) point out, Channel 4, the brightest new star in the public-service media, is no longer new, having been introduced in 1982, and that 'Since then, new technology has multiplied the number of television channels, yet these have all been defined by a market logic'.

There is a critical need to present considered alternatives to the market-based agenda, yet in the place where alternative, public-policy agendas should be there is presently a void. It is not necessary to believe in the apocalyptic vision that new technology will sweep away all existing media and communications systems, to see that technological development and change in the media, if left to markets or regulated only by essentially market-oriented mechanisms, is likely to reproduce or increase information inequality and fail to protect democratic values. It is therefore an immediate requirement that a coherent, alternative vision is arrived at and adopted by those serious about the furtherance of democratic ideals.

The law may have a potentially important role to play in the development and application of democratically oriented concepts, though as yet this potential appears to have been largely untapped. The next chapter addresses this issue, and in particular reflects on the significance of the relationship between law in media regulation and the constitutional context in which it operates.

PART THREE

Comparisons and Conclusions

CHAPTER 6

International Variations: Constitutions and Media Regulation

– 6.1 INTRODUCTION –

While previous chapters have considered a range of regulatory approaches adopted in recent years in Britain, in this chapter the geographical compass is wider, though the issues addressed remain very much the same. In essence, this chapter seeks to provide a succinct synthesis and analysis of research findings relating to a range of jurisdictions, in order to identify and understand commonalities, differences and, most importantly, the degree of success achieved against the various objectives for media regulation identified in Part One. In no way does this chapter set out to compete with the excellent comparative work by the likes of Barendt (1993) (considering five countries), Hoffmann-Riem (1996) (on six countries across the globe) or Humphreys (1996) (on Western Europe), but it draws on such material selectively in order to add a further dimension to discussion of issues in the British context.

It is obvious that the challenges to regulation associated with the growth of international media empires and technological convergence will occur regardless of national boundaries and legal jurisdiction. It is therefore potentially useful to consider the ways in which these issues are addressed in different constitutional, political and social contexts, and to attempt to identify the extent to which the regulatory regimes are informed by these variables. It is possible that models of best practice will emerge.

The UK experience will again be referred to, but now in a comparative context, in which developments in Germany and Italy – fellow EU Member States – and the USA apparently the source of much of the ongoing development in media markets – will be used to provide insight into possible ways ahead for Britain. The potential role of the EU, in itself an increasingly significant regional force, will also be considered.

In all of these jurisdictions, similar challenges are posed to conventional values and regimes of media regulation. While the USA, with an essentially commercial model of broadcasting, has not shared the common European tradition of primacy for public-service broadcasting, the US response to the developing pay-television market is relevant in the context of Britain and Europe's responses to the introduction of digital television. While Britain differs from the other countries by its absence of a written constitution, the benefits elsewhere of more certain constitutional ground in the context of the media revolution must be critically evaluated; they appear to promise a valuable fixed reference point in times of turbulent change, but whether they fulfil this promise in practice is open to question.

It is always important to bear in mind Kahn-Freund's caveats (Kahn-Freund 1974) when engaging in comparative law. In particular, anyone seeking to propose the transplantation of a legal measure or regime from one jurisdiction to another must be fully aware of the constitutional, political and socio-economic differences between the countries, and must take full account of them. That said, the focus of this brief comparative study is very much on these underlying differences and their effects on media regulation, rather than an attempt to draw up, by way of comparative study, a legal prescription for a future regulatory regime in Britain.

Across all of these jurisdictions, public-service values, especially universal access to media output are being challenged. In each of the countries, and within the EU, governing institutions have to make difficult decisions regarding the use of competition policy and law. They must engage in difficult cost/benefit analyses, considering the potential economic benefits of hosting major media players and setting these against ideals of pluralism and diversity in the domestic media. Humphreys (1996 and 1997a) argues that the emphasis on attracting media business has led to a process of 'competitive deregulation', running the risk of sacrificing national regulation for diversity and pluralism in favour of perceived economic benefits attaching to the growth of nationally based media empires. In Britain, in the changes from the Broadcasting Acts of 1990 and 1996, Humphreys identifies a marked deregulatory trend associated with an emphasis on regulation for competition to the exclusion, or at least diminution, of wider public-interest regulation. If this is the case, and if pluralism/diversity in so far as they relate to citizenship are acknowledged as public-interest components, then it becomes all the more urgent to establish mechanisms for effective regulation of the converging media markets, given, as Marsden states (1997b: 2) that 'mass communications [is] a uniquely sensitive industry prone to market failure'.

In essence, as Marsden (1997a and b) indicates, the choice to be made appears to be between, on the one hand, versions of competition-based regulation which emphasise the perceived benefits of markets and, on the other, policies directed at furthering specific public policy, or public-interest, values, such as furthering equality of access to information. In practice, this may be reduced to choosing between an emphasis on the media as commercial enterprise, or as cultural and democratic enterprise.

– 6.2 THE CONSTITUTIONAL CONTEXT AND REGULATORY PRACTICE –

Despite the fact that Britain has no modern, written constitutional document, it should not be thought that media regulation in Britain operates in a constitutional vacuum. Rather, the institutions of regulation are permeated with largely implicit constitutional assumptions which, as a result of their inexplicitness, are often difficult to pin down. This is but one aspect of a broader problem, identified by Harden and Lewis (1986) as the failure to develop, identify, articulate with reasonable clarity and protect the immanent expectations of the British constitutional scheme. One particular feature of this system is the consequent possibility that regulators and the judiciary may exercise discretion in ways which fail to accord with constitutional, democratic expectations, both in substance and procedure, though given the nebulous nature of such expectations, this will inevitably be difficult to determine. The limitations of judicial review as an accountability mechanism in this context have already been referred to in previous chapters, and will be returned to in the next; however, given the nature of the British constitutional arrangements, it is sensible to look abroad in an attempt to understand the significance of the constitutional background for the practicalities of media regulation. Whether the existence of constitutional requirements pertinent to media regulation tend to act as an encumbrance or a benefit, or are broadly neutral in terms of effective regulation, is a persistent theme in this chapter, in both the studies of individual jurisdictions and the comparative conclusions.

– 6.2.1 USA –

Media regulation in the USA must be viewed in the context of the constitutional protection of freedom of speech. The First Amendment freedom, that 'Congress shall make no law . . . abridging freedom of speech, or press', is not, however, unabridgable in the media context. For example, *Near* v *Minnesota* ((1931) 283 US 697), left open the possibility of the imposition of prior restraints, while *Pacifica* (*FCC* v *Pacifica Foundation* (1978) 438 US 726), referred to in Chapter 3, saw the court confirming the lawfulness of the higher degree of regulation applied to broadcast media when compared with the press, and in *Dietemann* v *Time Inc.* ((1971) 449 F 2d 244), the court was willing to place restrictions on 'news gathering' techniques (Wacks 1995: 125). The overall effect, however, remains that the onus is on the executive or legislature to justify, in the strongest possible terms, any restriction on freedom of expression.

McQuail (1992: 36) states that the USA 'has known three different types of media regulatory regimes, in succession, but now overlapping with each other'. Broadly speaking, these can be identified as a strong constitutional resistance to intervention in the press; the regulation of telecommunications infrastructure but not content; and the broadcasting model, which involves greater regulation, including to a strictly limited extent control over content. He notes also the 'strongly economic flavour' of media regulation in the USA, contrasting markedly with the traditional public-service emphasis in Britain.

Certainly, from the very start of broadcasting in the 1920s, the USA adopted a very different approach to that taken by most Western European states. Unlike Britain, where the airwaves were regulated and treated as a public asset from the outset, in the USA a strongly commercial, advertising-funded model of broadcasting was established from its earliest days. In Briggs' terms, 'no reasonable alternative means of securing revenue for broadcasting companies was ever proposed' and 'The methods later adopted in Britain – licensing and raising a levy on the sale of broadcasting receiving sets – were opposed by powerful interests and unpopular with the public' (Briggs 1985: 19).

In an excellent and succinct summary of the impact of the constitution on media regulation in the USA, Barendt (1993: 28) refers to the early development of radio there, in the 1920s, as 'anarchic', with advertising revenue based light-entertainment channels competing for the use of the frequencies made available, resulting in what Briggs (1985: 19) refers to as 'the chaos of the ether', in which 'The multiplicity of radio stations and the scarcity of wavelengths led to a "jumble of signals" and a "blasting and blanketing of rival programmes"'. Barendt records also how attempts to impose 'common carrier' obligations, requiring broadcasters to make channels allocated to them available to all comers, were rejected both at the time of the passage of both the Radio Act 1927 and the Federal Communications Act 1934, on the basis that this would improperly interfere with the licensees' freedom.

The Supreme Court did, however, in 1943 (*NBC v US* 319 US 190) find that the FCC's rules which were intended to prohibit exclusive ties between local broadcasting companies and national networks did not interfere with the freedom of speech of licensees. In the *Red Lion* case (*Red Lion Broadcasting Co.* v FCC (1969) 395 US 367), it confirmed as lawful the authority of the FCC to license broadcasters, stating that, in Barendt's terms, 'Freedom of speech did not entail a right to broadcast without a licence or un-conditionally with one' (Barendt 1993: 30). *Red Lion* also confirmed the lawfulness of the so-called 'Fairness Doctrine' dating back to 1949, which, although allowing licensed broadcasters to editorialise, 'required them to devote some time to the discussion of important issues and to present contrasting views on controversial topics' (Barendt 1993: 29; see also Hoffmann-Riem 1996: 34–8).

In connection with the extent of permissible regulation of communications media, the Supreme Court, in *Turner Broadcasting* v *FCC* ((1995) 114 S Ct 2445; see Vick 1995) restated the legitimacy of regulatory interventions so long as such interventions 'are justified on grounds unrelated to the content of expression' (Klingler 1996: 144) and that 'rules that specifically regulate entities engaged in editorial and speech functions must be justified by a heightened showing that the purported regulatory interest exists and that the regulation directly addresses that content-neutral objective' (145). In the new context of the Internet, the Supreme Court has shown itself willing, in pursuit of First Amendment objectives, to strike down measures intended to prohibit 'indecent transmission' and 'patently offensive display' (*US* v *American Civil Liberties Union* (1997) < http://supct.law.cornell.edu/supct/html/96-511.ZS.html >).

Thus, though by no means absolute, the First Amendment protection of freedom of speech, within the guardianship of the Supreme Court, establishes a norm which may be reversed only in strictly limited circumstances, and the constitutional expectation of freedom of speech undoubtedly accounts in part for the reluctance of the state to regulate the media to the extent familiar in Europe. In particular, the FCC has never sought to enforce programme standards on licensed broadcasters in the way that the ITC does in Britain, and Barendt (1993: 101) reports that even within the 'public' broadcasting system established in the late 1960s, freedom to take an editorial line remains, in stark contrast with strict 'balance' requirements imposed on British broadcasters. Under the deregulatory Reagan presidency, however, even the Fairness Doctrine, requirements to broadcast news and current affairs, and the limited restrictions on advertising were lifted.

The nature of the FCC's discretionary power has remained essentially unchanged since the passage of the Federal Communications Act 1934. The Act only requires the FCC to exercise its powers in the 'public interest, convenience and necessity', which Barendt (1993: 29) refers to as a 'vacuous formula'. It is also necessary to note that the Commissioners are appointed by the President, with the approval of Senate, and thus the FCC is vulnerable to executive capture. However, the reality is that the FCC is viewed in practice as also being highly vulnerable to lobbying by powerful interest groups (Barendt 1993: 85). In Schiller's very direct terms, 'anyone familiar with the industry-serving commission [has] to regard its alleged role as a protector of the public interest, and a scourge of the broadcasters, as a fantasy' (Schiller 1996: 53).

It should be noted, however, that the FCC's discretion is constrained by the supervision of the Supreme Court not only by reference to constitutional principles, as discussed above, but also by reference to Administrative Procedure Act, Sunshine Legislation and the Federal Freedom of Information Act, which together add an element of transparency and structuring to the FCC's exercise of discretion which may appear to compare favourably with British arrangements.

Despite the procedural safeguards imposed upon the FCC's actions, commentators consistently lament the quality of American television compared with that of Britain. Humphreys (1996: 312), for example, refers to European public-service broadcasters as having 'provided for a range and diversity of programming that the private commercial US networks have always been quite unable to match'. Certainly, the limited amount of publicly funded broadcasting in the USA operates at the margins of a highly commercial system, and Schiller (1996: 21) laments that in modern times, 'Public broadcasting for the most part has succumbed to commercialism and the imperatives that sponsorship demands' but notes also that despite this, the New Right continues to press for the final withdrawal of support for public broadcasting (Schiller 1996: 21 and 117).

Marsden (1997b), however, appears to believe that the American experience with the regulation of pay-television may offer insights into the challenges presently being faced by European regulators. In particular, he points towards the development in the USA of the 'essential facility' doctrine, a version of which can also be seen in EU law (see Prosser 1997), which addresses the problem of the potential for the owner of a utility infrastructure, or a key part of it, using the resulting power to exclude others from use of that facility and therefore from competing. As Marsden (1997b: 6) reports, the landmark Supreme Court case *of US* v *Terminal Railroad* ((1912) 224 US 383) established that purchase of an existing essential railroad facility would be subject to a requirement of access to that facility being granted to all competitors. Drawing on the Supreme Court's finding in *Associated Press* v *US* ((1945) 326 US 1), which extended the concept of public utility and therefore the essential facility doctrine to include the press, Marsden finds that 'There is thus expressly stated a presumption of access to essential facilities in the interest of media pluralism'.

Marsden (1997b: 5) reports that, in addition to the development and application of the essential facility doctrine, the US courts have been prepared to enforce compulsory licensing under the Cable Television Consumer Protection and Competition Act 1992. This Act ensured that programmes are made available to all competing distribution platforms, and has consequently allowed four independent DTH satellite broadcasters to enter a pay-television market previously dominated by cable companies.

Klingler (1996) believes that processes of technological convergence permit, if not demand, a reappraisal of the operation of the First Amendment in relation to the media, at least in the area of structural reform of the regulatory regime. In particular, he notes the challenge presented by new technology to the separate regulatory traditions applying to broadcasting (wireless point-to-multipoint), hard-wired communication (point-to-point) and 'packaged' media output in the form of books and videos; separate traditions perpetuated, and revised only marginally, he states (8), by recent legislation such as the Telecommunications Act 1996.

Clearly, however, the decisions referred to above, especially as regards essential facilities, mirrored in EU measures discussed later, are of potentially great significance in relation to control of the infrastructure of pay-television; for example, the CAS arrangements necessary for the introduction of DTT in Britain. The American approach would appear to demand open access arrangements to such existing facilities, but would, or should, it also apply to newly developed facilities? Would entrepreneurs be keen to sink the necessary funds into the development of such facilities if open access to the facilities for competitors would reduce the potential return on such investment?

In essence, the approach of the US Supreme Court in interpreting media regulation in the light of constitutional requirements has been to seek to separate structural regulation (which is viewed as legitimate) from content regulation (which is not). Marsden identifies certain similarities in the resulting competition-based approach adopted with that likely to be pursued by the EU, contrasting the US position with the broader public-interest model hitherto predominant in Western Europe. What is apparent from Marsden's work is that he believes that while the structural regulatory approach adopted in the USA 'has resulted in a broadly competitive market' (Marsden 1997b: 8) in pay-television, concerns remain regarding the quality and range of product offered in US broadcasting as a whole.

He concludes that, by way of contrast, 'European public service broadcasting goals of quality and diversity are not content neutral' and that 'European regulators, unhindered by US precedents for the unconstitutionality of content rules, should be explicit in their embrace of such content-biased policy' (Marsden 1997b: 9). It should be considered likely, however, that, given the central, 'constitutional' value embodied in the EU, namely economic integration, the agenda of the EU may bear a closer resemblance to the economics-based media regulation of the USA than to the public-service ethos represented in the regulatory traditions of most of its Member States.

– 6.2.2 Germany –

The German situation reveals both similarities to and differences from the US model, being based upon a modern, federal constitution which provides, says Blumler (1992: 2), 'a constitutionally mandated framework of overarching principles', but which operates in a context of a public-service broadcasting tradition. Given the post-war constitutional allocation of responsibility in this area not to the Federal State, but to the Länder (see Barendt 1993: 19), including, post-unification, the regions of the former East Germany, Germany may provide a useful comparator when considering the difficulties facing the EU in establishing an overarching European model of regulation while continuing to permit an element of freedom for individual Member States.

Following a common pattern in Western Europe, broadcasting in pre-unification West Germany existed as a public-service monopoly until the mid-1980s, though based upon regional rather than national foundations. Humphreys (1997a and b) notes that since that time, a high degree of concentration of ownership in commercial media has been allowed to develop, with the clear potential for perpetuation of this situation into the digital era in the absence of strong regulation. By way of contrast with Britain, cable especially, but also satellite broadcasting, have already achieved relatively high rates of penetration into the domestic household market.

The broadcast media in Germany have operated within a very specific and explicit constitutional framework established in the aftermath of Hitler's rule. Barendt (1993: 20) recounts how in the late 1950s, despite the support of business interests and the Federal Chancellor, the federal state lacked the power under German Basic Law to establish a national commercial television channel. He also points towards Article 5 of the Basic Law, which offers explicit protection to broadcasting free of censorship. As in the USA, therefore, the constitution in Germany inhibits significantly the regulation of programme content.

However, Barendt (1993: 23) notes that the *Sixth Television* case (83 BVerfGE 238 (1991)) made clear 'that the Basic Law does not prescribe any particular method of broadcasting', and the governments of individual

Länder may, for example, permit cooperation between private and public broadcasters, and permit lower standards of impartiality and comprehensiveness on private companies than public, licence-funded channels. The justification for this latter variation, states Barendt (1993: 76), is that 'as the German Constitutional Court has emphasised, the lower standards required of private broadcasters are only permissible because public broadcasters provide the basic service' which has strong requirements of comprehensiveness and impartiality. Thus, as in the USA, structural regulation is constitutionally permissible, despite strict limitations on regulation of programme content.

Another similarity with the USA is the extent to which the courts – in the USA the Supreme Court, in Germany the Federal Constitutional Court (*Bundesverfassungsgericht*) – play a significant role, though Hoffmann-Riem (1996) notes that in none of the other countries he studies has the law exerted such a significant force over the development of broadcasting as in Germany. Hoffmann-Riem summarises the position of the Court as follows:

> The fundamental assumption underlying the court's reasoning is that in all of its areas broadcasting can have an effect on the individual and collective orientations of citizens and may thus come to be of importance in all areas of life. Freedom of broadcasting serves the free formation of opinion, that is, the freedom of recipients to be able to inform themselves comprehensively. Since this freedom is endangered, it is in need of special protection. (Hoffmann-Riem 1996: 119)

As he states elsewhere (Hoffmann-Riem 1992b: 45), 'Broadcasting must not be left to the free play of forces, since, in the view of the Court, this free play – particularly in the economic marketplace – is incapable of preventing the concentration and abuse of power in the broadcasting sector'.

The practical effect of this approach, however, appears debatable, at least as far as concentration of ownership in the media is concerned. Humphreys (1977a: 5) notes that the commercial television market in Germany, which has been allowed to develop since the mid-1980s, is 'controlled by two powerful alliances which now account for well over 50% of total TV viewing time and almost 90% of German TV advertising market' and, these two alliances are 'backed by the country's two most powerful press concerns', Springer and Bertelsmann. Springer, in turn, is 'under the influence of the country's leading commercial dealer in entertainment films, Leo Kirch, who controls exclusive pay-television rights to the broadcasting in Germany of the products of five Hollywood studios. Humphreys reports also that the Kirch group, which introduced a digital pay-television service in 1996, is now left with a monopoly in this new market, following the collapse of a proposal to launch a rival service by Bertelsmann. In light of this, it is not surprising that Humphreys (1997a: 5) concludes that 'By any standards, the German private broadcasting sector has been allowed to become highly concentrated'. Any further link-up, for example between Deutsche Telekom, which controls the telecommunications infrastructure, and either or both of the media giants would, in effect, tie up the entire market in a very small number of hands. Inevitably, in accordance with the modern trends towards media markets being increasingly international, German broadcasters have also sought to expand their horizons; a Bertelsmann subsidiary merged with 'the giant Luxembourg based broadcasting multinational CLT' in 1996 to form a serious player in the European market (Humphreys 1997a: 6).

The degree of concentration exhibited in the German media market might be thought to be the result of a total absence of any attempt at regulation, though this is clearly not the case. On no fewer than three occasions in the last ten years, new settlements (*Staatsvertrag*) between the Länder have been drawn up, and Barendt (1993: 24) believes that 'The German Constitutional Court has exercised an enormous influence on shaping the contours of broadcasting law'. However, Humphreys (1997a: 6) dismisses recent attempts at revisions of the German regulatory regime as being 'formal – but largely symbolic – re-regulation', which he believes seem designed to accommodate rather than hinder the merger process.

More significant than the inter-Land agreements, according to Humphreys, is the pressure on the Länder to compete between themselves to attract or retain media investment. This politico-economic imperative leaves the large media conglomerates in a strong lobbying position in relation to the governments of the Länder, and effectively bypasses the formal regulatory powers of the Länder's media regulation authorities (*Ländesmedienanstalten - LMAs*).

In any case, Humphreys notes that the second *Staatsvertrag* of 1992, based on an ownership model rather than audience share, was weak, especially in relation to the investigative powers of the LMAs into, for example, the kind of warehousing arrangements where different family members might control different parts of a media conglomerate in an attempt to avoid ownership limits.

Under the third *Staatsvertrag*, effective from January 1997, the basis for limiting ownership is audience share – with a 30 per cent upper limit on national broadcasting – and a national Concentration Commission is established. This consists of nominees from the Länder and was a brief extending to cover not only broadcasting, but 'relevant markets' (i.e., cross-media ownership). It also assigns greater investigative powers to LMAs (Humphreys 1997b). In addition, in an arguably positive development in Nordrhein Westphalia, a requirement is imposed on broadcasters with more than a 10 per cent audience share to provide limited airtime ('windows') to independent broadcasters, though the extent to which this move genuinely facilitates pluralism or diversity will rely crucially on how it is interpreted, implemented and enforced. The third *Staatsvertrag* also seeks to adopt the EU Advanced Television Services Directive (95/47), thought it simply paraphrases the Directive and provides no new regulatory framework specific to digital broadcasting.

Just as in Britain, where questions have been raised increasingly regarding the continued legitimacy of licence revenue funding the BBC exclusively in an era of increased competition, so in Germany, notes Humphreys, the legitimacy of public-service broadcasting has been brought into question by the new market structures that have developed since the mid-1980s. However – no doubt bolstered by the position of the Federal Constitutional Court, which appears to recognise the risks of leaving broadcasting entirely to the free play of market forces – Humphreys reaches a fairly sanguine conclusion regarding public-service broadcasting in Germany:

> While some countries of Europe have seen a 'wild' deregulation of broadcasting in the 1980s (e.g. France and Italy), and in others neo-liberal ideology has inflicted great uncertainty and some damage (e.g. Britain), in Germany public-service broadcasting would appear to have an assured future and to enjoy an enviable degree of political underpinning. Even if regulation is encountering serious problems of implementation, . . ., there is still widespread acceptance that regulation is necessary. (Humphreys 1994: 328)

However, if the process of competitive deregulation that Humphreys describes were to be replicated on a Europe-wide basis and EU measures failed adequately to contain the understandable national interests underlying it, the likelihood of a heavily concentrated European media, along German lines, seems great. In Germany, Humphreys' confidence in the ability of constitutionally supported public-service broadcasting to provide balance and range in programming, even in the context of a heavily concentrated commercial broadcasting sector, might be justified. However, in Britain, public-service broadcasting is under an ongoing challenge from deregulatory, minimalist state philosophies, while within the EU, media policy is driven primarily by the agenda of economic integration, and in both cases the protection provided by an equivalent of the principles enforced by the German Federal Constitutional Court is absent. In an increasingly internationally integrated media environment, the German experience of media concentration suggests a strong case for arguing for effective regulation at the international level, if pluralism and/or diversity are not to be overridden by market forces.

– 6.2.3 ITALY –

If the German experience is, as Humphreys suggests, one of merely symbolic re-regulation in recent years, then it is difficult to find words to describe adequately the insignificance of regulation on the Italian media market. The starting point for post-war media regulation in Italy is the 1947 statute which, influenced no doubt by the experience of Mussolini's regime, sought to ensure the political independence of the state-monopolist broadcaster RAI, establishing a Parliamentary Commission to guarantee RAI's independence from the executive. In 1960, the Constitutional Court upheld the monopoly and denied the existence of rights for private television or radio broadcasting. The Court found, in Barendt's words, that 'In view of the shortage of frequencies broadcasting was a natural monopoly', that 'the public system was the best method to secure the access of all important political and social groups to the airwaves' and, prophetically, that 'Private broadcasting would inevitably be dominated by a few corporations' (Barendt 1993: 25).

Despite this promising constitutional starting point, Humphreys (1996: Chapter 5) describes how a relatively unconstrained market-driven system allowed the market to be dominated by Silvio Berlusconi. The context for this development was what Mazzoleni (1992: 79) describes as 'conditions of legislative anarchy', with broadcasting regulation being 'a source of continual discord among the government coalition parties'.

In 1976, though confirming RAI's national monopoly position, the Constitutional Court (202/1976) had legalised independent local broadcasting, in the interests of public service, acknowledging, suggests Humphreys (1996: 179), the market reality that local pirate stations had already established a high degree of popularity. By 1981, a number of publishing groups had moved not only into local broadcasting, but also into national broadcasting companies, though the Constitutional Court (148/81) confirmed RAI's monopoly at a national level, at least until such time as anti-trust laws could be developed to guard against the risks of private monopoly or oligopoly. However, immobility within Parliament resulted in inaction on this issue, creating the regulatory vacuum in which Berlusconi's growth could take place. By 1984, the best that Parliament could do was to legalise 'temporarily' all private stations and existing networks.

By this stage, Berlusconi had already taken over the vast majority of the networks owned by the publishing groups, acquiring a virtual monopoly of Italy's private broadcasting sector, including control of the three principal commercial networks, whose audience share was almost equal to that of RAI. The absence of policy-making had allowed the space in which Berlusconi's commercial television empire could develop – and commercial it was! Taking at least 75 per cent of all television advertising revenue, Berlusconi's channels featured advertising breaks sometimes amounting to 20 per cent of the length of a feature film, and the schedules were dominated by cheap entertainment shows (Humphreys 1996: 180).

Only in 1990 did Parliament introduce a meaningful Broadcasting Act, but by then the market had already been allowed to shape itself, and the law probably represented more a legitimisation or confirmation of the existing situation than anything else, tacitly approving the de facto 'partitioning' (Mazzoleni 1992: 79) of Italian broadcasting by Berlusconi and RAI. Following the allocation of licences in 1992, Berlusconi's Fininvest group obtained three national commercial licences and since then, Berlusconi has further strengthened his grip, combining with Kirch to launch a digital service in Italy. As Herman and McChesney (1997: 171) point out, 'With three channels apiece, together commanding over 90 percent of the national audience, Berlusconi's and the RAI system have constituted a broadcasting duopoly'.

Mazzoleni's outlook for protection of the public interest in broadcasting is not positive. He states that though RAI is supervised by a Parliamentary Commission, the effectiveness of this body is undermined by the fact that 'its composition mirrors that politico-cultural patchwork that has thwarted consensus formation over broadcasting for so many years' and that 'the legitimacy of such seemingly direct political control over broadcast expression is at least open to question' (Mazzoleni 1992: 92). In relation to private broadcasting (essentially Berlusconi), a one-person regulator, the Guarantor, is aided by a National Council of Viewers whose remit is to safeguard within broadcasting 'human dignity, pluralism, fairness, openness to diversity of opinions and to all political, social, cultural and religious standpoints' (Mazzoleni 1992: 94). Unfortunately, again Mazzoleni does not offer a hopeful prognosis, indicating that the requirements of the 1990 Act are unlikely to be enforced effectively, and suggesting that the National Council of Viewers, consisting of representatives of various pressure groups, is likely to be bogged down in the same conflictual stalemate that has dogged Italian Parliamentary politics.

While Humphreys noted the 'largely symbolic' nature of re-regulation in Germany, given the realpolitik of concentration of ownership, 'Italy', he states (Humphreys 1997a: 6), 'was a case of market *faits accomplis* in the absence even of formal or symbolic regulation'.

– 6.2.4 EUROPEAN UNION –

Herman and McChesney (1997: 64) state that 'nation states remain the most important political forces in communication and much else'. However, in some ways the rest of their work contradicts this claim, in so far as central to their thesis is a claim that, in reality, global media empires are increasingly coming to control the national and international media agenda, regardless of the efforts of national governments. At the same time, the drive towards competitive deregulation identified by Humphreys – in which individual states compete, by increasingly slackening regulation, to attract media companies to their jurisdiction – further suggests a reduced role for national regulation: certainly, the German experience outlined above indicates the powerful influence which negotiations and accommodations between media players and governments, in pursuit of common interests, can have in bypassing regulatory efforts. At a practical level, technological developments, especially satellite broadcasting, make national borders increasingly irrelevant; while more generally, the convergence of broadcast and telecommunications technology, and the growth of the Internet, may render national attempts at regulation increasingly futile.

All of these phenomena, combined with corporate structures in the media reflecting a general trend towards globalism, might suggest an increasing role for international, as opposed to national, regulatory regimes. Doyle (1997) identifies what she views as a particularly compelling argument in favour of European-level regulation namely that 'dominant media operators in Europe wield such significant political power in their own domestic market as to impede national regulators from instigating any effective curbs over their growth'.

For lawyers, the existence of both national and international legal regimes presents some interesting problems, especially where two or more concurrent legal regimes are simultaneously in play; for example, in relation to the satellite broadcast into Britain of sexually explicit materials, where domestic legislation, EC measures, and the Council of Europe's European Convention on Transfrontier Television all come into play (see Coleman and McMurtrie 1995). In addition to such measures, the ECHR, which the Labour Government only now proposes to incorporate into British domestic law, may also be of some significance in relation to media regulation.

On the basis of any construction of subsidiarity, it seems that there is a case for international and domestic regulatory regimes complementing each other. There will be matters best addressed at the international level, those most suited to national regulation, and, arguably, those best met by regional regulation. According to the principle of subsidiarity in EU law, matters should be dealt with at the lowest appropriate level.

It is important also to note that the potential provided for intervention by EU institutions in the area of media regulation is not unlimited. The areas in which the EU may exercise power are strictly limited by reference to the Treaty of Rome (as amended, for example, by the Single European Act and the Maastricht Treaty), which fulfils the constitutional function of laying down the areas of competence of the institutions. In this respect, it is clear that activities in pursuit of a 'single European market' in goods and services falls within the area of competence, and indeed comprises arguably the central *raison d'être* of the Union. This in itself appears sufficient to justify intervention by the EU in matters such as the Television Without Frontiers and Advanced Television Services Directives already referred to, both of which essentially address technical aspects of broadcasting. However, when it comes to regulating ownership in the media, it is questionable whether such matters fall within the specific single market agenda, or other areas in which the EU can legitimately exert influence.

As long ago as 1989, the EC legislated on the coordination of certain activities relating to broadcasting (Directive 89/552), including require-ments for Member States to ensure freedom of reception of broadcasts from within the EEC, to seek to achieve the predominance of European works in broadcasting, and to meet a quota for programmes made by producers independent of broadcasters. However, the Directive (Article 22) also affirmed the power of Member States to take appropriate measures to ensure that programme content does not 'seriously impair the physical, mental or moral development of minors'.

In relation to media concentration, however, action has been more hesitant. The Commission, in its 1994 follow-up (European Commission 1994) to the 1992 Green Paper (European Commission 1992) found that there was no necessary coincidence between the objectives of diversity and pluralism on the one hand, and the central EC objective of harmonisation on the other. As Hitchens (1994) notes, while the initial Green Paper from the Commission was rather vague in terms of objectives and possible methods to be adopted by the EC in relation to media concentration, the follow-up paper was highly suggestive of a Regulation or Directive aimed at harmonisation being the likely outcome, though with no clear indication of the level (highest or lowest existing level) at which harmonisation would take place.

It is reasonable, though, given the emphasis on the single European market, to predict the introduction of measures aimed at harmonisation in the not too distant future. A complicating factor, however, in any pan-European media regulation strategy, will be the competing claims of, on the one hand, cultural and linguistic diversity demanded by Member States and sub-national groups, and, on the other, the protection of European cultural integrity against apparent American imperialist tendencies. While the dominant agenda item for the EU may be integration into a single European market, both to encourage inward investment and to enable the growth of European media giants to compete with the powerful US players, as Doyle indicates, 'the *main* obstructions to cross-border expansion by European media companies are cultural and linguistic barriers, *not* disparities in national regulations' (Doyle 1997: 3, original emphasis). Taking these factors into account, it seems likely that a genuine single European media market will remain somewhat mirage-like, apparently retreating into the distance as it is approached.

As was noted in Chapter 4, internal tensions within the EU – between the European Parliament and the Commission, and between different Directorates General of the Commission (Harcourt 1996) – have not contributed to rapid progress in this field, and since 1994, as Doyle (1997) demonstrates, the Commission's agenda has changed somewhat. She views as symbolic of this change the different terminology used in earlier Commission documents, which refer to 'media pluralism', to that used in the title of the 1997 Draft Directive, which refers to 'media ownership'. Doyle views this as signalling 'a move to deflect the focus away from pluralism (where the Commission's competence would be in question) towards the aim of removing obstacles to the Internal Market', where the Commission can claim a legitimate remit. Verhulst (1997: 32) identifies a further underlying obstacle to progress within the EU, observing that while the European Parliament tends to view the media predominantly in cultural terms, the approach of certain Directorates General is to emphasise the media as a commodity, to be regulated by reference to the mechanisms of the single market.

The shift from earlier drafts to the 1997 Draft Directive is, however, more than just in the symbolic content of its title. As referred to in Chapter 4, the 1996 Draft Directive had included a 30 per cent audience share upper limit on ownership in one broadcast media sector in any one transmission area, with a total upper limit of 10 per cent audience of the total media market (television, radio and newspapers) in the geographical market in which the owner is operating. However, in response to objections from, amongst others, the German and British governments, the 1997 Draft, has included a 'flexibility clause' which, in Doyle's words, gives Member States the flexibility 'to exclude any broadcaster they wish from the upper limits, provided that the broadcaster in question is not simultaneously infringing these upper thresholds in more than one member state and, also, provided that other "appropriate measures" are used to secure pluralism' (Doyle 1997: 2.2). If the draft were to be implemented, as Doyle states, 'there would be no absolute requirement for member states to enforce the upper thresholds set out in the Directive, but the new measures would prevent any member state from adopting *more* restrictive domestic media ownership rules (which, arguably, could obstruct cross-border investments or distort competition)' (Doyle 1997: 2.2, original emphasis). While this response might address perceived difficulties arising from the great differences in size of media markets in the different Member States, strong lobbying against the proposal has continued to take place, especially from media companies.

Where the Commission goes from here on media concentration is unclear, as it seems likely, disregarding the interest-group opposition for the moment, that extensive use of the flexibility clause by Member States would largely undermine the effectiveness of the Directive and would certainly reduce the apparently desired objective of certainty and consistency across the Union. However, this begs an important question of precisely what the purpose of the proposal actually is.

While a further EU paper on media ownership may eventually emerge some time in 1998, its arrival has been overshadowed by the publication in December 1997 of the Commission's Green Paper *Towards an Information Society* (European Commission 1997), which focuses on the implications of technological convergence in media, telecommunications and information technology. Early comment on this document (see for example *The Guardian* 15 December 1997) indicates the problematic nature of responses to convergence, especially in terms of the hitherto different traditions in regulating the individual sectors. The degree of regulation has traditionally been much greater in broadcasting than in the information technology sector; moreover while broadcasting regulation in Western Europe has traditionally been centred on public-interest issues, including diversity of content and, in terms of ownership, structure, telecommunications regulation has predominantly focused on technical and, in terms of the market, behavioural issues.

There can be no doubt that the regulatory issues posed by convergence must be addressed, and if the consultation process arising out of this Green Paper results in a more considered resolution of the competing approaches than that which might be expected from the turf-war between Oftel and the ITC over DTT in Britain, then so much the better. The underlying policy dilemma is particularly acute in the developing pay-television field, says Marsden (1997b: 4), because of 'the hybrid nature of satellite and cable distribution', which brings together the television industry, traditionally regulated predominantly by structural measures (and control of content), and the telecommunications market where, since privatisation and deregulation, a behavioural basis for regulation has predominated.

Marsden's work is suggestive of a threefold agenda. First, to introduce media-specific measures which incorporate design features unashamedly for the purpose of ensuring quality and diversity. Second, to challenge the assumption that diversity and pluralism are compatible with an approach based on market-oriented competition law. Third, to consider actively, on broad public policy (as opposed to narrow, competition-oriented) grounds, the imposition of something like the US essential facilities doctrine on players who control crucial bottlenecks in the digital television market in Europe.

The Advanced Television Services Directive goes some way towards addressing this agenda as regards the specific issue of CASs in digital television, effectively requiring Member States to outlaw anti-competitive behaviour by those controlling the conditional access gateway. The natural reaction at a more general level might therefore be the adoption of the kind of essential facility doctrine and 'must carry' requirements applied in the US pay-television market. As Prosser (1997: 26) notes, an essential facilities doctrine already exists in EU law (see also Marsden 1997b), and its transferral to an integrated media/IT/telecommunications market can be readily envisaged. However, the clear implication of Marsden's work is that while the application of competition law techniques and devices can introduce or maintain competition in a market such as that for pay-television in the USA, this does not guarantee meaningful quality, or pluralism in media output; consumer benefits deriving from competition regulation may not equate with the interests of citizenship. Thus, suggests Marsden's work, the EU should not adopt the economic perspective underlying US communications regulation. This, puts the EU into a difficult position, however, as to intervene and seek to impose controls on Member States on grounds other than furtherance of single-market ideals would raise questions of competence, while to do nothing would be to allow the apparent failure of individual domestic regimes to continue, and spread into a Europe of highly concentrated media ownership.

No obvious way out of this dilemma appears open to the EU, as the only logical way forward seems to be in the direction of an explicitly public interest- or public policy-oriented agenda. The problem here, of course, is not only that the EU must justify its intervention on this ground and seek to establish competence, but also, as discussed in earlier chapters and to be returned to in Chapter 7, the identification of what is meant by 'the public interest'. In this respect, even in the absence of a decisive breakthrough in respect of substantive reform, the EU may be better placed than any individual state to take an overview. Also, given the inertia obvious within Member States, including Britain, in failing to act to address the regulatory issues arising from convergence, the EU may have a crucial role to play in consciousness-raising, agenda-setting, and provoking action.

– 6.3 Different but the Same? –

This brief survey of different jurisdictions demonstrates the interplay of media-specific measures, general competition law, and the influence of the constitution on the design and impact of media regulation. No two jurisdictions have shared precisely the same combination of influences, but common across all is an attempt to imbue the regulatory process with constitutional values. In each of the jurisdictions, the framework and objectives of regulation have been informed by reference to basic constitutional statements of intent, often concretised through judicial decisions over contentious issues.

Britain is different. This is not to argue that media regulation in Britain occurs in a constitutional vacuum, but rather to accept the reality that the values and their effects are so nebulous as to be difficult to identify with certainty. In particular, Britain has failed to see the judiciary making clear statements as to the democratic significance of the media, and therefore of the regimes which regulate them, a fact likely to be not unrelated to the relatively weak position of British judges compared with their American and continental colleagues, who enjoy the buoyancy that comes from being guardians and interpreters of explicit constitutional terms.

That said, it is clear from the experiences of Germany and Italy that the existence of a constitutional framework does not in itself result in a media regulation regime that successfully avoids substantial concentration of media ownership. Equally, the US experience is of an apparently competitive market which, it is generally accepted, has not produced a diverse range of quality programming. Though it must therefore be acknowledged that the mere existence of a clear constitutional framework does resolve all the tensions between different approaches to media regulation, it remains tempting to suggest that without it, a meaningful regulatory system, operating consistently in pursuit of identified objectives, is unlikely to be realised.

One of the problems here is that the constitutions under consideration seem to have operated largely in a negative way, limiting state activity in the specific field of media regulation rather than positively pursuing definite aims. In Germany and Italy, the constitutions date back to the immediate post-war era when, in the wake of Hitler and Mussolini's regimes, the primary concern of constitution writers was to ensure that central government could never again control the media for anti-democratic purposes. In the USA, the *Zeitgeist* which filled the founders of the nation, in a reaction to the perceived tyranny of the ancien régime in Europe, led to a constitutional emphasis on defined, positively stated freedoms, especially for the media, though with the same effect of severely restricting state intervention. Though admirable in many ways, such constitutional measures are not in themselves suitable for, and may even obstruct, the purpose of pursuing positively citizenship interests in a mass-communication age in which corporate media giants can utilise such rights much more effectively than the individual citizens for whom they were intended historically.

Probably the development of detailed provisions for the protection of citizenship interests in relation to the media should, quite properly, be the function of statute, secondary legislation and executive action, given the rapid change experienced in the media context; yet in the absence of long-term constitutional guidance, it appears too easy for governments to be tempted into the pursuit of short-term economic objectives, such as encouraging investment, in preference over longer-term, more fundamental objectives relating to the media's role in democracy. In the absence of effective constitutional safeguards, it is too easy for the media's function in cultural and democratic terms to be overridden by economic concerns and the pressures of commercialism. The emphasis on competition-oriented policies for the media, as opposed to broader, public-service perspectives, is typical of the policies of the Thatcher/Reagan years, with their particular view of society and government, and of their continuing hegemonic legacy.

Bearing in mind the findings of Chapter 4 regarding the British experience, a fairly consistent pattern of reactive regulation can now be seen across the whole range of jurisdictions considered, with the agenda driven by media giants and trends in technological development and corporate structures, rather than by governments – though the US experience of regulating pay-television, discussed by Marsden, provides one possible exception to this. In this case, regulation is bolstered by the Supreme Court's application of general competition principles which happen to mesh with broader, pluralism-related, public-interest goals. The key words here are 'happen to mesh', the important implication being that there is no *necessary* coincidence between general competition measures and broader public policy measures. As their name implies, competition measures are intended to promote competition, and their scope does not necessarily extend to the pursuit of broader, citizenship-oriented objectives. In most circumstance, therefore, such measures cannot, be a real substitute for focused, media-specific regulation.

The other potential exception to this general trend of reactive regulation lies in the EU. Although enmeshed in internal power struggles between its institutions and between the Member States, the Union provides the possibility of a body somewhat detached from immediate electoral concerns, which might be able to play an important role in agenda setting; the

December 1997 Green Paper on the 'Information Society' being an example of this phenomenon. Unfortunately, in addition to the internal political tensions, the EU also presents the problem (from the point of view of pluralism and/or citizenship-oriented goals) of being primarily concerned with single-market issues, and in particular the reduction of barriers to the free movement of goods and services between Member States. It is also explicitly committed to the encouragement of inward investment into the Union and, as such, is unlikely to impose a rigorous regime of regulation for pluralism for fear of driving investment by media giants elsewhere; it may find itself unable to resist being sucked into the process of competitive deregulation.

The application of market ideals of consumerism, if allowed to predominate over broader visions of the public interest, run the risk of legitimising and furthering the commodification of the media. In the case of products such as soap powder or baked beans, an apparently wide range of brand names, and therefore choice, serves only to mask what is essentially a wide range of undifferentiated products. In such cases, the purchasers' concerns are likely to relate primarily to cheapness or value for money. In relation to the media, however, a consumerist approach fails to acknowledge or capture the wider aspects of the political and cultural significance of the media to which the citizen, as opposed to 'the consumer', will have regard. If media regulation predominantly takes on forms from within the economic paradigm, as appears to be the case in the USA and EU, little or no opposition to commodification will exist, and important public-interest values will be quietly surrendered.

The process of competitive deregulation to which Humphreys refers, and which Doyle (1997: 1) acknowledges as occurring across Britain, Germany, the USA and France, confirms the reactive nature of the regulatory process, accepting and legitimising market trends rather than establishing positive targets for regulation. The degrees of concentration in the media of Britain, Germany and Italy suggest fundamental weaknesses in the regulatory regimes employed to date, and the lack of decisiveness on the part of the EU raises the prospect of the trend being repeated on a continental scale in the digital era, if prompt and effective action is not taken.

The impression gained from the brief survey of events in the countries considered suggests that even the presence of a constitutional framework for freedom of expression fails to arrest, and in the USA may have contributed to, the development of media markets dominated by private, commercial interests. There are clearly difficulties for governments and regulators in resisting the lobbying power of large-scale media interests, and Keane (1991) argues persuasively that the historically important principle of freedom of expression, leading to reluctance to regulate media, now serves predominantly to facilitate the growth of already powerful media concerns.

Serious concern should be noted also over what Humphreys (1997: 10) refers to as the 'special relationship' between Bertelsmann and the German SPD (Social Democrats); and, in Italy, 'an intricate enmeshing of political and media interests', where Herman and McChesney (1997: 172) state that 'The rise of the Berlusconi empire illustrates the intensifying politicization of the mass-media under the globalization-commercialization process'. To these examples might perhaps be added Blair's wooing of Murdoch in the run-up to the 1997 General Election. In Hamelink's terms (quoted by Lee 1995: 3), 'If the interests of the information and cultural producers and the powers that be are intertwined, a society's capacity for democratic government is seriously undermined'. In such a situation, public accountability, and especially transparency in the regulatory system, becomes more important than ever, and the need for clear, long-term, guiding principles becomes still more pressing.

Existing and proposed EU initiatives perhaps demonstrate most clearly some of the existing tensions regarding proposals for reform of the regulation of media ownership and control. Hitchens (1994: 585) summarises the position neatly, asking whether the purpose of such regulation is 'primarily to protect freedom of expression and to encourage a plurality of sources, or is it to provide a minimum level of control to facilitate trade and competitive activity?' As she observes, the answer to this fundamental question is likely to influence significantly the final form taken by any such regulation.

It can be argued that there is a certain air of unreality about the EU moves at present. The question of competence, alongside internal tensions seems to render rapid, decisive and effective action unlikely. In addition, though the single market is premised on the economic benefits of economies of scale, the media again must be distinguished from commodity markets. The cultural and linguistic impediments to a single European media market are huge, and while some countries, notably France, may attempt single-handed last stands against American cultural imperialism, it is unlikely that a coordinated defence could be launched on a Europe-wide basis. Indeed, a likely outcome of a real cultural single market in Europe would be the predominance of English, given its greater presence as a global language than any of its European counterparts. Given the deep-seated influence of American culture on British media, this would seem to amount only to closing the European garden gate while throwing open the back door.

At present, some of the resistance to EU action comes from Member States such as Britain, which plead the doctrine of subsidiarity in response to attempts by the EU to impose a uniform structure across the Union. In reality, there is some sense in this response, given the wide variations in size and form of media markets across the range of Member States. That said, it should be apparent that Britain, Italy and Germany have singularly failed to limit meaningfully concentration in their domestic markets, and the EU may be doing them all a service by forcing them to reconsider their approaches.

In reality, subsidiarity means not only the retention of power at a national level, but also the delegation of power to local or regional authorities where this is the most appropriate level for decision-making. For some, the idea of transferring authority for regulating local media to Scotland, Wales and perhaps the English regions is attractive, but as the German experience suggests, regulation at a regional level appears highly vulnerable to capture by the economic imperatives which may be pressed by huge media corporations. At the very least, such a measure would need bolstering by the establishment of clear, overarching substantive and procedural principles, and would also need coordinating with the national and international structures, which must be subject to the same requirements.

Despite the differences in constitutional form, and the different permutations of media-specific measures, general competition law and constitutional terms in the jurisdictions examined, the conclusion has to be that they are essentially 'different but the same'. Though Barendt (1991: 93) states that the constitutional courts in Germany and Italy have been very influential, in one respect or another, they have failed to protect the legitimate interest of citizens in a vibrant and varied media, diverse in ownership and political perspective. If they have failed, it is because of a lack of conceptual clarity in terms of specified citizenship outcomes; constitutional law has been utilised to prevent or to authorise state intervention, but not to require positive steps to be taken to further the democratic expectation of citizenship. As a result, generally speaking, the Europeans have failed to ensure pluralism in ownership, while the Americans have failed to ensure the delivery of a wide range of quality output. These trends can only be likely to continue in the digital era, though probably at an increased pace, unless effective measures are put in place now to arrest their progress.

Fundamental inequalities in access to information are not reduced, and indeed may be increased, by the application of market principles, though the implication of USO-type principles may to some extent ameliorate their effects. Competition between media owners does not guarantee diversity of output, especially where oligopoly already exists, while the commodification of the media unacceptably devalues their cultural and political significance.

Public-service values, which acknowledge and incorporate objectives of media pluralism and diversity, in tacit recognition of their role as a prerequisite of citizenship, have been sacrificed in the face of the onslaught of global commercialism in the media:

> Contrary to the idealized vision of commercialization, in which an impersonal market replaces a system under government rule or guidance, the process inevitably raises questions of excessive media power, and cross-border and cross-service alliances and encroachments arouse concern over both monopoly power and national sovereignty. (Herman and McChesney 1997: 172)

If this trend is to be halted, drastic measures will be required, which governments will find difficult to justify without reference to fundamental, democratic, citizen-oriented principles. It may be necessary to reverse the norm, to sacrifice the commercial imperative to the demands of a wider and defined construct of the public interest. It may even require the break-up, in pursuit of citizenship objectives, of existing power blocs, as otherwise, the very best that can be expected is a situation roughly equivalent to the existing, arguably unsatisfactory, one. It is unlikely that any single government would buck the trend by acting in this way, as to do so would lead only to a flight of investment away from its jurisdiction. As such, it becomes all the more important that the issue should be addressed on an international as well as national basis.

Perhaps the key lesson to be drawn from this chapter should be that, in relation to media regulation, while constitutional form is important – especially from the point of view of establishing norms and mechanisms of accountability – arguably it is not as important as conceptual clarity and the articulation of values and objectives which acknowledge and serve fundamental democratic expectations such as citizenship. Especially in an increasingly technologically determinist, market economics-driven era, the long-term consequences of failing to afford protection to such values may result in them being sacrificed on the altars of consumerism and short-term perceptions of national economic interests.

CHAPTER 7

Conclusions: Protecting Democratic Values

– 7.1 THE INCOMING TIDE –

This book set out to act as a guide for those wishing to view the landscape of media regulation and to offer suggested routes to desirable destinations. However, it is not easy to write a guidebook to an area when the incoming tide is in the process of changing the contours of the landscape, and perhaps even washing parts of it away. Observers are free to watch, with some combination of awe, excitement and trepidation, as waves of technological innovation and convergence, globalisation and cross-media conglomeration combine, and then appear to wash over familiar landmarks on the media scene. The height and ferocity of the waves are clear from wherever the observer stands, but for those charged with regulating the media, watching is not an option and instead they must intervene if the tidal forces are not simply to be allowed to take their course.

The conclusions to be drawn from Chapters 4–6, however, are that the regulatory mechanisms in place have to date singularly failed to address the threat posed by the media revolution. The regulatory forms applied have resulted in the trends of commercialism meeting with little resistance. In the mixed economy in which the media now operates, there is a significant risk, if commercial trends are not addressed, that public-service broadcasting and the values it represents will all too easily become marginalised. The consequence of such a development would be the diminishment of citizenship.

As the tide of change in the media sweeps in, Britain is also undergoing if not a sea change, a significant revision of its constitution. In addition to bringing about a degree of devolved power to Scotland and Wales, the 1997 Labour administration is introducing two measures long discussed by constitutional commentators. Both the proposed incorporation into domestic law of the ECHR, and the introduction of a Freedom of Information Act have implications for the media and their regulation. The precise extent of their significance is difficult to predict with any certainty, but in so far as the ECHR might encourage a more rights-centred jurisprudence and offer support for a more principle-based system of public law, and in so far as the

FOIA will increase the flow of information to both the general public and the media alike, both offer a degree of promise. How the measures are implemented, utilised and interpreted in practice will, of course, be crucial. Certainly, the incorporation of the ECHR will not in itself resolve all questions of media power, though it might play a fulcral role in raising expectations and providing the basis for greater use of the law in active pursuit of social objectives; provided that is, that legal reform follows from a meaningful and considered process of determining these objectives and the values that inform them.

While the change in general climate that might result from an FOIA and the incorporation of the ECHR appear positive, it will also be necessary for more specific measures to be introduced in relation to fields such as the media. In doing so, it would be consistent for the Government to adopt the same approach as it claims to have applied to education, namely to emphasise its impact on citizenship, and indeed to articulate the linkage between the two, identifying how one complements the other in respect of facilitating participation in society as a citizen.

If, in pursuit of this agenda, the fundamental issue for media regulation therefore becomes ensuring universal access to a wide range of quality media products, any move towards greater access to the media in terms of input is also to be welcomed. New technology does appear to offer the potential for increased citizen access to the media in terms of input. In this sense, it offers some attractions in terms of the ability of individuals and smaller groups to communicate their views directly, addressing some of the problems associated with the ability to access conventional broadcasting noted by, amongst others, Barendt (1993: Chapter 7). Transmission via the Internet, for example, shares some of the aspects of point-to-multi-point transmission traditionally associated with broadcasting and does not have the same cost barriers to entry, but it does not as yet, however, have the same reach as conventional mass media, and access to it is restricted largely to the socially advantaged. It does not equate with Curran and Seaton's model of 'Civic Media' (1997: 363), nor, given the absence of a genuinely mass audience, does it provide the advantages identified by Dovey (1995) in relation to 'authored' works transmitted under Community Programming obligations by existing public-service broadcasters, in terms of avoiding blandness and self-censorship in the traditional mass media. The key issue here is ensuring that access aspects of public-service broadcasting are integrated into the mainstream, as opposed to becoming marginalised in the way that the public broadcasting system has become in the USA (McQuail 1992: 53; Schiller 1996).

The potentially egalitarian aspects of electronic publishing will occur only, however, if gateway facilities are kept freely open and commercial interests are not allowed to dominate the new media. It will therefore be necessary to regulate the new media just as much as the old, if the potential benefits are to be reaped and the blight of domination by commercial interests avoided.

At the risk of underestimating the impact of new technology, it seems unlikely that new, interactive services routed through fibre-optic cable will, in the foreseeable future, entirely replace conventional broadcast and printed media. Rather, it seems more likely that, just as radio supplemented rather than supplanted print and television has, though reaching an extraordinary degree of prominence, not led to the demise of other media, so networked services via the information superhighway are likely to create and fill a new niche alongside other existing media. There is no evidence to suggest yet that the new technology will provide the range and quality of media products associated with public-service broadcasting, though it may, if used selectively, usefully serve to supplement them.

If, however, the new technology is to be central to our media and communications systems in the future, it is necessary to act now, to recognise key aspects of national and global information infrastructures as 'essential facilities' within communications and therefore democracy, and to claim them for the public before the claims to private benefit become too firmly embedded:

> US experience suggests that once a commercial system is firmly in place it becomes difficult to challenge, and as its economic power increases so does its ability to keep threats at bay and gradually to remove all obstacles to commercial domination of the media. (Herman and McChesney 1997: 148)

Unfortunately, this task of claiming new technology as a public resource is, however, much easier said than done, given the enormous power already wielded by the giant corporate bodies currently running the network, with all the synergistic strength identified by Herman and McChesney (1997), and the reluctance of governments to cooperate internationally against this trend.

If the information superhighway were to replace wholesale existing media, the damage to cultural cohesion would be significant, especially if its availability were limited to those with either the technical or financial ability to utilise it; the strongest forms of regulation would be indicated in such a situation. If, on the other hand, it formed only one part of the media, then it would have to be regulated alongside other media as part of a broader media market. The task of regulation will certainly be impeded by the international nature of the superhighway. Difficulties will also be encountered, as McQuail (1992: 305) suggests, in terms of identifying 'a media originator (what used to be called the "mass communicator") who has full responsibility for public performance or who might, in principle, be held accountable to "society", according to public interest criteria'. Nonetheless, these issues must form a necessary focus for regulators in coming years, and international cooperation must take place to resist the technologically determinist arguments of those with a vested, commercial interest in the technological infrastructure. Regulation must absorb and act upon the implications of technological development and convergence and of corporate conglomeration in the media, and must replace the traditional, sectoral approach to regulation with a more holistic view of the media.

There is little doubt that, as Dahlgren (1995:148) indicates, the institutional logic of corporate media players is that of commercialism or profit, rather than 'public sphering'. The extent to which the industry can be subverted, or converted, towards serving the public-interest goal of citizenship, traditionally associated with public-service broadcasting, is the pressing question.

Clearly, it will not be possible to preserve the entire media landscape in its present form; the power of the tide is too great, and much of what is valued, perhaps with a nostalgic glow, is already in the process of changing beyond recognition. In order to determine what should be sought to be preserved and what let go, a clear set of priorities must underpin any effective action. The history of media regulation to date, in Britain and elsewhere, has, however, been one of reactive, ad hoc response to technological and commercial innovation, with a focus on the mechanisms and institutions of regulation, rather than the reasons for their existence. To move beyond prescriptions from the past (Negrine 1994: 97) a radical reappraisal of the basic rationales for the regulatory endeavour is required. To avoid being left simply 'chasing the receding bus' (Elliot 1981), it is necessary to look ahead, have some idea when the bus will leave and be sure that it will take us where we want to go. Before identifying the policies and mechanisms that will be applied, clarity must be achieved as to the values and principles that lead to the conclusion that some outcomes are more desirable than others. In the absence of clearly articulated rationales and objectives for regulation, there can be no clear idea of where the process of regulation will or should lead.

Though citizenship has been heavily emphasised in this book, as the primary justification for regulation, it is also clear that the genuine economic importance of the media industries, in terms of GDP and employment, also demand the industries' regulation. Continuing to support independent production, via Channel 4, and the imposition of independent programme quotas may both prove useful in terms of continuing to stimulate this financially important secondary market as well as in main-taining a degree of diversity in output. However, too great an emphasis on the economics of the industry is likely to be at the expense of the protection of its democratic significance. In the absence of measures dedicated to the support of broader public-interest matters, the application of essentially economic forms of intervention, such as the mechanisms of competition law, appear to confirm rather than resist the commodification of the media.

It is clear that media output is not just another commodity, but rather part of the lifeblood of democracy, and therefore requires regulation going beyond the economic; this is recognised in the application of essential facilities doctrine and the consideration of USO-type measures. In Hoff-mann-Riem's terms, 'From the very outset, broadcasting regulation was not charged simply with the pragmatic role of "traffic police" but in addition by continual reference to a special public interest in freedom of communica-tion' (Hoffmann-Riem 1996: 335). To over-emphasise freedom of commu-nication is a dangerous strategy, however, given its vulnerability to 'capture' by corporate interests (Keane: 1991) and the fact that it may appear, as in the USA, to serve as a significant impediment to effective regulation for diversity of output via positive programme requirements and the like.

Much regulation relating to concentration of ownership tacitly acknowl-edges that the purpose of intervention is the maintenance of plurality of output, though its emphasis is clearly on plurality of ownership. However, as is apparent from studies of Britain, Germany and Italy, intervention measures have largely failed in both areas: and even where a degree of plurality of ownership has been maintained, this in itself does not necessa-rily result in diversity of output. If the key objective or justification for regulation is the achievement of universal access to a diverse range of high-quality media products, then it must be acknowledged that patterns of ownership are not significant in themselves, but only in their instrumental, and largely contingent, potential to result in output.

Even in the USA, where the Western European public-service broad-casting system is considered alien and where broadcasting has operated and been regulated from its inception on a commercial basis, the commercial outlook has justified the application of essential facility and 'must carry' doctrines which have averted the risks of the worst excesses of monopolistic power. Implicit in this approach is a recognition that the airwaves and gateways to the air comprise public rather than private assets. As has been indicated, the greater regulation of broadcast as opposed to print media can be identified as historically contingent; the development of broadcasting occurred predominantly in an era in which such activity was viewed as being legitimately within the role of the state. Since that era, however, the vision of legitimate state activity has become much narrower, and with it has come the privatisation, in various forms, of what was previously considered to be the public sphere. It is in this context that the information superhighway has developed, not in an anarchic manner as is sometimes suggested, but within the logic of the market paradigm, rather than regulated in a public-interest tradition.

The fact is, however, that there remains a clear public interest in regulating the media in all its forms. It derives substantially from the citizen participation approach to freedom of expression identified in Chapter 1, and is thus closely related to the citizenship rationale for regulation espoused by Collins and Murroni (1996). If individuals are cut off from mainstream media, they are denied the information necessary for them to participate in civic society, and they are denied access to an important element in the matter that holds society together *as* society. In this sense – like education, healthcare, food and housing – the availability of the media becomes, in effect, a prerequisite of any meaningful construct of citizenship. For a government such as Tony Blair's, said to be concerned with multiple deprivation and having established, within months of taking office, an inter-departmental 'Social Exclusion Unit', avoiding exclusion from the media must presumably be a high public-policy priority. Whether such rhetoric will be transformed into meaningful action will depend both on the degree to which the political will exists and also the recognition that the media is an area, from the perspective of citizenship, at least as important as other utilities (such as power and water), where regulation of the activities of recently created, private companies is considered important and justifiable. The fact that that failure to regulate can result in the privatisation of democracy, through corporate control of information flows and access restricted to those who can pay, suggests, however, that regulation of the media is still more important than regulation of other utilities and commodities.

When buying other commodities or utilities, it is possible to make choices based upon quality of product or service and cost. On the assumption that there is more than one supplier available, the choice is likely to be based largely on these criteria. In the case of the media, however, it is unlikely that I will have any choice over the supplier of information, given that a degree of exclusivity exists over particular products. If only one supplier provides worthwhile news coverage, I need access to that supplier. If I am a soccer fan, and only one channel broadcasts Premier League soccer, I will want access to that channel. Of course, my exclusion from such services will not occur if either they are freely available, or, if I have the means to pay for them on a subscription or pay-per-view basis. However, once exclusive control over information exists, I am at the mercy of the owner of those exclusive rights; and moreover, as concentration of media ownership increases, so the likelihood of exclusivity increases with it and the range of materials free at the point of reception may diminish significantly. Clearly, not all media products constitute material that can be identified as a prerequisite of citizenship. My unfulfilled desire for a channel dedicated to gardening programmes would not significantly impede my ability to operate as a citizen. That said, difficulties in defining where essentials end and luxuries begin must be acknowledged.

There is, however, enough evidence of the centrality of the media to democracy to indicate that the media require regulation, in the public interest, to a far greater degree than other commodities or services. Given the pronounced tendencies for media markets to tend towards concentration in private ownership, which presents the problems of exclusivity and, contingently, of lack of diversity of output, and given the perceived democratic and social need for diversity of content, it seems that regulation is both inevitable and desirable. It is also essential, though, that public policy interventions are premised on clearly articulated rationales.

The predominant form of regulation that has been considered is regulation of ownership and of behaviour, based upon economic, market principles. This is convenient, in terms both of the market-oriented *Zeitgeist* and the desire of governments around the Western world not to be seen to be involved in control of content, for fear of accusations of censorship. There are, however, severe limitations attaching to this approach. First, the relationship between ownership and diversity of content is contingent, and the problems associated with concentration of ownership could readily be addressed by the introduction of guarantees of journalistic and editorial independence (Gibbons 1992). Second, it is apparent that the measures adopted to date in Britain, Germany and Italy have singularly failed to prevent a high degree of media concentration, and the institutional structures require a radical overhaul if they are to meet the challenge of the ongoing revolution.

The failure of competition-oriented measures to maintain an apparently adequate level of diversity is, however, still more fundamentally problematic. In practice, the whole raft of competition-oriented provisions purport to ensure the benefits of markets while avoiding the perceived adverse consequences of monopoly. As has already been noted, it is perfectly possible for a monopoly or near-monopoly public-service system, subject to adequate requirements as to programming, to provide the supposedly market-related advantages of diversity and quality, and in this sense it may therefore be misguided to seek to adhere doggedly to market-oriented mechanisms. This is especially true if the US model is considered, where, as Schiller (1996: 85) notes, 'There has been no lack of *a certain kind* of competition between the dominant three, now four, national broadcasting networks' (original emphasis); but this competition has revolved around maximising audience share and therefore advertising revenue, and has resulted in a predominantly bland, commercial, homogenous television diet. However, market forces have been for some time, and look likely for the foreseeable future to be, flavour of the month on a near-global basis and, as a result, any move to an alternative model of broadcasting seems an extremely remote possibility. The empirical evidence of the failure of the existing approach in terms of diversity appears to have done little to dampen governmental enthusiasm for such mechanisms.

While this might be considered unfortunate, it seems very unlikely that any major divergence from this policy will occur. Given the commitment of governments to such an approach, the only hope for a different approach lies with international bodies, and in Europe – where the major regional power, the EU, is premised precisely upon a market philosophy – there seems little hope of an alternative vision emerging. As was suggested in Chapter 6, the EU is better placed than national governments to develop an anti-commodification agenda in relation to the media, but, given its politico-economic agenda, it is unlikely to act effectively in this respect.

Collins and Murroni (1996: 12) summarise the dilemma thus: 'A stronger competition policy, though desirable, is not sufficient to secure the public interest in media and communications. For the economic characteristics and political importance of media and communications are different from those of steel and shoes'. What is needed, they go on to say, 'is competition policy where competition can thrive in the public interest and regulation where it cannot'. Given the unreality of reverting to anything approaching a public-service monopoly position, the pragmatic use of market forces and public-policy based intervention, which Collins and Murroni advocate, appears the best available option.

Marsden (1997b) appears to offer support for the use of overtly content-biased policies. Here lies a problem, however, as the inherent shyness of governments to interfere overtly with media content is currently compounded by a strong belief in the efficacy of market forces. Hesitancy to exercise what, if it serves the public interest, would clearly be legitimate government power, is probably the major factor accounting for the failure of governments to take a considered and long-term policy-making process in relation to the media. However, as demonstrated in Chapter 5, it is clear that both overtly, for example via positive programming in public-service broadcasting, and covertly, via informal power and influence over public-service broadcasters and regulators, governments can and do regularly interfere with programme content.

It is not, however, the existence of such powers that is problematic, since these powers are legitimate in so far as such content-oriented regulation is demonstrably necessary in the public interest, in terms of diversity and quality of product, and in pursuit of social inclusivity for citizens. Where such powers are not exercised in the public interest and/or are not exercised accountably, they have no legitimate foundation, and should not exist. All that remains then is to establish adequately transparent and accountable mechanisms for the exercise of these powers.

The bottom line here, to return to Schiller (1996: 121) again, is that the pursuit of competition in this context, by national governments or international bodies such as the EU, 'signifies the relinquishment of national accountability to the play of market forces'. The adoption of market forces is a positive policy choice, though it may be presented as a non-policy, or at least a device for avoiding government responsibility by permitting the free play of supposedly value-neutral market forces. Of course, market forces are not neutral and indeed, as was noted in Chapter 3, they tend to generate results that reproduce or exaggerate social hierarchy.

Failure to intervene effectively in media markets, in pursuit of citizenship objectives, leaves everything of value in the public-service broadcasting tradition vulnerable to the tide of market forces. Some of the public-service landscape has already been washed away. Much top-level sport has already been lost and is probably irretrievable, given the need felt by most sporting bodies to maximise income from broadcasting rights, and the ability and willingness of, for example, satellite broadcasters to pay large sums in order to reap the benefits of using sport as one of the levers with which to open up for themselves an established place in broadcasting. Whether or not sports coverage is considered to be able to claim a place as a significant element of the public interest in broadcasting is debatable, though it does seem to form an important element in national, social cohesion. To some degree this is recognised by existing legislation, though the list of sporting events given statutory protection to which free-to-air coverage cannot be denied is limited, and subject to review by the Secretary of State; failure to 'list' live coverage of Premier League soccer and overseas cricket test matches are obvious examples of the limitations of this measure.

To some extent, the loss of such subject matter is in itself less problematic than the longer-term trend this appears to indicate. The more attractive material is provided by via pay-television, and the less the BBC and ITV companies have to offer, the greater the problems for the public-service broadcasters in justifying their existence. Amongst the likely consequences of this are attempts by ITV companies to go 'down-market' in program-ming, competing for audience share with lowest-common-denominator fare; and the increasing difficulty for the BBC in justifying its privileged, compulsory licence fee, basis for funding. As was seen in Chapter 5, the response of the BBC to intense pressure in the 1980s was to adjust itself to a more market-oriented style, but, primarily, to defend itself by continuing to provide a wide range of quality programming. The very fact that the BBC and the public-service values it epitomises were vulnerable to such poten-tially damaging pressure, however, suggests a failure in earlier times to articulate and legitimise adequately these values.

There is therefore, in the increasingly competitive world of broadcasting, a pressing need to reinvest the public-service tradition with a sense of legitimacy of purpose, and attempts to do this must be premised upon the fundamental public-interest values of diversity and quality in programme-making, and the pursuit of social inclusivity. Re-legitimising public-service broadcasting will need more than theoretical justifications, however, and an important part of the process will have to be a restructuring of the institutions of public-service broadcasting – notably the BBC and regulators such as the ITC and BSC – so as to ensure the maximum degree of transparency, accountability and therefore legitimacy in their operations.

The very fact that public-service broadcasting has not yet withered away entirely, and that the state continues to regulate, albeit rather ineffectively, in the name of the public interest (though it is rarely spelled out adequately) demonstrates a recognition of the value of the public-service tradition. Regulation has done just enough to ensure that a 'mixed economy' of public-service and commercial broadcasting now exists, though there is no doubt in which direction the tide is running.

If the public-service tradition is to be defended and reinvigorated, it is necessary to move beyond tacit and slightly apologetic defences of it against the market-oriented arguments, and instead argue loudly for an acceptance of the reality that *only* the public-service tradition alone has been proven to guarantee the range and quality of programming, and the reach to all sectors of society, that the public interest demands. Any other, market-driven alternatives are likely to fail in one or all of these respects, leading to an undermining of the public interest and ultimately, via the erosion of citizenship, the diminishment of democracy. Though the mixed economy in the media, and broadcasting in particular, is now established, this does not deny the potential for regulators to act effectively to protect and promote public-service and public-interest values. Indeed, regulation remains a necessity, if the mixed economy is not to transform into an entirely commercial media market.

If regulators fail to intervene effectively now, the future of broadcasting, a public resource, is abandoned to the tidal forces of commercialism. It cannot be certain what will remain of the media landscape when the waters recede sufficiently to allow a view, and thus, if there is anything considered worthy of protection, steps must be taken without delay.

The power of the incoming tide is immense, and artificial sea defences offer protection only for a limited period. Over longer periods, coastal erosion will take its course, and conservation of the landscape, be it England's east coast, the National Parks or the media 'landscape', will not be successful if attempts are made simply to preserve it at a static moment in history. Just as farming, land management practices and demography will change, influenced by wider social and technological developments originating outside the local area, so with the media, where information technology and global commercial imperatives represent forces that cannot simply be excluded or ignored. Just as the landscape of a National Park must be allowed to develop in accordance with changing wisdom on land use and tourist policies, though hopefully in a way that preserves its essential qualities, so the media cannot be insulated from technological and commercial change, but, again, with good management it should be possible to maintain, in a modernised form those aspects of it that are most highly valued.

– 7.2 Rising Above the Waves –

Building new structures that rise above the incoming tide is a more attractive proposition than learning to live underwater. Designing new institutional structures that hold back the tide in places and rise through the waves in others is the primary task now facing would-be institutional architects. The key to success in this respect is to build upon foundations sufficiently deep and strong to support a structure in the turbulent waters above. In this context, it may be that the law and its constitutional basis in democracy offer a solid base upon which to build; it may be far from perfect, but may be the best available option or indeed, in effect, 'the only game in town'. Different positions will provide observers of the incoming tide with different perspectives, rendering certain features more or less prominent. The standpoint of the public lawyer offers one view of the key management issues for those involved in media regulation in the current context of the in-rushing tide.

The history to date of ad hoc, reactive change in response to developments associated with corporate and technological change is not encouraging. The failure to legislate effectively is a result of a congeries of factors, which include political fashions such as adherence to market values and concepts of the 'rolling back of the state', and also, importantly, an unfounded hesitancy to pursue unashamedly content-biased policies for fear of breaching democratic expectations of freedom of expression. This latter factor is in particular observable in the USA, where intervention to achieve a minimum range of pluralism in the media (in pursuit of a particular concept of competition) is deemed lawful, but any attempt to control content would be struck down as a breach of the constitutional promise of freedom of speech. Thus, the American public is fed an unremitting diet of lowest-common-denominator, audience-maximising television, but is able to supplement this, if it so desires, with a readily available supply of constitutionally protected pornography.

As Schiller (1996: 43) observes, 'Historically, the threat to individual expression has been seen to come from an arbitrary state', and therefore it is not surprising that there are clear and inevitable tensions between the state and the media. The media claim to act as the fourth estate, subjecting state power to scrutiny and, in an era of mass political communication, to provide the information necessary for citizen participation in democracy. Modern-day governments are therefore understandably wary of intervening openly, especially given their heavy dependence on the media's roles in disseminating their policies and forming public opinion, raising the likelihood of quiet, corporatist, symbiotic accommodations between the media and the regulatory state. However, it is also necessary to be aware of Keane's more general warning (1991: 130) about how regulation premised upon freedom of expression may be utilised by corporate giants not as intended, as a shield to protect citizens from state repression, but as a sword to attack state attempts at regulation, citing freedom of expression as a just cause.

It should also be observed that the consequence of historical lack of effective regulation of the media by the state has been the modern realpolitik of media, under the control increasingly of international, corporate, profit-oriented giants, controlling information flows subject only to the vagaries of market forces. It seems unlikely that any serious commentator would argue that this is sufficient to ensure that the enormous power wielded by the media is adequately controlled to ensure the fulfilment of the fundamental, liberal-democratic principle that power should not be unlimited. The fact that the media are increasingly privately owned should not blind politicians to the reality that the media, with their central place in democracy, continue to form an essential public resource, and should therefore be subject to adequate accountability mechanisms ensuring that this public function is properly carried out.

Public lawyers are therefore charged with the task of devising mechanisms that ensure that the media fulfil the provision of a diverse and high-quality range of material to all, in order that citizenship may be furthered. However, given the important role of media freedom in scrutinising the activities of government, other organs of the state and powerful private concerns, devices must also be put in place to ensure that the exercise of regulatory power over the media, and especially any government role in the media-regulation process, is also exercised in an accountable and legitimate manner.

It is first necessary to reassert, as the fundamental, democratic principle that justifies or legitimates media regulation, the objective of ensuring that a diverse, high-quality range of media are made available to all citizens, in the interests of seeking to avoid social exclusion. Though this construct does not in itself provide practical answers to all the many issues which must be addressed, it does provide the foundations upon which answers can be built, and the values which must be reflected and embodied in institutions.

One particularly troublesome issue which cannot be avoided is that citizenship implies a degree of equality, and therefore raises a question, in terms of both substantive and institutional arrangements, as to the degree of equality which must be sought or protected. While there can be little doubt over the impropriety of privatisation of significant civic communication (such as election coverage), the answer is not so clear-cut in relation to popular cultural material such as soap operas or sport, though these serve an important social function and therefore seem, arguably, to form part of the public sphere. This raises a range of essentially sociological questions regarding the cultural and social significance of the media which it is not the place of this book to attempt to resolve. It is, however, reasonable to note here that, as in relation to other aspects of media regulation, the pattern of intervention by governments into cultural events has developed in a largely pragmatic and unprincipled manner.

Though loath to interfere with marketplace agreements between sporting bodies and broadcasters, the British Government, as was noted in Chapter 3, over many years sought to support British cinema via a levy, and latterly through the presence of Channel 4 in the broadcasting field, where the policy of independent production has delivered positive financial spin-offs for the film industry, with a number of huge commercial successes resulting from association with Channel 4. In addition, governments have consistently subsidised 'high' but commercially unviable art, in the form of opera and ballet, in a way that would not occur in relation to more populist culture. If intervention in relation to elitist art is considered legitimate (in the public interest), it is consistent to argue that populist culture may also be the legitimate subject of state intervention, using state power and influence to avoid social exclusion. Though relevant to it, this does not in itself, however, resolve the question of how equal access to media output must be. To a limited extent, comparisons can be drawn with the regulation of privatised utilities, where USOs have been utilised (see Graham (forthcoming)) to seek to avoid some of the potential consequences of the free play of market forces in terms of cherry-picking and social exclusion. Crucially, to support even a minimum standard of equality of access to media output, and therefore information necessary to permit participation as a citizen, an adequate range of media must be available to all at an affordable cost. As McQuail (1992: 4) notes, even the liberalising Peacock Report (1986) 'endorsed the importance of public service purposes, especially in respect of providing universal service'.

Despite the promise of new technology providing the potential for an unparalleled number of channels and services becoming available, as Collins and Murroni (1996: 79) note, 'without regulatory intervention the broadcasting market is likely to provide *fewer* radio and television programmes and services free at the point of use' (original emphasis). As Charlesworth and Cullen state (1996: 31), citizenship issues may easily be marginalised if not provided for explicitly when basic USO requirements are drawn up.

In Keane's terms (1991: 176), 'Democracy requires informed citizens. Their capacity to produce intelligent agreements by democratic means can be nurtured only when they enjoy equal and open access to diverse sources of opinion'. With the new technology for delivering the multi-channel future, however, come also the facilities to restrict access in ways impossible with conventional, analogue broadcasting. Digitalisation means that those receiving broadcasts must do so via decoding equipment, with the possibility of incorporating facilities for charging – on either a subscription or pay-per-view basis – therefore being readily available. The public-good characteristic of conventional broadcasting, the practical difficulty of allocating charges to individual recipients, does not therefore apply to digital broadcasting. In addition, if technological gateways are not kept open, undue power to control who can transmit (and what, and when) will be handed to those corporate interests controlling the gateways. Here, something akin to the essential facilities doctrine may need further development, with specific application in areas such as CASs. It should be apparent, however, that regulation founded exclusively on economic rationales is unlikely to be enough, in itself, to guarantee the meeting of citizenship expectations.

However, it is still necessary to respond to the question of how equal access must be to offer effective guarantees that equality of citizenship is furthered or protected. In McQuail's terms, the difficulties here

> Stem mainly from disagreements about what features of mass communication are essential (many are clearly not) and about whether special arrangements, interfering in the free market, are needed at all to secure a fair and efficient provision of those services which are agreed to be essential. (McQuail 1992: 21)

In the final analysis, it seems impossible to draw a clear 'line in the sand' on this issue, not only because of inherent difficulties in determining which aspects of media output are and which are not prerequisites of citizenship, but also because of the rapid and unpredictable nature of ongoing technological development. Collins and Murroni are undoubtedly right to seek to ensure the continuation of what they term 'community service obligations' via:

- the continued existence of publicly funded services and notably the BBC
- must carry requirements for the services [public-service broadcasting] which conform to positive (and negative) programme requirements on alternative delivery systems [and]
- the granting of priority access to networks of limited capacity to services which are free at the point of use. (Collins and Murroni 1996: 81)

Without question, these are all, sound principles, and in a sense their adoption can already be seen in the regulatory mechanism applied to the allocation of multiplex licences for DTT discussed in Chapter 4. However, rather than attempt to prescribe precise limits, based on specific examples of output which will inevitably be transient and are likely to be arbitrary, it seems sensible to grant regulators sufficient discretion to take action in this area, but with the discretion structured by reference to the fundamental long-term principle informing the overall regulatory agenda. The question which regulators must consider and give reasoned justifications for the answers they reach is whether their decision will lend support to the maintenance of availability to all of a wide and high-quality range of media products (as a pre-requisite of citizenship). This allows and indeed requires regulators, quite properly, to reflect on the media as a whole as opposed to any particular media sector. It allows regulators, subject to the rigorous accountability mechanisms discussed below, the flexibility to determine new cases in light of current circumstances and foreseeable future developments. It does not bind regulators, nor does it permit regulators to bind themselves, to considering an issue in a narrow context. In these circumstances, the substance of the regulators' decisions are legitimated by reference to the fundamental, citizenship justification for intervention, while requirements of transparency and accountability ensure the legitimacy of the procedures they should be required to adopt.

In terms of more specific procedural and substantive developments, the example of the licensing regime introduced in relation to licensing of the forthcoming British DTT service demonstrates some improvements in regulation but also, ultimately, confirms weaknesses. The introduction of Oftel into the arrangements for licensing CASs, with experience of regulating telecommunications against USO requirements, is probably a positive step forward, and the degree of alertness shown to the potential threat posed by a BSkyB interest in a consortium seeking multiplex licences is a hopeful sign in terms of regulating media markets. The arrival of Oftel on the media scene appears to suggest the likelihood of an appropriately increased emphasis on behavioural measures as telecommunications and the media converge. It also appears to offer support for the Collins and Murroni proposals for a single media/communications regulator, positioned to take an overview of the field as a whole. That said, the fact that control of CASs is not factored into the calculations of limits on cross-media ownership demonstrates an ongoing weakness in the system. While the focus of the Broadcasting Act 1996 provisions on cross-media ownership comprises an attempt to limit the growth of such empires, the failure to incorporate into such calculations and thresholds any control of crucial technological gateways indicates a somewhat blinkered approach to the modern cross-media context. Media cannot be regulated meaningfully in isolation; and, in assessing the degree of concentration in the market as a whole, control over gateways and pinch-points in the technological infrastructure (such as CASs and electronic programme guides) needs weighing alongside control over newspapers and broadcasting corporations.

The privileging of existing terrestrial broadcasters in the allocation of multiplex capacity is a positive sign, appearing to acknowledge Collins and Murroni's demand for priority access being granted to services free at the point of use where limited capacity exists. That said, space in the allocation is one thing, but ease of use, and therefore the degree to which access to these services is readily utilised by viewers, will be significantly influenced by those controlling the allocation of channels, and electronic programme guides. The risk of such mainstream public-service broadcasting services being marginalised, lost within a morass of competing, commercial services, must be vigilantly and actively regulated against. The point just made regarding the need to regulate power in the media on a genuinely cross-media basis, including power over delivery mechanisms and gateways as well as broadcasting licences, is re-emphasised. Again, appropriate, precise limits on ownership are hard to define, especially given the difficulties inherent in defining markets and measuring market share, offering further support to a shift towards the pragmatic use of behavioural rather than structural regulation. However, the exercise of discretion by regulators, or preferably a regulator – charged with examining the media on as wide a basis as possible from the perspective of citizenship, and maximising the quality and range of available products, and required to consult widely and openly and provide meaningful reasons for decisions – would focus regulatory attention on the crucial informing issue, yet permit flexibility in addressing new technological developments.

Such developments as have been seen in relation to DTT do nothing to reduce the need for a general acknowledgement of the purpose of regulation: to further the public interest in terms of the affordable and widespread availability of a range of quality media products. As competition for viewers grows from an increasing number of pay-television broadcasters, so the need for protection of those aspects of public-service broadcasting that are valued most is greater. The BBC and Channel 4 in particular, but also the ITV regional companies, should continue to play an important part in the mixed economy of broadcasting, ensuring the continuation of a range of quality output which the market alone is unlikely to deliver. Pay-television is likely to extend usefully the range of broadcasting at the margins, creating and filling new niche markets, but is not likely to offer the core of high-quality, innovative, informative, educative and entertaining programming that public-service broadcasters have traditionally provided, given the lack of commercial prospects in this area. With this in mind, the BBC must be re-legitimised by reference to its central democratic function; but, if necessary, governments could legitimately bolster its funding beyond the licence fee, and ensure its future success, by providing a financial safety net in much the same way as Channel 4 was protected in its early years. On this occasion, however, it might be more reasonable to impose such provisions on niche satellite and cable companies, exempted from the panoply of public-service requirements, rather than on the ITV regional companies with which the BBC is very much in competition. Such 'play or pay' type provisions are perfectly consistent with the legitimising justification of furtherance of citizenship which underpins public-service broadcasting.

The foregoing has largely examined issues of regulation of media markets rather than media content, though the emphasis on range and quality of programming implies an acceptance of the advisability of overtly 'content biased' policies as suggested by Marsden (1997b). It must be accepted that it is rather far-fetched to expect the imposition on individual newspapers of the kind of balance requirements that public-service regulation applies to broadcasters. However, the public-interest justification for media regulation, as defined above, appears to permit or indeed encourage intervention to prevent political or cultural homogeneity in the press just as much as anywhere else in the media. Though it is only proper, and consistent with the line espoused here, that the press must be viewed in the context of the wider media, to the extent that a lack of diversity existing in the press sector distorts the balance of views in the media as a whole then intervention targeted at the press is perfectly justifiable. While it would seem unlikely that the present Government or any likely successor would be keen to intervene to offer press subsidies to newspapers representing minority interests (and therefore not commercially viable) in the way that Humphreys (1996: 92–3) refers to in Scandinavia, to introduce guarantees of journalistic and/or editorial independence, restricting the potential influence of newspaper owners (Gibbons 1992), would not necessarily offend the spirit of the age.

It remains to be seen whether the revision to the PCC code of conduct following the death of Princess Diana, taking effect in January 1998, takes the heat out of the privacy issue. Certainly, this is the outcome the press would prefer as, despite the apparently intractable definitional problems involved in a criminal or civil offence of invasion of privacy in Britain (if not elsewhere in the world), for the PCC to fail again to be seen to offer an effective scheme of self-regulation would surely create an irresistible case for the imposition of legal regulation, either by statute or perhaps by judicial decision under the auspices of the newly incorporated ECHR. However, as is evidenced by the example of the ASA, the question of who regulates is not as important as whether they do so effectively and accountably, though in the case of self-regulatory regimes, a clear collective self-interest, seemingly absent from the newspaper industry, seems crucial.

The so-called 'self-regulatory alternative' is, however, as Prosser (1997: 271) indicates, something of a misnomer, confusing the techniques of self-regulation with the 'prescription for overall institutional design'. As study of the PCC and ASA indicates, self-regulation is neither to be necessarily wholeheartedly embraced nor deprecated. It is merely a technique, which may be adopted to achieve regulatory objectives. Provided that it is accountable and effective – and Curran and Seaton's proposal (1997: 369) to link its use with a greater 'professionalization' of the media appears useful in this respect – it is no more or less problematic than any other mode of regulation. But to be effective and legitimate, it must operate accountably within an overall institutional design which is premised upon clear regulatory rationales and objectives. The use of self-regulation is not an acceptable alternative to the establishment and articulation of such institutional goals.

Self-regulation, however, also raises questions of more general application to media regulators, of accountability in the exercise of regulatory power. This is no constitutional or legal nicety, but fundamental to establishing the democratic legitimacy of regulatory regimes.

Chapters 4 and 5 essentially formed a catalogue of examples of regulators exercising unnecessarily wide and unstructured discretion without meaningful checks on the exercise of their powers. Government ministers were seen to exercise wide-ranging discretion over newspaper acquisitions, to have the ability to exert both formal power and informal influence over broadcasters and, via powers of appointment, the regulators; for an organisation such as the BBC, the claim of real independence from government is severely challenged in such circumstances. Regulators such as the ITC act in pursuit of only the vaguest public-interest tests, without a clear idea of underpinning values or future objectives, and subject to review by the courts only if they err significantly in procedure or commit the most egregious substantive errors. They are under minimal duties to give reasons. All of these bodies are distanced from the public, are run by government appointees, and rarely engage in wide-ranging or open consultation. In this respect they have much to learn from regulators of the utilities, such as Oftel, whose consultation processes appear by comparison innovative, wide-ranging, meaningful and transparent (Prosser 1997).

In terms of clarity and simplicity, there is much to be said for a single media regulator which combines the relevant functions of, amongst others, the DCMS, ITC, BSC, Oftel, DTI and the MMC; and, given the context of technological overlap and convergence, the brief should probably include the telecommunications industry. Whether one regulator is formed or many are retained (see Collins (ed.) 1996), the same risk apples, of regulatory capture by the industries it is intended to regulate. The risk would presumably be proportionately greater in the case of a single regulator and therefore requirements of transparency would be still more important.

The remit of any single regulator must explicitly cover the whole of the media, and should incorporate regulation of both media markets and media content. The apparent enthusiasm for a single regulator on the part of the increasingly influential Oftel (Oftel 1995) is to be welcomed in principle, though to move to a unified scheme of regulation that excludes regulation of content would be fundamentally misguided, given that the behavioural and structural aspects of media regulation serve essentially as surrogates for regulation directly targeted at diversity of content.

However, if the preferred approach is to maintain a range of sector- or subject-specific regulators, then it seems necessary to establish a body – probably, though not necessarily, independent of the DCMS – to develop and monitor the application of the fundamental rationales for media regulation, ensuring the consistent application by regulators of the citizenship-oriented approach outlined above. The increased role of a semi-independent Bank of England in relation to interest rates, and proposals to establish an independent Food Safety Agency, suggest that the Government understands the potential advantages of independence for agencies in areas of public interest.

From the point of view of the public lawyer, but more generally from the point of view of democracy and constitutionalism, a key issue in the reform of the media regulation regime is the development and application of hard-hitting requirements of accountability. Legitimacy in the exercise of power requires it to be limited, and thus media regulators should be subjected to requirements of transparency in their operation that should lead to both greater clarity in the decision-making process, and a greater sense of legitimacy for regulators in their actions.

The introduction of FOI measures should help here but is only part of the story. Availability of information on demand, such as is likely for much information covered by an FOIA, does not achieve as much as the automatic publication and widespread dissemination of information. Greater public representation on regulatory bodies is probably desirable, though not in principle a necessity, given that whoever is making the decisions should be rendered subject to public scrutiny and accountability, though transparency in the appointments process is clearly appropriate. Widespread consultation by regulators going beyond directly interested parties and extending to the general public is certainly indicated as necessary; though to avoid the risk of tokenism, such consultation must be carried out early in decision-making processes (before alternatives have been closed off) and supported by the provision of sufficient information to allow meaningfully informed responses to be made. Though the consultation exercise by the DCMS and RA in relation to DTT (DCMS 1998a), launched in February 1998, is helpful, being accompanied by the publication of a study on the predicted economic impact of the government's policies (DCMS 1998b), it has come awfully late in the day and long after a clear decision had been taken by the Major Government, and endorsed by Blair's, to opt for DTT, as opposed to other delivery mechanisms, as the chosen future mainstream platform for delivering television. In many ways, such late consultation typifies the approach of treating citizens as consumers, with the limited rights and interests that this entails, rather than as citizens, which would involve expectations of informed consultation and involvement at the formative stage of policy-making.

By way of contrast with current norms in regulatory practice, meetings of regulatory bodies should be widely publicised, open to the public and the media, except only where particularly sensitive material (and not all commercial material is confidential) is being discussed; in such defined exceptions, detailed justifications must be provided. Most important of all, regulators must be required to give reasons for their decisions, identifying why one option has been preferred over others, and justifying their chosen course of action in terms of the public-interest criteria of citizenship and the range and quality of media output.

There is nothing particularly innovative or unusual in these recommendations within public-law scholarship. In particular, anyone familiar with Harden and Lewis (1986) or indeed Keane (1991) will recognise their basis in US public law, in the provisions of the constitution, the Administrative Procedure Acts, 'Government in the Sunshine' legislation and the judicially developed 'hard-look' doctrine. Though ever wary of 'legal transplants', and conscious of the underlying constitutional, social and political differences between Britain and the USA, the problems identified in relation to the accountability of regulators in Chapter 5 demonstrate the need for equivalent measures in Britain. Though the ultimate success or failure of such measures will inevitably depend to some degree upon their interpretation and development by the judiciary, it is to be hoped that the incorporation of the ECHR will encourage British judges to develop a more principle-oriented approach to public law, and in any event, the presence of a clearly articulated citizenship orientation for the reformed media-regulation regime would provide a relevant focus for review activity.

The requirements outlined above are intended primarily to improve the quality and legitimacy of decision-making. However, were measures to be introduced that require decision-makers to operate transparently, and to justify decisions against the objective of maximising the universal availability of a wide-ranging media output, a side effect of such reforms would be likely to be more meaningful standards of judicial review of regulatory activity. Judicial process would enjoy greater purchase than where those exercising discretion do so in the absence of developed or articulated criteria, and the existence of such a principle would also help to structure judicial discretion.

The public interest in furtherance of citizenship, via universal access to a diverse range of quality media products, demands and justifies much more than structural regulation. It justifies regulation of output, in terms of the imposition on broadcasters of positive programme requirements, and perhaps the imposition of 'play or pay' levies to support public-service broadcasting, on those broadcasters exempted from such comprehensive requirements. It justifies also regulation of carriage, in terms of open access through gateways or essential facilities, and the imposition of 'must carry' requirements in relation to public-service broadcasting transmissions. It also justifies behavioural regulation, especially in terms of addressing the abuse of dominant positions; and, perhaps, the need to guarantee journalistic independence so as to reduce the influence of either private owners or government. It may even justify public subsidy of media not otherwise economically viable, along the lines suggested by Curran and Seaton (1997) in relation to 'Civic Media', or already seen in Scandinavia (Humphreys 1996).

As should be apparent, there is no neat single answer to how the media regulation regime should be reformed. There is a place for structural regulation, given the contingent relationship between concentration in media ownership and lack of diversity in output. There is a place for behavioural regulation, in terms of restricting the ability of those controlling gateways to exercise undue influence, especially given that behavioural regulation may link more closely than structural regulation to the ultimate objective of achieving diversity in output. However, to be effective, regulation must be focused upon a single, organising principle, and if universal availability of diverse media output is adopted, then both structural and behavioural regulation must be viewed properly as merely surrogates for direct 'imperative', content regulation, which focuses more clearly on the central issue and offers a more direct route to diversity.

This book has revolved around two central issues: conflicts between different rationales for media regulation, and a degree of concern regarding the use of discretion and accountability in its exercise. However, it is clear that both these tensions can be used to creative ends if activity is channelled towards a clear goal, and if the exercise of discretion is rendered accountable by making its exercise transparent and ensuring that it is properly 'confined, structured and checked'. In resolving these tensions, conceptual clarity is of the utmost importance.

The general trends identified by Hoffmann-Riem (1996: 340 et seq.) from cultural to economic emphasis, from freedom of communication to freedom of entrepreneurship in broadcasting, from comprehensive to limited regulatory responsibility and from programming-oriented (content) to allocation-oriented (licensing) regulation, form part of what he identifies as a paradigmatic shift in media-regulation policy. Certainly, all these trends can be observed in British reforms in recent years, and though they may appear piecemeal, they constitute in their totality a fundamental change of emphasis in the regulatory machine away from regulation for public-service values, and towards regulation of economic activity.

The changed view of the state, and the extent of its legitimate activity, brought about during the Thatcher and Major years and now accepted by the Blair Government, has introduced significant additional complications to an already confused agenda regarding media regulation. To borrow Osborne and Gaebler's terms (Osborne and Gaebler 1992), in many areas of public life, public bodies have moved away from 'rowing' (meaning the actual provision of services) to 'steering' (meaning control over the direction such services will take). In relation to the media, though the BBC and to some extent Channel 4 and the ITV broadcasters continue to provide a public service, this is in an environment increasingly hostile to public-service broadcasting values, while the range of regulators, often pulling in different directions, fail to provide a clear direction in which to travel. Thus, in the present sea of change, instead of moving towards identified, desirable goals that serve the public interest in the media, the media 'ship' moves in whatever direction the tidal forces of the market, globalisation and technological development wash it. Piecemeal reform of regulation in this environment appears to be rather like rearranging the deck chairs on the *Titanic* – it may provide a comforting impression of tidiness, but will do nothing to avert impending disaster. In this sense, not only is the media no longer rowed by public bodies, it is not even steered on a safe and prudent course.

Reflecting in particular the fourth 'law job', identified in Chapter 1, Ranson and Stewart state that:

> The public domain has to determine which activities are essential to maintain and develop the 'common-wealth'. It may be defending the boundaries of the realm, developing an efficient infrastructure for private transactions, or more actively pursuing the public purpose of an active citizenship. (Ranson and Stewart 1989: 12)

This agenda is applicable both to the activities of the media, operating as a pubic resource, and to media regulators, whose activities are legitimated by reference to these purposes. Citizenship and democracy will not be protected if effective regulation of the media and meaningful accountability of the media and their regulators are not achieved, and they will not be achieved without the adoption and application of a clear, organising conceptual framework. Thus, both substantive and procedural reform are indicated, but such reform must take into account a clear conceptual basis.

While it might be expected that constitutional values would provide such foundations, the evidence of Chapter 6 is somewhat inconclusive. While constitutions such as those of Germany and Italy, and statements from the respective constitutional courts, appear to promise much, in practice they have failed to halt wholesale concentration of ownership in commercial media. In the USA, the constitution appears to have served as an obstacle to intervention relating to the achievement of diversity in output. In Britain, the relevant constitutional values are hopelessly ill-defined. However, while neither the existing arrangements nor the constitutional reform programme on which the Labour Government has embarked provide straightforward answers to this problem, it can still be argued that both constitutional values and legal concepts may provide some limited assistance.

Discussing regulation of the airwaves in the USA, McQuail notes that 'there is no doubt that the legislation, in the name of the "public interest", and in return for the grant of a licence to operate was intended to place the broadcaster in a position of public *trustee*' (1992: 50, original emphasis). Hoffmann-Riem (1992b: 46) states that the German Federal Constitutional Court 'apparently does not believe that private, market-oriented broadcasting can in the long run serve as a trustee for all societal interests and protect vulnerable values sufficiently, and it has therefore taken great pains to ensure such a lasting, trusteeship role for public broadcasting to provide sufficiently broad, high-quality programming for all sections of the population'. Elsewhere, Hoffmann-Riem (1996: 77) specifically attributes a concept of 'trusteeship' to the activities of the BBC and broadcasting regulators in Britain, though describes (1996: 340) the recent paradigmatic shift in media regulation as being essentially away from the trustee model towards a market model. Though it has to be expected that neither author necessarily intended the concept of 'trusteeship' to be understood in the peculiar sense attributed to it in English law, it is interesting to compare the implications of their statements with the meaning of 'legal trusteeship', which is very different to 'ownership' as generally understood.

Under a trust, a legal or natural person – a 'settlor' – will grant property to trustees who will then hold this property *for the benefit of others*, specified in the trust deed as beneficiaries either individually or as a group. The trustee, by virtue of the fiduciary duties associated with their position, will be responsible to the beneficiaries for the maintenance of the value of the asset held, and for payment to them of benefits as prescribed by the terms of the trust. Though essentially a private-law concept, it is also applied in situations such as charitable and educational trusts, where large numbers of potential beneficiaries exist who will receive benefits as and when they come forward and are approved as being within the valid class of beneficiary as identified by the trustees or, in the case of dispute, the courts.

Examples of legal trusteeship do exist within the British media, most notably the Scott Trust, established in 1936 by the family of the former owner of the *Manchester Guardian*, to run what is now *The Guardian* and since its acquisition *The Observer*. In essence, the trust mechanism operates to preserve a degree of passivity in proprietorship, avoiding the degree of interference with editorial line sometimes associated with ownership (see Gibbons 1992).

However, the legal essence of a trust is that property is held *for the benefit of others*, the property subject to the trust being held by a body of trustees who exercise some though not all of the 'incidents of ownership' (Honoré 1987), and the legal concept of a trust is therefore difficult to apply in the context of the media as whole. In relation to privately owned media, a legal trust will occur only if the existing owner chooses, voluntarily, to hand over property to trustees for the benefit of others; they cannot be forced to become unwilling settlors. Even in relation to a publicly-owned body such as the BBC, however, the legal concept of the trust is not readily applied, as the duties of the Board of Governors do not extend to the delivery of specific benefits to an identifiable group of specific individuals. The individualistic, private-property based concept of the trust does not transfer easily into the context of public resources such as the media.

Though the legal concept of trusteeship is not widely applicable in this context, therefore, the principle of exercising power over property for the benefit of others manifests itself also in a second concept: 'stewardship'. This appears to be hinted at by Gibbons when he argues that

> The special status of freedom of the press is based on its association with editorial autonomy and that, whatever grounds owners may have for resisting regulatory intervention, it will not be sufficient for them to assert their property rights. Indeed, it may be that the only way to protect freedom of the press is to limit those interests. (Gibbons 1992: 279)

In the concept of 'stewardship' may be found an answer which avoids the legal complexities of trusteeship, while emphasising the media's function as a public resource and the resultant public-interest values. It acknowledges the 'right' of media owners to benefit from their private property, while simultaneously pursuing Keane's agenda that 'communications media should be for the public use and enjoyment of all citizens and not for the private gain or profit of political rulers or businesses' (Keane 1991: 127).

In discussing the concept of stewardship, in the context of a discussion of theory of property in relation to the finite and non-renewable resource of land, Lucy and Mitchell state that

> An abstract account of stewardship maintains that the holder, or steward, has some control and rights over the resource, but that control must in the main be exercised for the benefit of specific others. Since the steward's control must *in the main* be exercised in favour of others, it is not the case that he must be completely selfless, an island of altruism in a sea of self-interest. (Lucy and Mitchell 1996: 584, original emphasis)

The task of regulating the media has already been compared to that of managing a public asset, considered unique, or at least finite and non-renewable, such as a National Park. In Britain, landowners in National Parks are placed under what amounts to a limited duty of stewardship, supervised by a planning authority, whose explicit duty is to manage the potential conflicts of interest between those who own land in the area, those who want recreational access to the area, and the conservation of the area's outstanding natural features for future generations. National Park planning authorities in Britain are not granted ownership of all land in the area, but rather, in the interests of those of present and future generations who wish to use the area for recreation, powers to restrict the activities of those who do own the land, replacing what in Honoré's terms are the full set of 'incidents of ownership' with a more limited set of incidents of stewardship. Thus, planning controls on building and industry are strictly enforced in such areas, while efforts are also made to prevent or repair damage done to the area by the many visitors who will come each year.

The explicit objective of such a planning authority is to resolve the conflicts of these competing interests. The extent to which such conflicts are successfully resolved can be debated, on a practical, technical, legal or a theoretical level (for example, in relation to access to land, see Barker 1994, and Barker and Lucy 1993), – though there can be little doubt that the result better serves the perceived public interest than would a total absence of regulation, abandoning all to the unrestricted commercial property rights and interests of the landowner. Similarly, while the application of steward-ship principles to the media would not resolve all existing challenges to regulation, it might assist substantially in breaking the contingent link between ownership and output.

Arguably, the media are at least as important to democracy and citizen-ship as conservation of our wild and open spaces and maintenance of access to them. As the mixed-media economy appears to tend to privilege unduly the commercial, and marginalise the public-interest, elements, it therefore seems necessary to reclaim some of this territory for the legitimate public interest. It is impossible, given the ongoing non-interventionist rhetoric of Government, to imagine the present or any foreseeable Government taking steps to nationalise or renationalise sectors of the economy in pursuit of public-interest claims. However, it is possible to envisage a new govern-ment, with citizenship explicitly at the centre of its agenda, imposing stewardship arrangements in relation to national assets that form essential aspects of citizenship and democracy.

Though it might be argued that digital technology has ended any scarcity of resources in the media, and especially has ended the frequency shortage justification for regulation, to argue for stewardship is not to revert to this argument. Rather, it is to recognise that in certain areas of media activity, for example technological gateways in DTT, the resource is effectively unique and finite, but also that, *as a whole*, the media form a unique democratic resource in which public interest, as well as private property rights, deserve recognition. We are all stakeholders in both National Parks and the media.

Though 'stewardship' is not a 'black letter' legal concept in English law, it is clearly embodied, in the context of National Parks, in the activities of planning authorities and the restrictions upon landowners enforced by them. In a sense it can also be seen in relation to the regulation of privatised utilities, where the activities of regulators serve to limit the freedom of companies to act entirely in pursuit of commercial interests. It is also embodied in relation to more general restrictions on corporate governance of companies, where the primary, profit-maximisation duty of directors to shareholders can be tempered by measures demanding a responsibility to the broader public in the management of the company (Parkinson 1993).

It has been argued consistently in this book that the power and democratic significance of the media justify its regulation in the public interest. It can now be seen that there is nothing unique in this proposition which can also be applied to other large businesses:

> The reason large companies should be viewed as social enterprises relies, it is suggested, on a political theory about the legitimacy of private power. That theory holds that the possession of social decision-making power by companies is legitimate (that is, there are good reasons for regarding its possession as justified) only if this state of affairs is in the public interest. Since the public interest is the foundation of the legitimacy of companies, it follows that society is entitled to ensure that corporate power is exercised in a way that is consistent with that interest. To describe companies as social enterprises is thus to make a claim about the grounds of their legitimacy, and its practical significance is to hold that the state is entitled to prescribe the terms on which corporate power may be possessed and exercised. (Parkinson 1993: 23)

In relation to the media, the recognition of stewardship obligations by those who regulate, and their enforcement on those who own and control, though it may appear a flimsy basis on which to regulate (having no clear legal foundation), serves precisely the function which has been identified as necessary throughout this book and reflects closely the social responsibility model of Siebert *et al.* (1956). It simultaneously acknowledges the rights of media owners to make profits, thereby avoiding any significant blight on entrepreneurship, while limiting their rights of ownership in pursuit of citizenship-related objectives such as universal access and diversity of output.

It promotes the decommodification of the media, and protects against the risks to citizenship, and therefore democracy, posed by exclusive ownership of key aspects of the public-communication mechanisms, just as steps to regulate the computerised reservations systems for airlines (Goh 1997), noted in Chapter 4, protect competitors and consumers from the system controller. In the application of measures such as the essential facility doctrine, and must, carry requirements, which restrict the nature of private proprietorial power, the spirit of stewardship is already present in media regulation.

Stewardship-type duties can also be found in other areas of regulatory activity, for example in the enforcement on licensed commercial broadcasters of positive programming and other licence requirements by the ITC, and in attempts to regulate the new gateways and pinch-points involved in DTT. There are, of course, problems which have already been identified in relation to the practical exercise of these powers; however, what is more important from the point of view of a stewardship-type agenda is that the remit is extended to apply to the media as a whole, rather than to discrete aspects of it.

Thus, regulators, in enforcing a stewardship agenda, must be empowered to ensure that ownership whether of broadcasting or print or both – in so far as it impacts on diversity of output, is not allowed to run counter to citizenship interests. It requires an acknowledgement that the public interest in the airwaves and other media demands at least as much recognition as commercial interests, and that the property rights of those who develop and own new technology must be limited by reference to the public interest in the media's role as a public resource.

The principle of stewardship appears to offer a coherent foundation for the exercise of regulatory power in pursuit of citizenship-related public interests in the media. It helps to give effect to underlying constitutional values, and fills a gap in the existing conceptual framework of law.

Those regulating to further stewardship of the media might legitimately be empowered to require corporate bodies to divest themselves of assets where their ownership of them is deemed to run counter to interests of citizenship; or to require the implementation of effective guarantees of editorial or journalistic independence from proprietorial interference; or – in order to support those broadcasters that continue to provide the full range of public-service output – to impose financial levies on those who do not offer a full range of programme services or do not make them universally available. The regulators might also be permitted to allocate public funds to subsidise new or existing media which serve to extend the range of media output.

From the point of view of consistency, a single regulator able to take an overview may well prove preferable to the multiplicity of loci of regulatory power currently existing. Crucial to all of this, however, must be an element of institutional design which ensures that powers of those regulating for stewardship are exercised transparently and accountably; that the widest possible range of views is taken into account, and that fully detailed reasons are given publicly for decisions; that the discretion of regulators is no wider than it need be, and that it is adequately structured, by standards deriving from expectations of citizenship; and that adequate internal and external checking mechanisms are imposed.

All of this presupposes, however, the acknowledgement and adoption of citizenship as the logical, legitimate, central organising principle for the democratic endeavour of media regulation. In more concrete terms, this will require spelling out via the imposition on regulators of a duty to act in pursuit of, and justify their actions in terms of, the furtherance of universal access to a diverse range of media output. At the same time, it must be accepted that ownership of the media, so essential a part of the fabric of democracy, must not be subject to the full power of private ownership, but rather to a stewardship model that reflects the public interest. While such reform might appear revolutionary, it does not require the total abandonment of all existing regulation, but merely a refocusing of the entire mechanism onto the clear and unambiguous objective of citizenship.

The alternative to fundamental reform of the media-regulation system is to persevere with the current system, and to amend it incrementally to follow technological and corporate change. The dangers of such a reactive process, where the regulatory regime serves only to legitimate the market-derived *fait accompli*, were illustrated vividly in Chapter 6 by the Italian experience.

The existing situation in Britain already amounts, arguably, to a failure in previous and current regimes of media regulation. Ongoing technological and commercial change threaten to render existing mechanisms of regulation, both in Britain and elsewhere, entirely obsolete, and responses to date have been disappointing largely because of their persistent failure to identify, acknowledge and support adequately the values underlying regulatory intervention. In the absence of clarity regarding these fundamental values, regulation will remain unfocused and essentially reactive to technological change and commercial development, resulting in uncertainty and ad hoc responses.

The present circumstances of ongoing revolutionary change in the media and the degree of constitutional change occurring in Britain appear to form precisely the conjunction of events identified by Blumler and Gurevitch (1995: 204) as representing the opportunity for a fundamental overhaul of regulatory arrangements, and the replacement of ill-suited and poorly structured, historically contingently designed institutions with a new generation of regulator appropriate to the modern context and equipped with a clear, overarching philosophy. The law, like other aspects of media regulation, has developed in an incremental and pragmatic fashion, and the potential it offers for providing procedural and substantive fairness and support for fundamental constitutional and democratic principles has hardly begun to be harnessed.

While the ongoing media revolution provides the conditions in which it is possible for change to be 'captured' by the state and forced into the service of the public interest or of citizenship, the absence in Britain of a developed concept of the state, and therefore public law (Prosser 1982) or even public service (Prosser 1997: 287), form major obstacles to this task, given the significant relationship noted by Humphreys (1996) between media regulation and historical, constitutional tradition. Thus, any move to a single, unified media/communications regulator, even assuming its operation to be adequately transparent and accountable, along the lines suggested by Collins and Murroni, would be unlikely to be of assistance unless it were accompanied by a fundamental reappraisal of the conceptual basis for regulation. Undoubtedly, a Royal Commission on the media and its regulation, as recommended by Curran and Seaton (1997: 358), has its attractions in providing a forum in which the identification and development of underlying concepts might take place. Unfortunately, however, speed is not one of the attractions and any findings of a Royal Commission might come too late to prevent the further, and perhaps ultimate, erosion of the public interest in the media. The revolutionary moment may have passed.

In relation to regulating the media both in terms of content and in respect of media markets, via controls on structure and behaviour, the regulatory structures have been reactive to technological and corporate change, with a consequent failure to take opportunities to reappraise and reassert the values and purposes of the regime. The opportunity must be taken now to reinvest the media-regulation process with purpose and legitimacy, via overt recognition of the public interest in the universal provision of a wide range of quality media output. In pursuit via regulation of citizenship objectives, however, it is crucial to ensure that the regulatory process meets the highest standards of transparency and accountability. If this opportunity is missed, there can be little doubt that the last remnants of diversity in the press and what remains of the uniquely valuable, public-service broadcasting tradition in Britain will be lost to future generations, and along with them will be lost a crucial element of democracy.

Bibliography

Abel, R. (1994), *Speech and Respect*, London: Sweet and Maxwell.

Ainsworth, L. and Weston, D. (1995), 'Newspapers and UK media ownership controls', *Media Law and Practice*, vol. 16, no. 1, p. 2.

Annan Report (1977), *Report of the Committee on the Future of Broadcasting*, Cmnd 6753, London: HMSO.

Bagdikian, B. (1992), *The Media Monopoly* (4th edition), Boston: Beacon Press.

Baldwin, R. and McCrudden, C. (1987), *Regulation and Public Law*, London: Weidenfeld and Nicolson.

Barbalet, J. (1988), *Citizenship*, Milton Keynes: Open University Press.

Barbrook, R. (1995), *Media Freedom: the Contradictions of Communications in the Age of Modernity*, London: Pluto Press.

Barendt, E. (1985), *Freedom of Speech*, Oxford: Clarendon.

Barendt, E. (1991), 'The influence of the German and Italian Constitutional Courts on their national broadcasting systems', *Public Law*, Spring, p. 93.

Barendt, E. (1993), *Broadcasting Law: a Comparative Study*, Oxford: Clarendon.

Barker, F. (1994), *Private Property, Public Access – a critique of the legal framework governing the enforcement and exercise of public rights of access to land*, unpublished Ph.D. thesis, University of Hull.

Barker, F. and Lucy, W. (1993), 'Justifying property and justifying access', *Canadian Journal of Law and Jurisprudence*, vol. VI, no. 2, p. 287.

Birkinshaw, P. (1993), ' "I only ask for information" – the White Paper on open government', *Public Law*, Winter, p. 557.

Birkinshaw, P. (1994), *Grievances, Remedies and the State* (2nd edition), London: Sweet and Maxwell.

Birkinshaw, P. (1996), *Freedom of Information: the Law, the Practice and the Ideal* (2nd edition), London: Butterworths.

Birkinshaw, P., Harden, I. and Lewis, N. (1990), *Government by Moonlight: the Hybrid Parts of the State*, London: Unwin Hyman.

Blumler, J. (ed.) (1992), *Television and the Public Interest: Vulnerable Values in West European Broadcasting*, London: Sage.

Blumler, J. (1992), 'Introduction: current confrontations in West European television', in Blumler, J. (ed.), *Television and the Public Interest: Vulnerable Values in West European Broadcasting*, London: Sage.

Blumler, J. and Gurevitch, M. (1995), *The Crisis of Public Communication*, London: Routledge.

Blumler, J. and Madge, J. (1967), *Citizenship and Television*, London: PEP.

Bollinger, L. (1990), 'Freedom of the press and public access', in Lichtenberg, J. (ed.), *Democracy and the Mass Media*, Cambridge: Cambridge University Press.

Briggs, A. (1985), *The BBC: the First Fifty Years*, Oxford: Oxford University Press.

Calcutt, D. (1990), *Report of the Committee on Privacy and Related Matters*, Cm. 1102, London: HMSO.

Calcutt, D. (1993), *Review of Press Self-Regulation*, Cm. 2135, London: HMSO.

Charlesworth, A. and Cullen, H. (1996), 'Under my wheels: issues of access and social exclusion on the information superhighway', *International Review of Law, Computers and Technology*, vol. 10, no. 1, p. 27.

Coleman, F. and McMurtrie, S. (1995), 'Red hot television: domestic and international legal aspects of the regulation of satellite television', *European Public Law*, vol. 1, issue 2, p. 201.

Collins, R. (ed.) (1996), *Converging Media? Converging Regulation?*, London: IPPR.

Collins, R. and Murroni, C. (1996), *New Media, New Policies*, Cambridge: Polity Press.

Congdon, T., Graham, A., Green, D. and Robinson, B. (1995), *The Cross Media Revolution: Ownership and Control*, London: John Libbey.

Curran, J. and Seaton, J. (1991), *Power Without Responsibility: the Press and Broadcasting in Britain* (4th edition), London: Routledge.

Curran, J. and Seaton, J. (1997), *Power Without Responsibility: the Press and Broadcasting in Britain* (5th edition), London: Routledge.

Dahlgren, P. (1995), *Television and the Public Sphere: Citizenship, Democracy and the Media*, London: Sage.

Daintith, T. (1979), 'Regulation by contract: the new prerogative', *Current Legal Problems*, vol. 32, p. 41.

Davis, K. C. (1971), *Discretionary Justice: a Preliminary Inquiry*, Urbana: University of Illinois Press.

Department of Culture, Media and Sport (DCMS) (1998a), *Television: the Digital Future*, < http://www.culture.gov.uk/CONS.HTM >

Department of Culture, Media and Sport (DCMS) (1998b), *A Study to Estimate the Economic Impact of Government Policies Towards Digital Television*, < http://www.culture.gov.uk/NERA.HTM >

Department of Culture, Media and Sport (DCMS) (1998c), *Guide to Schedule 2, Broadcasting Act 1996*, < http://www.culture.gov.uk/m1.HTM >

Department of National Heritage (DNH) (1995a), White Paper, *Media Ownership: the Government's Proposals*, Cm. 2872, London: HMSO.

Department of National Heritage (DNH) (1995b), White Paper, *Privacy and Media Intrusion*, Cm. 2918, London: HMSO.

Department of National Heritage (DNH) (1995c), White Paper, *Digital Terrestrial Broadcasting: the Government's Proposals*, Cm. 2946, London: HMSO.

Department of Trade and Industry (DTI) (1996), White Paper, *Spectrum Management: into the 21st Century*, Cm. 3252, London: HMSO.

Dovey, J. (1995), 'Access television', in Dowmunt, T. (ed.), *Channels of Resistance: Global Television and Local Empowerment*, London: Channel 4/BFI.

Dowmunt, T. (ed.) (1995), *Channels of Resistance: Global Television and Local Empowerment*, London: Channel 4/BFI.

Doyle, G. (1997), 'From "pluralism" to "ownership": Europe's emergent policy on media concentrations navigates the doldrums', *Journal of Information, Law and Technology*, < http://elj.warwick.ac.uk/jilt/commsreg/97__3doyl/ >

Ehrlich, E. (1922), 'The Sociology of Law', *Harvard Law Review*, vol. 36, no. 130.

Eldridge, J., Kitzinger, J. and Williams, K. (1997), *The Mass Media and Power in Modern Britain*, Oxford: Oxford University Press.

Elliott, M. (1981), 'Chasing the receding bus: the Broadcasting Act 1980', *Modern Law Review*, vol. 44, November, p. 683.

European Commission (1992), *Pluralism and Media Concentration in the Internal Market. An Assessment of the Need for Community Action*, Com. (1992) 480.

European Commission (1994), *Follow-up to the Consultation Process Relating to the Green Paper on 'Pluralism and Media Concentration in the Internal Market – an Assessment of the Need for Community Action*, Com. (1994) 353.

European Commission (1997), *Towards an Information Society Approach*, < http://www.ispo.cec.be/convergenceg >

Feintuck, M. (1994), *Accountability and Choice in Schooling*, Buckingham: Open University Press.

Feintuck, M. (1995), 'Good news for the media? Developments in regulating media ownership in Britain and Europe', *European Public Law*, vol. 1, issue 4, p. 549.

Feintuck, M. (1997a), 'Regulating the bogey man', *Utilities Law Review*, vol. 8, no. 2, p. 29.

Feintuck, M. (1997b), 'The UK Broadcasting Act 1996: a holding operation?', *European Public Law*, vol. 3, issue 2, p. 201.

Feintuck, M. (1997c), 'Regulating the media revolution: in search of the public interest', *Journal of Information, Law and Technology*, < http://elj.warwick.ac.uk/ jilt/commsreg/97__3fein/ >

Ferguson, M. (ed.) (1990), *Public Communication: the New Imperatives*, London: Sage.

Foster, R. (1992), *Public Broadcasters: Accountability and Efficiency*, Edinburgh: Edinburgh University Press.

Gamble, A. (1994), *The Free Economy and the Strong State: the Politics of Thatcherism*, Basingstoke: Macmillan.

Gibbons, T. (1991), *Regulating the Media*, London: Sweet and Maxwell.

Gibbons, T. (1992), 'Freedom of the press: ownership and editorial values', *Public Law*, Summer, p. 279.

Gibbons, T. (1996), 'Commentary on the Broadcasting Act 1996', in *Current Law Statutes Annotated*, London: Sweet and Maxwell.

Goh, J. (1997), *European Air Transport Law and Competition*, Chichester: Wiley.

Goldberg, D. and Verhulst, S. (1997) 'Legal responses to regulating the changing media in the UK', *Utilities Law Review*, vol. 8, no. 4, p. 97.

Golding, P. (1990), 'Political communication and citizenship: the media and democracy in an inegalitarian social order', in Ferguson, M. (ed.), *Public Communication: the New Imperatives*, London: Sage.

LIVERPOOL JOHN MOORES UNIVERSITY
LEARNING SERVICES

Graham, C. (1994), 'Self-regulation', in Genn, H. and Richardson, G. (eds), *Administrative Law and Government Action*, Oxford: Clarendon.

Graham, C. (forthcoming), 'OFTEL as a competition versus sectoral regulator', in Doern, B and Wilks, S. (eds), *Regulatory Institutions in Britain and North America: Politics and Paths to Reform*, Toronto: University of Toronto Press.

Graham, C. and Prosser, T. (eds) (1988),*Waiving the Rules: the Constitution Under Thatcherism*, Milton Keynes: Open University Press.

Hall, S., Chritcher, C., Jefferson, T., Clarke, J. and Roberts, B. (1978), *Policing the Crisis: Mugging, the State, and Law and Order*, Basingstoke: Macmillan.

Hamelink, C. (1995), 'The democratic ideal and its enemies', in Lee, P. (ed.), *The Democratization of Communication*, Cardiff: University of Wales Press, pp. 15–37.

Harcourt, A. (1996), 'Regulating for media concentration: the emerging policy of the European Union', *Utilities Law Review*, vol. 7, October, p. 202.

Harden, I. and Lewis, N. (1986), *The Noble Lie: the British Constitution and the Rule of Law*, London: Hutchinson.

Harlow, C. and Rawlings, R. (1997), *Law and Administration* (2nd edition), London: Butterworths.

Held, V. (1970), *The Public Interest and Individual Interests*, New York: Basic Books.

Herman, E. and McChesney, R. (1997), *The Global Media*, London: Cassell.

Hitchens, L. (1994), 'Media ownership and control: a European approach', *Modern Law Review*, vol. 57, July, p. 585.

Hitchens, L. (1995a), ' "Get ready, fire, take aim". The regulation of cross media ownership – an exercise in policy-making', *Public Law*, Writer, p. 620.

Hitchens, L. (1995b), 'Fit to broadcast? Fit to decide?', *Media Law and Practice*, vol. 16, no. 3, p. 115.

Hoffmann-Riem, W. (1992a), 'Defending vulnerable values: regulatory measures and enforcement dilemmas', in Blumler, J. (ed.), *Television and the Public Interest: Vulnerable Values in West European Broadcasting*, London: Sage.

Hoffmann-Riem, W. (1992b), 'Protecting vulnerable values in the German broadcasting order', in Blumler, J. (ed.), *Television and the Public Interest: Vulnerable Values in West European Broadcasting*, London: Sage.

Hoffmann-Riem, W. (1996), *Regulating Media: the Licensing and Supervision of Broadcasting in Six Countries*, New York: Guilford Press.

Hogan, D. (1997), 'The logic of protection: citizenship, justice and political community', in Kennedy, K. (ed.), *Citizenship Education and the Modern State*, London: Falmer.

Home Affairs Committee (1987–8), *The Future of Broadcasting*, HC 262.

Home Office (1997a), White Paper, *Rights Brought Home: the Human Rights Bill*, Cm. 3782, London: HMSO.

Home Office (1997b), White Paper, *Your Right to Know: Freedom of Information*, Cm. 3818, London: HMSO.

Honoré, A. (1987), *Making Law Bind*, Oxford: Clarendon Press.

Humphreys, P. (1994), *Media and Media Policy in Germany: the Press and Broadcasting Since 1945*, Oxford: Berg.

Humphreys, P. (1996), *Mass Media and Media Policy in Western Europe*, Manchester: Manchester University Press.

Humphreys, P. (1997a), 'Power and control in the new media', paper presented at the ECPR Workshop, *New Media and Political Communication*, Berne, 27 February – 4 March 1997.

Humphreys, P. (1997b), 'Media concentration and policy in Germany', unpublished paper presented at University of Manchester Workshop, *Directions in the Regulation of Media Ownership*, 17 October 1997.

Hutton, W. (1995), *The State We're In*, London: Jonathan Cape.

Independent Television Commission (ITC) (1997), News Release, *ITC Announces its Decision to Award Multiplex Licences for Digital Terrestrial Television*, < http://www.itc.co.uk/factfile/dttnr.htm >

Itzin, C. (1995), 'Pornography, harm and human rights – the European context', *Media Law and Practice*, vol. 16, no. 3, p. 107.

Jones, T. (1992), 'Judicial review of the ITC', *Public Law*, p. 372.

Jowell, J. (1994), 'The rule of law today', in Jowell, J. and Oliver, D. (eds)., *The Changing Constitution* (3rd edition), Oxford: Oxford University Press.

Kahn-Freund, O. (1974), 'On uses and misuses of comparative law', *Modern Law Review*, vol. 37, no. 1, p. 1.

Keane, J. (1991), *The Media and Democracy*, Cambridge: Polity Press.

Kennedy, K. (1997), *Citizenship Education and the Modern State*, London: Falmer.

Klingler, R. (1996), *The New Information Industry: Regulatory Challenges and the First Amendment*, Washington, D.C.: Brookings Institute Press.

Lawson-Cruttenden, T. and Addison, N. (1997), *Blackstone's Guide to the Protection From Harassment Act 1997*, London: Blackstone Press.

Lee, P. (ed.) (1995), *The Democratization of Communication*, Cardiff: University of Wales Press.

Lee, P. (1995), 'Introduction: the illusion of democracy', in Lee, P. (ed.), (1995) *The Democratization of Communication*, Cardiff: University of Wales Press, pp. 1–14.

Le Grand, J. (1991), 'Quasi-markets and social policy', *Economic Journal*, vol. 101, p. 1256.

Lewis, N. (1975), 'IBA programme contract awards', *Public Law*, Winter, p. 317.

Lewis, N. D. (1996), *Choice and the Legal Order*, London: Butterworths.

Lidbetter, A. (1994), 'The Advertising Standards Authority, the Committee of Advertising Practice and Judicial Review', *Media Law and Practice*, p. 113.

Longley, D. (1993), *Public Law and Health Service Accountability*, Buckingham: Open University Press.

Lucy, W. and Mitchell, C. (1996), 'Replacing private property: the case for stewardship', *Cambridge Law Journal*, vol.55 no. 3 November, p. 566.

McQuail,D. (1992), *Media Performance: Mass Communication and the Public Interest*, London: Sage.

Marsden, C. (1996) 'Judicial review of the Channel 5 licence award', *Nottingham Law Journal*, vol. 5, part 1, p. 86.

Marsden, C. (1997a), 'Structural and behavioural regulation in UK, European and US digital pay-TV', *Utilities Law Review*, vol. 8, no. 4, p. 114.

Marsden, C. (1997b), 'The European digital convergence paradigm: from structural pluralism to behavioural competition law', *Journal of Information, Law and Technology*, < http://elj.warwick.ac.uk/jilt/commsreg/97__3mars/ >

Marshall, T. (1964), *Class, Citizenship and Social Development*, New York: Doubleday.

Mazzoleni, G. (1992), 'Is there a question of vulnerable Values in Italy?', in Blumler, J. (ed.), *Television and the Public Interest: Vulnerable Values in West European Broadcasting*, London: Sage.

Munro, C. (1991), 'Press freedom – how the beast was tamed', *Modern Law Review*, vol. 54, no. 1, January, p. 104.

Munro, C. (1997), 'Self-regulation in the media', *Public Law*, Spring, p. 6.

Negrine, R. (1994), *Politics and the Mass Media in Britain* (2nd edition), London: Routledge.

Oftel (1995), Beyond the Telephone, the Television and the PC, < http:// www.oftel.gov.uk/superhwy/multi.htm >

Oftel (1996), *Conditional Access: Consultative Document on Draft Oftel Guidelines*, < http://www.open.gov.uk/oftel/oftelwww/oftelhm.htm >

Oftel (1997a), *Submission to the ITC on Competition Issues Arising from the Award of Digital Terrestrial Television Multiplex Licences*, < http://www.oftel.gov.uk/ broadcast/dtt.htm >

Oftel (1997b), Press Release, *Oftel Publishes Advice to ITC on Bids for Digital Terrestrial Television Licence*, < http://www.coi.gov.uk/coi/depts/GOT/coi9865c.ok >

Oftel (1997c), *The Regulation of Conditional Access for Digital Television Services. Oftel Guidelines*, < http://www.oftel.gov.uk/broadcast/conacc.htm >

Oftel (1997d), *Conditional Access: Consultative Document on Draft Oftel Guidelines*, < http://www.oftel.gov.uk/broadcast/condacc.thm >

Ogus, A. (1994), *Regulation: Legal Form and Economic Theory*, Oxford: Clarendon.

Osborne, D. and Gaebler, T. (1992), *Reinventing Government*, New York: Addison-Wesley.

Page, A. (1987), 'Financial services: the self-regulatory alternative?', in Baldwin, R. and McCrudden, C., *Regulation and Public Law*, London: Weidenfeld and Nicolson.

Parkinson, J. (1993), *Corporate Power and Responsibility: Issues in the Theory of Company Law*, Oxford: Oxford University Press.

Peacock Report (1986), Report of the Committee on Financing the BBC, Cmnd 9824, London: HMSO.

Peak, S. and Fisher, P. (eds) (1996), *The Media Guide 1997*, London: Fourth Estate.

Prosser, T. (1982), 'Towards a critical public law', *Journal of Law and Society*, vol. 9, no. 1, p. 1.

Prosser, T. (1994), 'Regulation, markets and legitimacy', in Jowell, J. and Oliver, D. (eds), *The Changing Constitution* (3rd edition), Oxford: Oxford University Press.

Prosser, T. (1997), *Law and the Regulators*, Oxford: Clarendon.

Ranson, S. and Stewart, J. (1989), 'Citizenship and government: the challenge for management in the public domain', *Political Studies*, vol. 37, no. 1, p. 5.

Robertson, G. and Nicol, A. (1992), *Media Law* (3rd edition), London: Penguin.

Rudenstine, D. (1996), *The Day the Presses Stopped: a History of the Pentagon Papers Case*, Berkeley: University of California Press.

Sadler Report (1991), Inquiry into Standards in Cross Media Promotion, Cm. 1436, London: HMSO.

Schiller, H. (1996), *Information Inequality*, New York: Routledge.

Seymour-Ure, C. (1996), *The British Press and Broadcasting Since 1945* (2nd edition), Oxford: Blackwell.

Siebert, F., Peterson, T. and Schramm, W. (1956), *Four Theories of the Press*, Urbana: University of Illinois Press.

Skouris, W. (ed.) (1994), *Advertising and Constitutional Rights in Europe*, Baden-Baden: Nomos Verlagsgesellschaft.

Tehranian, M. and Tehranian, K. (1995), 'That recurrent suspicion: democratization in a global perspective', in Lee, P. (ed.), *The Democratization of Communication*, Cardiff: University of Wales Press, pp. 38–74.

Thomas, N. (1995), 'Linguistic minorities and the media', in Lee, P. (ed.), *The Democratization of Communication*, Cardiff: University of Wales Press, pp. 173–182.

Tunstall, J. and Palmer, M. (1991), *Media Moguls*, London: Routledge.

Veljanovski, C. (1987), 'Cable television: agency franchising and economics', in Baldwin, R. and McCrudden, C., *Regulation and Public Law*, London: Weidenfeld and Nicolson.

Veljanovski, C. (1989), *Freedom in Broadcasting*, London: Institute of Economic Affairs.

Verhulst, S. (1997), 'Public service broadcasting in Europe', *Utilities Law Review*, vol. 8, no. 2, p. 31.

Vick, D. (1995), 'The First Amendment limitations on broadcasting in the United States after *Turner Broadcasting v FCC*', *Media Law and Practice*, vol. 16, no. 3, p. 97.

Wacks, R. (1995), *Privacy and Press Freedom*, London: Blackstone Press.

Whish, R. (1993), *Competition Law* (3rd edition), London: Sweet and Maxwell.

Index

accountability, 5, 8, 16, 34
  defined, 120
  of media, 39, 133–5, 198
  of regulators, 39, 40, 49, 122–3, 139, 153, 156, 159, 199, 204, 206
advertising, 64, 121, 129, 141, 151–5
  on television, 37, 38, 151, 175
Advertising Standards Authority (ASA), 50, 141, 151-5, 158–9, 204
Annan Report, 60, 61, 98, 129

Barendt, E., 11–13, 42, 62, 63, 69, 70, 71, 78, 79, 99, 107, 139, 140, 167-8, 170-1, 174
behavioural regulation, 51, 53, 56, 74, 91, 208
Berlusconi, S., 18–19, 55, 174–5, 184
Birt, J., 130, 131, 132
Blair, T., 34, 79, 152, 184, 192, 206, 209
British Board of Film Classification (BBFC), 10, 31, 50, 63, 126–7, 136, 139
British Broadcasting Corporation (BBC), 3, 24, 36–7, 39, 45, 60, 64, 65, 80, 81, 85, 135–6, 158, 173, 195–6, 202, 203, 205, 209, 210, 211
  Charter, 50, 61, 85, 125, 127, 134, 136–8
  duopoly with ITV, 3, 22, 36, 37, 64, 99, 124, 128
  Governors, 60, 118, 122, 123, 126, 127, 133, 205, 211
  reform of, 22, 36, 129–34, 157

Broadcasting Acts, 34, 43, 50, 61; see also Television Act 1963
Broadcasting Act 1980, 98–9, 124
Broadcasting Act 1981, 125, 129
Broadcasting Act 1990, 10, 53, 94, 99–101, 107, 119, 121, 124, 125–6, 128, 129, 150, 164
Broadcasting Act 1996, 58, 94, 103, 105–6, 107, 110–12, 116–17, 121, 126, 135, 137, 164, 202
Broadcasting Complaints Commission, 135, 137, 139; see also Broadcasting Standards Commission
Broadcasting Standards Commission (BSC), 117, 118, 126, 135–6, 137–8, 139, 140, 149, 158, 160, 196
Broadcasting Standards Council, 135, 136, 138, 139; see also Broadcasting Standards Commission
BSkyB, 4, 17, 22, 23, 54, 65, 99, 109, 114–15, 117, 202

cable, 22–3, 26, 40, 52, 64, 70, 101, 108, 109, 116, 123, 128, 169, 189
Calcutt Reports, 145–6
Carlton Television, 114, 117
censorship see content, regulation of; prior restraint
Channel 3 see also ITV
  licence allocation, 53, 98, 100–1, 105, 110, 117, 124; see also ITC

–225–

50, 126, 146, 148, 151, 156,
158, 176, 187–8, 204, 207
European Union (EU), 8, 21, 46,
59, 69, 71, 76, 92, 94, 103–4,
109, 112–13, 139, 157, 163,
164, 168, 169, 170, 173, 175–
80, 182–3, 184, 185, 194, 195;
see also subsidiarity
Commission, 50, 102, 177, 178–9
competition law, 51, 91, 103
Directives, 46, 67, 102, 103–4, 110,
113, 139, 151, 173, 177, 180

Fair Trading Act 1973 (FTA), 94–8,
103
Federal Communications
Commission (FCC), 5, 63,
166–8
Feintuck, M., 19, 26, 28, 84, 87,
107, 141
France, 41, 45, 70, 77, 144, 173,
183, 184
freedom of communication, 9–14,
15, 26, 40, 43, 79; see also
citizen participation; self-
fulfilment; truth
freedom of information, 33–4, 122,
149, 159, 168, 187–8, 206
frequency scarcity, 24, 40, 41, 43,
62, 64, 212–13

Germany, 16, 41, 45, 55, 70, 77,
102, 163, 170–3, 178, 181, 183,
185, 191, 193, 209, 210
Gibbons, T., 28, 93, 96, 97, 103,
105, 112, 128–9, 143, 211
global information infrastructure
(GII), 21, 122; see also
information superhighway;
Internet
globalisation, 5, 8, 18–21, 67, 121–2,
176
Golding, P., 81–2, 84, 86
Graham, C., 140, 152, 159
Granada Television, 114, 117
Guardian, 44, 95, 210

Harden, I., 30, 33, 80, 116, 165
Harlow, C., 99, 100, 116, 119
Herman, E., 5, 14, 18, 19, 20, 23–4,
42, 67, 82, 109, 175, 184, 186,
189
Hitchens, L., 28, 49, 57, 87, 107,
112, 177, 184
Hoffmann-Riem, W., 51, 56, 64, 91,
99, 171, 191, 208, 210
Humphreys, P., 21, 41, 42, 47, 94,
102, 139, 143–4, 164, 168, 170,
171–3, 174–5, 176, 183, 184,
204, 208, 216
Hutton, W., 16, 93, 99, 132, 157

Independent, 95, 127
Independent Broadcasting Authority
(IBA), 60, 98, 99, 121, 124,
127, 128–9; see also ITC
Independent Television (ITV), 3, 20,
37, 47, 48, 64, 65, 81, 99, 123,
124–5, 126, 128, 129, 195–6,
203, 209; see also Channel 3
duopoly with BBC, 3, 22, 36, 37,
64, 99, 124, 128
Independent Television Commission
(ITC), 116, 117, 118, 121, 125,
126, 128, 129, 153, 205; see also
IBA
licensing, 58, 91, 99–102, 105–6,
108, 110–12, 114–15, 123, 124,
135, 156
regulation of programme content,
52, 136, 138, 139, 141, 158,
167, 179
information superhighway, 23, 24,
67, 189, 192; see also GII;
Internet
integration, 5, 20, 67
Internet, 23–4, 26, 63, 84, 117, 122,
160, 167, 176; see also GII;
information superhighway
Italy, 18–19, 36, 37, 55, 70, 77, 163,
173, 174–5, 181, 183, 184, 185,
191, 193, 209, 215